9113

"Willie played each and every game like it was his last. A great center fielder and leadoff hitter and one of the best base runners I ever played with. He turned singles to doubles doubles to triples and triples into inside-the-park home runs."

**—George Brett,**
**former Royals third baseman, Hall of Fame 1999**

"I am proud of Willie's revitalization in Kansas City! His current involvement with underserved sectors of the community incorporated with years of experience on the ball field, provide inspirational life lessons."

**—Helen Mohr,**
**Event Director,**
**Willie Wilson Baseball Foundation**

"Willie and I were teammates for over 10 years with the Kansas City Royals. We had the opportunity to play in numerous championships including being a part of the Royals World Series winning team in 1985. Willie was a great teammate and player and is a very good friend of mine."

**—Frank White,**
**former Royals second baseman,**
**member Royals Hall of Fame**

"Willie Wilson was simply the fastest man in the game and his play electrified Royals baseball for many years. His life is full of cherished triumphs and a few struggles overcome – and in 'Inside the Park' he tells the tales of both. Willie was a joy to watch and his story is a joy to read."

**—Curt Nelson,**
**Director, Kansas City Royals Hall of Fame**

"Having Willie Wilson in center field is like having four outfielders, which says something about the range and speed right there."

—**Billy Scripture,**
**Wilson's first minor league manager**

"I think he could have made it in pro football directly out of high school as a wide receiver or a defensive back, but not as a running back."

—**Howie Anderson,**
**Wilson's football coach at Summit High School**

"He's a walking double. When I'm in right field I hope he doesn't get a hit in my area because he'll be running around the bases laughing while I'm juggling the ball."

—**Reggie Jackson,**
**former Yankee right fielder, Hall of Fame 1993**

"There's no question Wilson is the best No. 1 draft pick we've signed. He could be the next Willie Mays."

—**Royals GM Lou Gorman**
**after signing Wilson**

"Men grow as trees, through many phases of life. Some trees wilt and die in the face of adversity, some thrive as they grow older and stronger. Willie Wilson has grown into a towering, strong oak … one resilient to the seasons of life, providing shade and protection to all."

—**George H. Richter,**
**President and Chief Operating Officer,**
**Smithfield Foods, Inc.**

"Few athletes have ever electrified a crowd the way Willie Wilson did when he ran the bases and patrolled the outfield at Kauffman Stadium. It was simply a thing of beauty!"

—**Bob Kendrick,**
**President, Negro Leagues Baseball Museum**

# Inside the Park

## Running the Base Path of Life

### with Kent Pulliam

Requests for permission should be addressed Ascend Books, LLC, Attn: Rights and Permissions Department, 12710 Pflumm Rd., Suite 200, Olathe, KS. 66062.
10 9 8 7 6 5 4 3 2 1

Printed in the United States of America
ISBN- 978-0-9889964-2-7
ISBN: e-book 978-0-9889964-3-4

Library of Congress Cataloging-in-Publications Data Available Upon Request

Publisher: Bob Snodgrass
Publication Coordinator: Beth Brown
Editor: Jim Bradford
Dust Jacket and Book Design: Rob Peters
Sales and Marketing: Lenny Cohen, Dylan Tucker

All photos courtesy of Willie Wilson unless otherwise indicated.

Every reasonable attempt has been made to determine the ownership of copyright. Please notify the publisher of any erroneous credits or omissions, and corrections will be made to subsequent editions/future printings. The goal of the entire staff of Ascend Books is to publish quality works. With that in mind, we are proud to offer this book to our readers. Please note, however, that the story, the experiences and the words are those of the author alone.

Printed in the United States of America

www.ascendbooks.com

# CONTENTS

Dedicated to the memory of
Madear Annie Mae Timothy
Ma Dorothy Lynn and
Buck Anthony Lynn

# FOREWORD
## BY KENT PULLIAM

Willie Wilson was an integral part of the Royals teams of the 1980s. He, George Brett, Frank White, Amos Otis and Hal McRae were the nucleus of Royals teams that went to the World Series in 1980 and won the World Series in 1985.

Over the next 43 chapters that fit with the year-to-year arc of Willie's career and life, you'll learn how he has met and overcome many challenges in life.

Some would characterize Wilson as a "Punch-'n'-Judy" hitter – he ranks second on the team for most singles in a career. But when Wilson reached first base he was in scoring position. Brett knocked him in 321 times – the second highest total of one teammate batting in another since 1950.

In 1980, the first season the Royals reached the World Series, Wilson had the most prolific year ever for a Royals' batter, and it went largely unrecognized because Brett was chasing a .400 batting average that season. Wilson had 55 more hits than Brett that year. He had the most hits ever by a Royals player in a single season that year, the most plate appearances, most at bats, most singles and most multi-hit games from that season alone.

He still holds the Royals record for stolen bases with 83 in the 1979 season. He holds the single-season record for triples with 21 in the 1985 season.

In the '80s, Wilson was *the* Royals hitter, collecting 1,639 hits to Brett's 1,446. His total ranked second in the Major Leagues to Robin Yount, who had 1,731 hits during the 1980s. In the 1980s Wilson scored

865 runs. That's 12.6 percent of the runs the Royals scored in the decade, and nearly 100 more runs than the next closest player.

Brett remains the iconic hitter in Royals history. His Baseball Hall of Fame status reflects that, and Brett is atop virtually every career batting record in Royals history. Wilson ranks in the top 10 of virtually every batting category the Royals keep – save home runs – and is in the top five in most categories.

Twice during the 1980s Wilson was selected as the Royals Player of the year – 1981 and 1984. Ironically, both seasons came after epic failures. The 1981 award followed the dubious record of 12 strikeouts in the World Series against the Philadelphia Phillies. In 1984, Wilson was coming off a winter in jail following a three-month prison sentence for his part in the drug scandal that rocked the Royals through the latter half of the 1983 season. He missed the first 45 days of the season and still played in more games than all but two other Royals.

He played in two All-Star games, won a Gold Glove and with his speed made catches in center field that other outfielders waved at.

Baseball is the reason people know about Willie Wilson, but the events in his life away from baseball and how he dealt with them are the things that make his story interesting.

—Kent Pulliam

## WILSON'S SINGLE-SEASON RECORDS

| CATEGORY | NO. | YEAR |
|---|---|---|
| Most stolen bases | 83 | 1979 |
| Most at bats | 705 | 1980 |
| Most plate appearances | 745 | 1980 |
| Most hits | 230 | 1980 |
| Most hits by switch hitter | 230 | 1980 |
| Most singles | 184 | 1980 |
| Most multi-hit games | 71 | 1980 |
| Most triples | 21 | 1985 |

## WILSON'S ROYALS CAREER RANKING

| CATEGORY | RANK | NUMBER |
|---|---|---|
| Games played | No. 5 | 1,787 |
| At bats | No. 4 | 6,799 |
| Runs scored | No. 3 | 1,060 |
| Career hits | No. 4 | 1,968 |
| Career doubles | No. 6 | 241 |
| Career triples | No. 2 | 133 |
| Runs-batted-in | No. 9 | 509 |
| Batting average | No. 9 | .289 |
| Walks | No. 9 | 360 |
| Strikeouts | No. 2 | 990 |
| Hit by pitch | No. 5 | 54 |
| Stolen bases | No. 1 | 612 |
| Total bases | No. 5 | 2,595 |
| Extra-base hits | No. 6 | 414 |
| Inside-the-park home runs | No. 1 | 13 |

## CATEGORIES/YEARS IN WHICH WILSON LEAD THE LEAGUE

| CATEGORY | YEAR | NUMBER |
|---|---|---|
| Batting average | 1982 | .332 |
| At Bats | 1980 | 705 |
| Plate appearances | 1980 | 745 |
| Runs | 1980 | 133 |
| Hits | 1980 | 230 |
| Triples | 1980 | 15 |
| | 1982 | 15 |
| | 1985 | 21 |
| | 1987 | 15 |
| | 1988 | 11 |
| Stolen bases | 1979 | 83 |

## MILESTONE HITS

| HIT | DATE | OPPONENT |
|---|---|---|
| 1 | September 10, 1976 | At Minnesota |
| 500 | May 16, 1981 | At Boston |
| 1,000 | June 24, 1994 | Vs. Oakland |
| 1,500 | May 30, 1987 | Vs. Texas |
| 2,000 | June 20, 1991 | At Boston* |
| 2,207 | April 23, 1994 | At Colorado ** |

* With Oakland Athletics; ** With Chicago Cubs

# 1

# IT'S IN YOUR HANDS

I don't really know how I can explain being at the highest of highs and the lowest of the lows.

I was sitting in the quietest room of my rented duplex – the bathroom – in the winter after I had been selected for to the Royals Hall of Fame. My mind was racing, thinking of the 1985 World Series one second and suicide the next. I mean, a lot of stuff was going through my brain.

I was clean again, and sober, but I had no idea what my next step was going to be. I had no job. I had no college degree. My marriage was in trouble. I couldn't provide financial support for any of the people I loved.

I was lost. Everything was weighing on me. I didn't have a positive thought in my brain. "You were one of the best baseball players in Royals history … you lost your house … you won a batting title … you've downsized twice and are renting a two-bedroom duplex with five other people, and you can't even afford that … you just got elected to the Royals Hall of Fame … your World Series ring is sitting in another man's safety deposit box because you had to sell it."

So there I was sitting in the bathroom where nobody will bother you when you close the door. I was confused. How am I supposed to survive? All this stuff was going through my head. I'm crying a little bit just trying to figure out what the hell is going on.

When you' are sitting there like that, you think you are a victim. Any time you get in a bad mood you think you're a victim. So I was going over it, trying to figure out why people were doing things, and why it was being done to me. It's always about you when you are as down as I was right then.

Maybe if I can do this, … or that. Maybe that will make a difference. My brain is just going as fast as it can, and then after a while I just figure that it isn't going to work. Then I came to the conclusion that this is how it's going to be.

There is so much stuff going through my brain. While I am sitting there I am thinking about a million things,: "Is it worth it? If I kill myself, how will it affect my children? Men don't kill themselves. Just go back to the basics."

That's when I just looked up, closed my eyes, and said, "It's in your hands, God."

All of a sudden I heard, "It will be all right, my son."

I can't explain how I heard it. Maybe it was a voice in my brain coming back because I hadn't said anything out loud. But when I heard it, I started looking all around. I'm telling you, it was as clear as if you were standing next to someone talking with them. It was really clear.

I just got a really warm feeling. I got up and walked out of the bathroom, and I felt really different. I had a really calm feeling. I was still worried, but it was different. It wasn't like everything went away, but it didn't seem like I had the weight of the world on my shoulders. I realized little things are more important than big things, spending time with my kids instead of worrying about where money is coming from. I was putting the emphasis on money more than anything else. I learned that through heartache and pain.

I don't know if that was a miracle. I don't know if people think I'm crazy when I say this, but I really don't care. There are things that happen in your life that you have no explanation for. The very next day I got a call from the Arizona Diamondbacks to be a minor league coach.

Was that a coincidence? I don't know. But from that point on it would get better and better and better. It's weird, man, because when you believe in something you can make up all kinds of stuff to help you believe in it. I thought God was saying, "OK, now I'm going to take care of you. But you have to know it's coming from me, and if you don't know, then every now and then I'm going to give you a little sign."

I was always spiritual, but I had never experienced anything like that. Then tiny little things started to happen.

After the Diamondbacks hired me, Fred White – who had been a Royals broadcaster – got me in the BAT (Baseball Assistance Team) program. They help former players who are having financial trouble pay their bills and get back on their feet. It was only for six months, but I was able to save my other money. Without Fred helping me get the bills paid and all of that stuff I could hardly see a light.

There were still some hard times. I coached for the Diamondbacks for two years, and during that time my wife moved our family to Toronto, where she is from. I tried to go back to the basics. I remembered when I was a kid, I had to work hard. I had to sacrifice. When I went to Canada that's what I did. I tried to get as much money as I could by doing little jobs. In Toronto I was a coat check guy. My pride went out the window. That's something I couldn't have done here because everybody knew me, and it would have been embarrassing.

It was a real different time in my life.

I got back to the basics.

What I have finally come to grips with is that I was the culprit for everything that happened in my life. I can accept that now. I don't like it, but I accept it, which makes me deal with it every day a little better. I made some bad choices. But they are life choices. That's what happens in life.

I'm at a much better place in my life right now. I don't think I like the old Willie Wilson very much. I like the new Willie Wilson much better. The journey has been a long one. I would like to share my story of reaching great heights and falling to the deepest of deep holes and show that you can come back from it when you take responsibility for your actions.

2

# BOBBIE LEE

I was born in 1955 in Montgomery, Alabama, when so much was going on in the South. Rosa Parks moved from the back of the bus six months after I was born. Martin Luther King was marching in Montgomery. I eventually moved away from the South to New Jersey.

I had an unusual childhood.

The first six years of my life I thought my name was Bobbie Lee. That's what everyone called me. So I thought it was my name. There wasn't any reason to question it. That's just what I was called. I was around my cousins and aunties and uncles in an area of Jackson Heights in Montgomery. I was living in a loving family with my grandmother Annie Mae, my aunt Martha, my aunt Salley, my uncle Tim and my great grandmother. It wasn't until I went to live with my mother when I was 7 years old and she started calling me Willie James that I learned my name was Willie James Wilson.

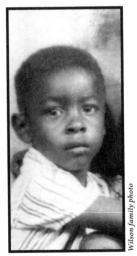

Wilson family photo

I didn't learn until we were writing this book why people called me Bobbie Lee. My aunt Martha says it was my great grandmother who gave me the nickname.

"My grandmother used to call his momma 'Bobbie,'" said Martha Gardner. "I don't know where that came from. Willie's momma's name was Dorothy, and we didn't have any Bobbies in our family that I know of. My grandmother called her Bobbie, and everyone else did, too.

The only photo of me as a child.

19

*When Willie was born my grandmomma said Willie looked just like his momma when she was a baby. So she started calling him Bobbie Lee."*

My grandmother wasn't that old at the time, and I just thought she was my mother. Nobody ever really talked about my mother or my father that I can remember. That's just the way it was. Later, it was kind of confusing, but I was just a kid at the time. I wasn't going to question anything.

There were only two entrances into Jackson Heights. They led into a semicircle of apartment buildings. The entrance on the south went straight out to the main highway, and the other ran to the neighborhoods. We were in a black neighborhood. All the stores were black-owned. All the nice houses were owned by black people. We all knew everybody around that part of town and all looked after each other.

We lived on the second floor of two floors. It was my grandmother, my uncle Tim, my aunt Salley and my great grandmother. I don't know if we were poor. When you are a kid you don't know that. We always had food and a roof over our heads.

My cousins all lived in the neighborhood, and we were together a lot of the time. My auntie Martha lived up the street with her husband Frank – we called him "Slick." Their apartment backed up to a juvenile delinquent facility. We didn't really know what it was, but when we would be eating watermelon outside, you could see those kids, I don't know, 10 yards away.

My grandmother worked for people who didn't live in Jackson Heights, so I spent a lot of time at my aunt Martha's house growing up with her children.

We played outside all the time, and everybody in the neighborhood watched out for each other. I remember I stepped on a piece of glass once, and the mailman took it out because nobody was at home at the time. One time I was riding a bike and got my foot caught in the spokes, just got it stuck crosswise right in there. To this day I don't even know how I'm still walking because it just stuck right in there. We didn't have any health insurance, we didn't have any of that stuff. There were just a lot of home remedies that everybody used.

We never really talked about my mom and I really thought that my grandmother was my mom. For some reason down there, you don't talk about that stuff … you know "papa was a rolling stone." Wherever he laid his hat was his home. But our family history was never really questioned. Us kids just accepted what was going on. I never questioned anyone about my father. I guess it was confusing, but I never really thought about it.

*Wilson family photo*

*My grandmother, Annie Mae Timothy, was the first mother I really knew.*

"*I was mostly raising Willie after his mother left town,*" *Martha said. "Dot (Willie's mother Dorothy) left and went to Cincinnati when there were no jobs here. She stayed in Cincinnati for a few years, but she came back when my momma got sick. She stayed a while, but she still couldn't find a job.*

"*Back then there were agencies looking for people who wanted what they called 'sleep-in jobs.' Jobs here in Alabama were very scarce, and you didn't make much to live on and raise a family. Willie's momma was a single parent, and she left here to do better. She sent money back to help my momma and things. Most everybody in Alabama, if they got a chance to leave Alabama, they left.*

"*I just couldn't see nobody leaving their kids behind. I do understand why she did it, but at the time I guess I didn't. So I always sort of felt like Willie was my child. I was the one who started him in school down here at George Washington Carver Elementary.*"

The school was on the outskirts of Jackson Heights, and everything was black. The school had a big jet plane in the front yard. Across the street was a Catholic school – all white. But there was never any interaction with the white kids across the street. The black high school was right next door to the elementary school, just separated by a couple of pillars. When you finished elementary school, you just walked across the hall to the high school.

I didn't know anybody who was white. The school was a black

school. Where I lived was a black neighborhood. Everybody I hung around with was black. We didn't have but a black and white TV, and everybody was black or white.

I only went as far as second grade there. I remember every day that my grandmother would give me and my uncle Tim 50 cents, she would toss us a couple of quarters out of the back of the bus as she was going to work. On weekends we would go back to the school. In the back they had a recreation center and at the recreation center we would watch Wile E. Coyote, Daffy Duck – all the cartoons that now they call violent with Acme safes falling on everybody. Those were great cartoons.

Montgomery is where I first learned to stand up for myself. My auntie Salley was the one who taught me that. She was a tomboy. I had to be 5 or 6, and I was playing outside in front of the apartment. I came upstairs crying, and she said, "Who hit you?" I went to the kitchen window – I don't even remember the kid's name – but I said "he did" and pointed him out. She said to go back downstairs and hit him.

I said, "What?"

She said, "Go back downstairs and hit him."

So I go back downstairs, and I'm just sort of shuffling out there, and I pushed him. The crazy part was the kid just stood there. So I pushed him again. She opened that window and shouted down to me and said, "I said HIT him."

So I go "BOOM!" and just smoked the kid, and then I took off running.

Afterwards, she said – in these words – "As long as you're black don't you ever let anybody push you around." Well that (black) was going to be forever. She said, "When you hit somebody, show them you hit them." That's how I learned to stand up for myself and fight if I needed to.

"Willie wouldn't fight," Martha said. "Everytime somebody would fight, Willie would run home crying. My sister Salley was back from California by then. She would go out with him and meet the boy and tell Willie to beat them up. I guess they would call it bullying now, but they used to just call it fighting. She would be standing there and say, 'Don't you run from him. Hit him. Don't you run.'"

As I look back at it now, all these people who were bringing me up were teenagers themselves, my aunties Salley and Martha and my uncles. There was uncle Slick, which is Frank – I never called him Frank. I never even knew his name, he was just Uncle Slick, Frank Gardner. There was Uncle Nathaniel and Uncle Richard. They were all influential in my life. All of them are dead now.

Jackson Heights is where I first found out I was fast. There were these two guys named Paul and Nanny. They would go into stores and have me stand outside the store. They would come out and give me stuff, and I would run up the street where they would come and meet up with me. To this day I remember that, and that was a long time ago. Funny thing is that the first time I was in Detroit playing in the big leagues, Paul and Nanny were in Detroit, and they came to one of the games. That was probably my first year in the big leagues.

*"He used to hang out with them and steal candy," Martha said. "I used to try and keep Willie away from them. Anything they said, Willie would do. I never liked them that much. They were in trouble, and they stayed in trouble.*

*"But I knew he was fast. He was always running. He never walked nowhere. He would run. When he would get out of school, that boy didn't want to come home. He wanted to stay outside and play all the time. I used to go look for him. He would see me coming when I was driving the car, and Willie would beat me home by running there. I always thought he would be on the track team and do well. He always loved the outside. I don't care, cold or what, Willie was outside playing."*

Anyway, I was living in Jackson Heights with all my cousins, and then all of a sudden – without a word or knowing anything – my bags were packed and I was in a truck driving to downtown Montgomery, which I had never been to before. I mean we never went out of that area around Jackson Heights. Now I was looking out the back of the truck and seeing my cousins running toward me and waving their hands.

I didn't know it, but I was moving to New Jersey. I kept in touch with my Alabama family, and in the summers I would go back to Alabama to see them. When I got a little older I worked with my uncles on the little farm they had. The South was going through a big change by the time I was getting to be 6 or 7 years old. Montgomery was where a lot of the civil rights movement was happening. I would hear about Dr. Martin Luther King marching down the street. I knew that my grandmother had gone on the bus strike in Montgomery in 1955-56. I knew about the civil rights movement because of my aunties and what they were saying. They were young, and they wanted to participate in what was going on. I knew about prejudice because I would overhear my grandmother and my aunties talking. I never experienced any prejudice growing up there as a child because the only people I was around were other black people.

If I had stayed there, I hope I would have grown up like my cousins did. They all have good jobs and good lives. I'm pretty sure I wouldn't have had the same chances of being an athlete. Sports just wasn't in my repertoire as a kid growing up in Alabama. Work was the important thing. Working and education were stressed. It was all about working to do something, putting a good day's work in, working hard, feeling good about yourself and what you accomplished. It was all about work, not about playing games.

I know my grandmother and aunties were bringing me up to know what was right and what was wrong. I look at my cousins now, and they are doing great. They have it together – which is really impressive now as I look back. I realize that my aunties were so young when they became mothers, really only teenagers themselves. My aunt Martha is only 12 years older than I am. So think about it, when I am 5 years old – she was married and had two kids.

When I moved to New Jersey I was taken out of that highly-charged environment. I have a bit of a temper, and that wouldn't have been the best thing to have in the South and in Montgomery when I would have been a teenager.

I would go back to Alabama in the summertime. After a few years I really didn't want to go back there because I had to go back to being Bobbie Lee. By then I was way past Bobbie Lee. I was making something of myself. I knew I loved my aunties. I knew they loved me. I knew they were helping my mom.

So I never said I wouldn't go – even though I didn't want to. I never said to my uncle Slick or anybody that I didn't want to work on the farm – out at the shack where I had been born. Dirt roads. Cows walking down the street. They would catch chickens in the coop and that's what we'd have for Sunday dinner.

"Nobody liked to work on the farm," Martha said. "My sister Lula Mae was the one who had the farm. She had come back from Indiana. It wasn't a big farm, just some land where they would grow vegetables and stuff. They would have him digging in the garden and cutting down trees.

"Willie's brother Anthony came down one year. By the end of the summer Anthony had lost a bunch of weight because he was working. He wouldn't come back no more. You couldn't get Anthony back down here."

I keep in touch with all the Montgomery family. I see my uncle Tim every now and then … I don't talk to him that much, but I want to get better at that. He and my grandmother moved up to New Jersey with us. A year or so later after he got out of high school, Tim got drafted and went to Vietnam. He made it back. He's a little quiet, but he's back. I think he worked three jobs for a while so he didn't have to think about what he went through.

At one point I was really mad at him. He's a Jehovah's Witness, and when my grandmother died he didn't enter the church. I was really angry. I mean, to me, she was my mom, and she was his mom. But I didn't know what he was going through. So probably 10 years later, early 2000s or so his daughter was getting married. I went to the wedding and said to him, "You know I have forgiven you. I love you."

He knew all those years I was mad at him. From that point, we have been a little bit closer.

# 3
# WILLIE JAMES

**A**s my cousins chased the truck down the street I was on my way to a whole new world. For the next few days we rode a Greyhound bus from Montgomery to Newark, New Jersey. We stopped like every hour going through the South, and it seemed like we were on the bus "fooooor-ever." I was sick the entire time.

We were sitting on the right side of the bus three or four rows from the back. I never thought about why we were sitting closer to the back of the bus. What I was thinking about was that's where the gas fumes came up from under the bus and it made me sick. I was lying in my grandmother's lap the whole time. I didn't know where I was going. I was just going because my grandmother and my uncle Tim were taking me.

*My aunt, Martha Ann Gardner.*

Wilson family photo

When we got to New Jersey, there were people everywhere. That was my first experience of seeing a great deal of white people. It was the train/bus station in Newark. Just walking in there was an eye opener for me. The South is easy going, we just moseyed along. Then, I got to Jersey, and they're going "Whoosh! Whoosh! Whoosh!" There were people everywhere.

I'm just a little black kid holding my grandmother's hand and looking around at all these people just flying past. No one discussed with me why we were going there. We get there, and there is this lady waiting. We walked up to her and my grandmother said:

"I want you to meet your mother."

I went, "But you're my mother."

She said, "Nope. This is your mother, honey. I'm your grandmother." All those years I thought she was my mother and that my cousins were my brothers.

My mom started calling me Willie James. That's when I learned my name was Willie James. I was Bobbie Lee for the first six years of my life, but that day I became Willie James.

My mother took my hand. We got in the car and went to Union, New Jersey, which was called Vauxhall at the time. Mother had married a guy named Gene Lynn. My baby brother, Anthony Lynn, had been born in May, so he was just a few months old. All of a sudden, my grandmother said, "goodbye," and I was just hanging out with this lady I didn't know, this guy I didn't know and a little brother I didn't know.

*"I never really understood why my momma went up there, too,"* Martha said. *"Henry was in 9th grade – that's uncle Tim. I always had it in my mind that they wanted momma to baby sit Anthony because they were both working. And I guess Dot knew that my momma wasn't going to leave my brother. So that's how they got up there.*

*"That's what I always thought it was. The idea about them going up there wasn't until after she had Anthony. Then she wanted them up there. But my momma didn't stay with them when they were in Vauxhall. She stayed with another woman in Newark. Then, when they moved to Summit, she was closer to them."*

I stayed at the house my mother and her husband had. I don't really know where my grandmother and my uncle Tim went. It was just me, my mother, my brother and my stepfather. That's when I kind of got really quiet and went into my shell.

I wasn't really scared, just sort of confused by everything that was going on. Nobody had ever talked about my mother in Montgomery. They just didn't. In Southern cities in those days, everything was so hush-hush. I don't really know why my mom had left. I have a feeling why she left. I think she left to find my dad – who I found out much later was living in New York City. But I don't know. We never really talked about it.

Within, maybe, a month, we moved from Vauxhall to Summit because the schools were better. Gene, my stepfather, was a window washer, and he had a great job in Summit. Summit was a small little town, lots of windows and a lot of stores. He would wash all the windows. We never knew where he was going to be in town, but when we walked to school, we could always find him and he would give us our lunch money.

I never met my real father. I talked to him two times. My mom never really talked to me about him. We were down in Alabama when my grandmother was celebrating her 80-something birthday. We were at a family reunion, and this guy came up to my mom and said, "You know that young man sure looks like my brother." She talked with this guy, and somehow they figured out that his brother was my father. He gave her his brother's number, and my mother gave it to me. When my mother got pregnant, I guess she was going out with two different people.

I called him, and we talked a little bit. I wasn't looking for anything. I wasn't trying to get money or anything. I just wanted to say, "hello." The third time I called, his wife answered the phone, and she recommended I never call him again. I don't know what she thought I was doing or whether she thought I was trying to break up his home, or what. I know she wasn't a very nice lady who didn't have any sympathy for someone who didn't know his dad.

I don't think my father ever knew that I played baseball. It turns out I have two half-sisters and a brother. I don't know any of them.

My mom was really cute. That's one of the first things I thought about her. She was a really pretty lady. She was very slim. We were only 17 years apart, and she was a really good looking lady, but she was demanding.

She wanted it "this way" or "that way." She didn't want any lip. I learned very early that my mom had a quick right hand. I mean it was quick, man. She would just "whap," like that. So I would get on her left side so I could see it coming.

I was really quiet, and knew that if I did what she said, I got no problems. My little brother, Anthony, was the complete opposite. He would question, "Why? Why? Why?" My mother would say, "Because I said." And he would say, "Why?" I would just be like "Anthony ... be quiet." ... "Well why?"

One thing I could do was make my mother laugh. She would be so mad at me sometimes, and I would say something funny. Then, she would say, "Don't you make me laugh!" And I was like "C'mon, ma." That was after I got to know her. Later on, she would be like Gestapo some times. She would come in the house, and would start putting her fingers on all the furniture or the windows looking for dust. When we got home from school, we knew we had to wash dishes, dust, vacuum, do all that stuff. On weekends, because she worked two jobs, I learned how to wash clothes, iron clothes and make my bed.

I do that to this day, and I can make a mean bed. I can make a bed where I can take that quarter and "boing!" But that's how she was. She was so demanding.

She got divorced from my stepfather when I was in elementary school about 6th grade. My brother actually left with his father to go to Buffalo, N.Y., after they got divorced. When I was a 9th or 10th grader, he came back and started staying with us. My mom just kept fighting and fighting to get him.

So for a while I really didn't have a father figure. Even when they were together, him and my mom used to get into some knock-down fights. He liked to drink, and he liked to gamble. My mom didn't like to drink or gamble.

*"None of us drink," Martha said. "Momma didn't drink. I don't smoke. I don't drink. Henry don't smoke. He don't drink. I guess we weren't able to ever buy it, so we didn't do it."*

My stepfather would be having these card players over at the house and there was a lot of drinking. I was the guy running, the go-fer. I would go for the food at the Summit Diner. Back in those days you could go get cigarettes as a kid because the store clerks knew you. I would run in there and get cigarettes, come back and all that.

The last time I saw my stepfather, he and my mom got into a fight. My brother and I jumped in. I jumped on his back, and my brother had his legs. So you have three people in the mix-up, and my mom is going "Boom! Boom! Boom!" just whaling on him. That was the last time I saw him.

When they were together my grandmother wasn't living with us. After he left we were all together.

My mom was a good mom. She did everything she could for us to be fed, clothed and living in a great spot. Summit was not cheap. It was an expensive little area. Even though we weren't in the high-priced area, it was not a cheap place. But she knew the school system was good, and then when I became a sports star in 9th grade, everybody starting telling her how much potential I had, so she stayed for that.

I didn't like Jersey that much when I first got there. Within two days I was in a fight. We didn't live in Summit right away, I didn't move to Summit until a month or so later when school started. My mom and stepfather picked out a place. My grandmother and my uncle Tim were downstairs. We were up stairs on the other side.

I still don't really know why we went to Jersey. My grandmother and uncle Tim stayed because he was going to go to school there. I guess they thought it was going to be a better life for us, a better way. My aunties and my grandmother had all discussed it and figured out what was going to be the best for us three. They all couldn't go to New Jersey because they were married and had kids and were set in their ways. My mom had left – whether it was to find my father or just go up there for a better opportunity because she was just 18 years old. I don't know what the discussion was, but I'm sure there had to be quite a discussion knowing my aunties.

I do know this. To this day when I smell gas, I go back to riding that Greyhound bus those two days to New Jersey – sick the whole way.

# 4
# HILLTOPPER

**S**trangely enough the first friends I made in New Jersey were because of my auntie Salley. I was on a playground near our apartment in Vauxhall, and there were these two guys who jumped me. They were both hitting me. I grabbed a rock and put it in my hand, and I just started hitting one of the guys. Then all of a sudden I couldn't feel the other guy hitting me from behind anymore.

I turned around and Betty Ann Hill had him on the ground and "Boom! Boom! Boom!" she was just beating the crap out of this guy. I was like, "Wow." So we became friends. It turns out when we moved to Summit, her cousins lived right down the street from us. So I would see her pretty often even after we moved to Summit. She was the first friend I had in Jersey, and we were close for a while.

Then when we moved to Summit within two days I was in another scrap. This was with Anthony Zachary and his sister, Wendy. I don't remember why it started, but I didn't want to hit Wendy. So every time she would swing, I would turn her away from me like a karate move, then I would wheel back around and hit him. Later Zach and I became pretty good friends. We were on the football and basketball teams together when we got to high school.

Then school started, and that was a shock, as well. We had moved to Summit

*My senior photo.*

Summit High School Yearbook

33

because the school system was better. What I wasn't prepared for was that it was almost all white. Every school in Summit was integrated.

In Montgomery, I was in an all black school. My first experience of even being around white people was on the bus and in the bus station when we came to New Jersey. But when I got to Lincoln Elementary School, all the teachers were white. Everybody was white. Our classes, starting in elementary school averaged two, maybe three black kids.

I had this really thick Southern accent, and because of that they told me they would be giving me speech lessons. I think you were considered kind of dumb or "slow" if you had that Southern accent, and all that. So I had speech lessons for almost two years because the school was so rich. After my first year I had a C average, but my mom didn't think it was good enough so she told them to hold me back. She said, "Keep him until he gets A's and B's." This is the mother I've only known for a few months, and she's telling them to hold me back.

So, I stayed back in the third grade, and that's when I met the twins, Bobby and Sammy Gregory. These two guys would become my two best friends. I don't know why, but the twins hooked on to me, and I hooked on to them. They were just so easygoing. I'm trying to think of some way to explain how the whole family was. They had a lot of money, but they were one of those families that you never knew had money. They came to school in jeans and T-shirts just like everyone else. Mrs. Gregory made them do everything normal. They weren't that "richy-rich" kind of family.

Their family looked like the Kennedy's, I'm telling you, man. If you were to look at Sam and Bobby, that's what you would have thought. Sam is a lawyer now, Bobby runs the family business. They kind of adopted me, and another kid named Kenny Shamblee. Kenny stole something from their house, and they disowned him. But their house was almost like a second home for me from that time all the way through high school. Color was never mentioned in their house. They never talked about black and white, and Mrs. Gregory treated me with the utmost respect. When you were at their house, you were family.

They were the kind of people who were in my life from the time I got to Summit until I left. I got to know people who just looked at you as a person, not whether you were black or because you were white. I think that's why even to this day I don't judge anyone by whether they are black or white. I judge people by how they treat me.

My high school football coach, Howie Anderson was the same way. He was a man of honor. Mr. (Dominick) Guida, who was the first one to get me to play baseball, he was a man of honor. He was a man of integrity. All the coaches I had were that way. If you could play, they didn't care if you were black, white or indifferent. Every man that was in my life at that point was a positive influence, a good human being. Those guys are positive guys, and it was really great to deal with that.

I thought, you know, once I got into this game (baseball) that I would run into the same kind of people. It didn't work out that way. This game is a business. But here's what I don't understand. The good ones don't treat it like a business, and they get the very best out of their players. The ones who treat it as a business are the ones who don't get the best out of their players because the players begin treating it like a business. I would learn that later when Tony LaRussa was my manager with the A's.

I started playing organized sports about the fifth grade in the Pop Warner League. It was football, not baseball. I needed to buy a uniform … here's an example of what I'm telling you about the Gregorys. Mrs. Gregory bought my first football uniform for me. I don't know what happened. I don't know who talked to who. But one day, Mrs. Gregory just said, "Here. Here's a uniform." We all played – Sammy, Bobby, me. Later, in high school Sammy was a wrestler. Bobby was a wrestler, too, but he was more of a football player.

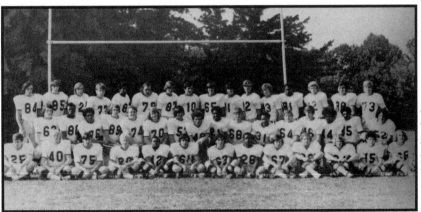

*Football was THE sport in Summit. This was my senior-year team. I'm wearing No. 21 in the middle of the second row.*

*Summit High School Yearbook*

*I signed a letter to play football at Maryland where I hoped they would give me the same No. 21 I wore at Summit.*

I was the quarterback on our youth teams. And everybody was happy around us. There was this running back named Mike Montgomery. He was happy, and his dad was happy. I just played quarterback. This is when I first learned about jealousy and how it affects people.

When we got to high school, the coach already had a junior and senior who were first and second quarterback. Coach thought I could be a better running back. That's when the Montgomerys got mad because I beat him out for running back. He quit. His father never really forgave me.

Summit is a small town. I attended three schools: Lincoln Elementary School, Summit Junior High and Summit High School. Because it was a small town, there were these little cliques. I don't know what it was, but I seemed to get more flack from the black people than I did from the white people. I don't know whether it was jealousy or not … that's what I think.

I didn't start playing baseball until the summer after my 8th grade year. That was the first summer I didn't go back down to Alabama. That was when I met Mr. Guida down at the recreation center. He had seen me playing football, and for some reason he must have seen something in me. He was always preaching the positive. I was hanging around the recreation center, and he said, "Why don't you get off that bike you are riding and go do something constructive." Being a smartass, I said, "What would you have me do, Mr. Guida?"

He said, "Why don't you go play baseball?" So I said I would go over and give it a shot. It was a summer league, and it was first come, first serve. If you played last summer at a certain position, you played that position. If someone was better than you, it didn't matter. If you were there first, you got to play. The only position that was open was catcher. So I started off being a catcher ... well, I didn't play. I sat on the bench and was a pinch runner that summer. But it was so cool to have something to go do in the summertime instead of just riding your bike around.

I always thought I had a weird body. I didn't have a chest. But they knew I was quick. We had our T-shirts, the baggy baseball pants and our socks. The shoes were given to us. So I would sit on the bench and pinch run. Then, the next year, I made the 9th grade team, and I was the catcher. The next summer I was the starting catcher.

I loved it. If you want to know how to play baseball you should become a catcher. Fortunately for me, one of our coaches in high school had played Triple-A for the Philadelphia Phillies and he was a catcher. So he taught me how to be a catcher.

I was a catcher until I turned professional. I loved catching, man. My idol was Manny Sanguillen. You know, (cocking his leg out to the side) he had that leg out there, and he would have that one hand tucked behind his back. Elston Howard was with the Yankees, but I hated the Yankees. At the time, Pittsburgh was winning, and we would occasionally get some Pirates games – you know you only got so many games back in those days because there were only three channels. I fell in love with Manny Sanguillen because he was the only other black catcher I could see. And also because of the way he

*Summit High School Yearbook*

*Memorial Field in Summit didn't have any fences. All the home runs I hit were "inside the park."*

batted. That's why I loved him, for real (laughing). You throw, one right down the middle, and it was a strike. He would just look at it. You throw, one up here by his eyes and he would go, "A-ha!" I liked that guy. He swung at everything. That's what I did. I swung at everything. So, Manny was my guy. In football it was the Kansas Comet, Gale Sayers. I didn't even know he was from Kansas at the time. He was already with the Bears.

I played sports all the time. I played football. I played basketball and I played baseball. In high school they ran into each other, and you just went from one right into the other. At that particular time baseball was the No. 3 sport. Football was the No. 1 sport. As it turned out, in football I was a two-time All-America and in baseball, I was a two-time All-America. But basketball was my second favorite sport.

I didn't know I was a really good athlete in the beginning. I knew I was OK, and everything came to me pretty easily, but then when I was in the 11th grade and we went undefeated in football it was cool. I kind of knew I was pretty good at basketball with the older guys around the playground. There was this guy named Brent Cromwell, who played for Winston Salem. He was the sixth man on the team with Earl "The

*My second favorite sport after football was basketball when I was in high school.*

Summit High School Yearbook

Pearl" Monroe. He was left-handed and tall. I would play with them starting in 9th grade, and he was the one who said I was pretty good, so I kind of had an idea.

Our football team won the championship when I was a junior, I was All-American. I think I was on the All-America second team. I was All America in football and baseball my senior year, and an all-state basketball player.

I had an idea that I might be drafted in baseball because my basketball coach was one of the summer league baseball coaches, Eddie Lyons. Eddie had told me a lot of scouts said I was going to be the No. 1 draft choice in America. Philadelphia had the No. 1 draft choice. But I didn't really want to play baseball. I was a football player in my brain. I wanted to go to school.

I was going to get a free ride, study business, carry a briefcase and wear a tie. That is what I wanted because I saw all the rich people in Summit carrying briefcases and wearing a tie. They were the ones with pretty big houses. So, I wanted to do what they were doing.

In high school was also the first time I ever felt the pressure of expectations. After we won the state championship in my junior year I felt like I had the pressure of not letting anybody down.

Can't let my mom down.

Can't let my high school coach down.

Can't let the kids down.

Can't let the teachers down.

Can't let anybody down.

When you feel like you can't let anybody down, you take everything so hard. I took losses really hard. Because of the coaches I had, I never flaunted it when we won. I wasn't one of those guys strutting around saying, "We won! We won!" But if we lost I really took it hard. I didn't know how ... I don't think anybody who is really a winner in high school ever takes losing easy. You might accept it a little better as you get older. But when I was in high school I didn't want to accept losing. I didn't like losing. I took it to the point where I never wanted to feel that way again.

*Summit High School Yearbook*

*I didn't wear a baseball cap too often because I was a catcher. I wore what would keep me warm. Spring baseball in New Jersey could be cold.*

*Summit High School Yearbook*

*When I was a senior we won the Suburban Conference championship.*

When I got to be a baseball player, you play 162 games. You're going to lose 70 or 80 games. So you learn. But I'm telling you, it's a learning process. It was hard for me to learn that. So I was mad every day we lost for about the first five or six years of my baseball career. You know how hard it is to be angry every day. It is really hard, man.

I was a B student in high school. I could have been an A student, but I didn't want to be. It seems like sometimes the more successful I was the more flack you got. I needed a B average to get into Maryland, and my mom wanted me to have Bs, so when I got a B or above, I was good. She would go crazy if I got a C. But I wanted the B's because of Maryland.

# 5
# ROLE MODELS

It was very difficult for me to be a role model in the beginning – heck, I didn't even think I should be. I thought your parents should be your role model for everything except, maybe, how someone approached their job.

I had two athletic role models when I was growing up. It wasn't a guy who said the right thing or by what he did off the field. My guys were role models because of what they did on the field, how they played the game, what they did in the game and how exciting they were.

The two guys I had were Gale Sayers and Manny Sanguillen.

I don't know why, but Pittsburgh used to be on television back in New Jersey a lot. You had Roberto (Clemente) and Willie (Stargell). You know there weren't a whole lot of channels back then, but their games would come on.

I was a catcher, so for me there weren't too many catchers who were black. I hate to say that because I'm not a prejudiced person, going to an almost all-white school, but I wanted to see people like me on the field. The Pirates had people like me. The Yankees had Elston Howard, but for some reason I just didn't adapt to the way he caught. He caught the most proper fundamentals, by the book.

But Manny ... he had that right foot hanging out. He would get way down low, and it was like he always had fun back there. And he could just hit. You throw a ball down the middle and he would take it for a strike. You throw it eye high, and he would just go, yeow, and slash at it. For some reason, I just liked him.

I never met him until years later, after I retired. We were doing an event down in Puerto Rico. I was participating in Roberto Clemente's family event. And I got to sit at a table with Manny Sanguillen. I was like a kid in a candy store. I asked him everything. I was like, "Manny, you were my idol." He was smiling and having a good time. He was just my guy in baseball.

In football, it was Gale Sayers, the Kansas Comet. When I would watch games I would watch how he would anticipate a guy coming at him and making a move. When he cut, he never cut on his toes. He cut on his heels – bet you didn't know that. When I would practice running, that's how I would cut. You can go a lot more quickly on your heels. And I would watch how he would go through holes and how he would juke people and all that. Again, his teams were on TV.

Gale came to visit me when I was in high school. I had cracked a bone in my back, and I was in a hospital. I'm lying down, propped up on a pillow. My coach walked in the door first, and right after him is Gale Sayers. My eyes just lit up. I'm trying to sit up straight, lean up so I can talk to Gale Sayers, man. I mean, this is Gale Sayers. I'm like "Wow, man!" He said just stay there. He shook my hand and started talking about recruiting me to play at Kansas for football. Really, I don't think I heard a word he said. I was just staring at him. I mean this was Gale Sayers.

I was never really involved in a lot of Yankees games. They were just too, "establishment." Eventually, I became a Mets fan because of the Miracle Mets. I started loving Jerry Grote – I actually got a chance to play with him in Kansas City when he was near the end of his career – I really liked Bud Harrelson, too. The guy on the Mets I really had respect for was Felix Milan, the second baseman. He and Pete Rose got into at least one fight, and I hated Pete Rose as a player. I thought he played kind of dirty sometimes. I met Pete Rose later on, and he's all right, but when you are a kid, you got your guys that you like.

I can sort of relate to how kids stare at me now. I mean I just stared at Gale Sayers when he came to see me. I mean, I was just looking at him from the head to the toes, his fingers, his hands, everything. So, I can sort of realize now how kids might have looked at me back in the day. But I never thought of myself like that. I never put myself in that category. I always thought if you did that it made you seem like you were big-headed or cocky. I never wanted to be perceived like that.

But it turned out I was like that in a lot of ways.

The real role models in my life and (people who taught me) how I should live were not athletes.

My grandmother (Madear), of course. Madear taught me the basics.

My auntie Martha Ann was a big role model, and my aunt Salley. My mother taught me the value of hard work.

My mom used to say every now and then, "You aren't the sharpest knife in the drawer." But she was a good role model. Almost before I even got to know her for a year she had them hold me back because the Cs I got in second grade weren't good enough. She taught me how to work hard because she had to work hard. She worked two jobs to keep food on the table for two kids and my grandmother.

My uncles in Alabama were good role models. My mom was smart enough to send me down there for the summers. My uncle Frank (Martha's husband) Gardner and my uncle Richard (Salley's husband) Calhoun were in my life toward the beginning. Slick (Frank) used to get up and go to work. He worked at a dairy place, and on the weekends he worked on a farm outside the town. For me, I did what they said to do. I never questioned anything, I just did it. They were very positive from the beginning.

When I got to Summit it was Coach (Howie) Anderson, Mr. (Art) Cottrell, Coach Lyons and of course, Mr. Guida.

Mr. Guida, Dominick Guida, treated everybody the same. He was head of the recreation center, and you had kids coming from everywhere all over Summit. He just treated everybody the same. That

*Wilson family photo*

*The women in my life. From left: aunt Martha, aunt Salley, aunt Lula and my mother, Dorothy Lynn. They were all great role models growing up.*

was something I always treasured. It didn't matter who you were, what color you were. If you were a good person, he treated you the same. If you were a bad person, he didn't want you around. That's what I got from Mr. Guida. He never called me Willie, always called me Will. Even after the drug thing happened in 1983 and 1984, he was always the same. He never changed.

Howie taught me to win, and he let us have fun winning, but he also taught me to turn the other cheek in high school. There were certain times I wasn't going to turn my cheek. But there is that old saying: You have to pick your battles. In high school I had to turn the other cheek. If a guy hit you hard after the whistle blew, I learned not to get up and do something. He would always say to me, "Will, you are more valuable on the field than off the field. So, if someone hits you, you walk away."

I would go, "Why should I walk away?" He would very patiently say, "You are more valuable on the field than off the field." So, he taught me to stay on the field. Later on in the minor leagues he wasn't there, and you don't have that guidance. You just have other dudes. Now you are going all macho. I'm a macho guy, and I'm not going to let someone do that to me. In the minor leagues you are fighting for your life. In the major leagues you are fighting when it is appropriate. If a guy is throwing at your head, I'm going to fight. If he is throwing at your legs, I'm going to steal second and third. I'm going to get back at you that way.

Those coaches were all positive role models. Summit was a city where there weren't a whole lot of black people. That city could have been a whole lot different if they had been prejudiced. I'm sure there were some areas where there was prejudice. But I never saw it. I think maybe I never saw it because I was good in sports.

I think they looked out for me, too. I don't mean cheat like, "I'm going to give you a grade," what they did was lay out very clearly, "You have to do this to get there." They were showing me in little ways what I had to do to dedicate myself to being successful.

One of the teachers who had a big influence was Mrs. Meskin, Leslie Meskin. She helped me understand that with social issues there also was a right and wrong way. She was a young lady who had just got out of college, probably in her early 20s. I remember one time I had gone out with this girl, a white girl, and it was taboo back in the day, in the

'70s. She noticed how sad I was sitting in her room, and she asked me to talk. I told her what happened, and I remember it as clearly as if she was sitting right beside me today. She said, "Well they can't do that." I think she was letting me know that some people who are not black are pretty good people.

That's why I think when I had somebody tell me I couldn't do something, in my mind I could hear her say, "Well they can't do that." She was very influential for me.

And there was "Mr. B" – Wally Binford, a little small black man. Mr. B lived in Summit, and he was a friend of our family. I don't know how old he was, but if he was 70, you would swear he was 50. He just had that much energy. He exercised every day. When I was playing football, there was a track around the football field. I would be running for a touchdown, and he would be running right along beside me on the track.

For some reason, he kept showing up wherever I was in baseball. I don't know if my mom was sending him to keep an eye on me or what, but about two or three weeks before the season would end he would just show up, and he would end up driving home with me. He wouldn't drive. He would sit on the passenger side, and I would drive. He wore a Royals cap and a Royals jacket. I don't think he ever paid to get in a game. He would show up some place like Yankee Stadium and just walk in.

He would tell me he saw Babe Ruth, Josh Gibson, all the great players. He would tell me, "Now, Will, the good athletes, the good superstars, could play in any era, but you guys are bigger, stronger faster." One time I remember he was talking to me – and I will never forget this – he was asking me why I didn't dive for a ball. He said, "If you don't dive how do you know you can't catch it? You gotta try. If you never take a chance, you won't know when you should and when you shouldn't. You gotta take a chance and dive for a ball that first time. Then later on you will know I can get it or I can't get it."

He was always in my ear, about baseball, about athletics, about everything. He would always pump me up, and always give me little life lessons like that.

# 6
# I'M GOING TO
# PLAY FOOTBALL

"*T*he night before the draft I stayed out real late because I
*wanted to avoid the phone. I prayed that I wouldn't be drafted. It all
seems so clear to me. I was going to a good college where I'd be a big man,
have a lot of fun and help build a power.*"
—Willie Wilson, Newark Ledger Star, 1974.

So the day of the baseball draft comes, and the phone starts ringing
about 7 o'clock in the morning. My mother had gone to work, and my
grandmother was tired of answering the phone. So it was me.

"Hello"

"This is so and so"

"I'm going to play football."

Click.

Over and over. I did that about 10 or 12 times. Click. Click. Click.
So I'm thinking I have told everybody I was going to play football.

I get to school, and I'm walking down the hallway and here comes
basketball coach Eddie Lyons, who also coached baseball in the summer
league. He is smiling real big, and I say, "What's up coach?"

"Congratulations, you just got picked No. 1 by the Kansas City
Royals."

I go, "Where's Kansas City?"

I was so mad. The only team that didn't call was the Kansas City
Royals. I guess they thought they would just take a chance and draft
me anyway. Then I was really upset because I thought that disqualified
me from playing football in college. Coach Lyons said, "No, this is great

47

because you can negotiate." I thought if I was drafted, I couldn't play college football. They had just changed the rule that you could be a pro in one sport and go to school in another sport.

I had decided to go to Maryland earlier in the year and signed a letter of intent. It was exactly what I pictured a college campus would be like. It was also the first place I visited, and I think I compared everything against Maryland on all my other visits. When I visited Michigan and Ohio State, they were like cities in themselves. At Michigan they were driving me through campus, and we had been going for like 20 minutes and I asked where we were, and they go, "We're still at the university." I thought, "How can you go to school at a place like this?"

So for me it was Maryland. It was three hours or so from New Jersey where my mom could just drive down and watch a game. It would be a lot easier for my coaches and my friends to come down and see me. And I was an East Coast guy. They also were going to let me play baseball in the spring. The last reason I wanted to go to Maryland was that they stressed education. Growing up in Summit, I had a lot of positive figures who stressed education, from my mother, who had them hold me back in 3rd grade with a C average to all the coaches at the school.

*My mother, Dorothy Lynn, and Royals GM, Lou Gorman, were with me on signing day at Royals Stadium in 1974.*

*Wilson family photo*

The university sold itself.

It almost freaked me out on my visit down there, though. I had never been on an airplane. They pick me up at the Newark Airport in a helicopter that took me over to LaGuardia. Then I got on a flight from New York to Baltimore. When I got there, they picked me up, and the first guy taking me around is Walter White, who later played for the Chiefs and still lives in Kansas City. He was my guy. I met him and Randy White and a couple of other guys who made the NFL. Maryland had a great basketball team with Lefty Driesell. So it was going to be pretty cool.

Maryland coach Jerry Claiborne was another truthful man. He told me I was going to start as a freshman, so I figured I had a real shot at playing. Then I met Randy White. That kind of changed my mind about a lot of things. That guy was huge. I did not want to run into that guy every day in practice. So that at least opened up my mind about considering other options when I got drafted.

*This shirt was all the style when I signed with the Royals in 1974.*

Wilson family photo

After I knew I could negotiate with the Royals and still play college football, if I wanted, we decided to do that. My football coach Howie Anderson hooked me up with Gill Owren, an attorney in Summit. Gill had been a quarterback for Howie on one of his first teams at Summit High School, then he had gone on to be a lawyer. So Howie asked Gill to do my

> *"I think he could have made it in pro football directly out of high school as a wide receiver or a defensive back, but not as a running back"*
>
> *—Howie Anderson, high school coach*

contract, and he also told him not to charge me for it. Gill is a great guy. I see him when I go back to Summit.

So now I'm thinking, "OK, if I can go back to school let's go check this out." So I am thinking what does a No. 1 get? When I found out it was about $100,000 my mom says, "Child, if you get that I can pay my bills."

Al Diez was the Royals scout on the East Coast. A couple of years earlier he had convinced the Royals to draft Dennis Leonard in the first round. So Al is scouting me, talking to my baseball coach, who was Art Cottrell. Cottrell was letting Howie know that teams really were interested.

Al came to the apartment in Summit to try and get me signed. They were trying to lowball me in the beginning. He said he could only go so far with the contract. But Gill had done his homework, and he said as a No. 1 draft choice, $50,000 wasn't going to cut it. Al said, "Well if you're really interested we will have to bring you out to Kansas City." So it ended up being Howie, Gill, my mother and me. They flew us out here.

It was really a weird negotiation. I wasn't allowed to speak to the Royals because of the college rules. It was like if I talked to the Royals I wouldn't be eligible to play in college. You could be a pro and play college in a different sport, but you couldn't actually do the negotiating with them.

So we are sitting in this room upstairs in the Royals offices, and I'm listening to everything they're saying. But they're not talking to me. They are talking to Gill. Then Gill turns to me and he says the exact thing to me. I answer Gill – and they're

*A lot of people felt let down when Willie signed a baseball contract because they wanted to see him play football. He was better in football than he was in baseball. I've seen a lot of football players and he was the best I've ever seen ... the best prospect anyway"*
*—Gill Owren, his agent*

listening. Then Gill tells them what I was saying – even though they heard me saying exactly the same thing.

So we go back and forth on numbers. He was asking for $100,000 – which is what he got. But they had to work their way up to it, and they promised to pay for college if I still wanted to go. I could probably still go to college today, and they'd have to pay for it. But I never really did think about it after I signed with the Royals. The other thing is that the contract said is that I would get to come to spring training the very next year with the big team. After that I had to do something to get on the 40-man roster.

But the really funny thing was how my mother reacted to the whole thing.

We had negotiations the one day we were in Kansas City. We were getting close. So, they had us stay overnight, and they put us up in the old Muehlebach Hotel downtown. So, we are in the hotel and talking about the contract. My mom had lost her job the year before when she got fired for taking off work to watch one of my games. She had gotten permission, then her boss decided to change his mind and have her work. But she took off anyway. So, she had been out of work since then.

I knew she didn't have a job, but I wasn't consciously aware that she owed a bunch of money. I think maybe subconsciously I was. But when we started negotiation, she let me in on how much she owed. And of course I said: "Well if we get this, then we will just pay all that off."

Sometime that night, the tornado sirens started going off. We're in the Muehlebach downtown, and my mom is trying to read the back of the door, trying to figure out what is going on. She didn't read too well, but she's trying to figure this out. So I look at it and I say: "They say go into the bathroom and get into the tub." So here we are, sirens going off and we're standing there in the tub.

It was me and my mom, and we're having a conversation, "You think they are really going to give you all that money."

I was saying, "I don't know Mom, but I hope so." This was all new to me.

As far as the physical aspect, it was a great decision comparing football to baseball. But one of the main reasons I chose baseball was because my mom was in financial trouble. My stepfather and my mother divorced when I was a child. She was doing the best she could, working two jobs part of the time. But when you have kids, they have needs. So, I imagine there were a lot of things that piled up in those few months.

But gawd, that was funny. The sirens were going off, and we're standing there in the tub hanging onto the shower rod just talking about it. It was just crazy. The very next day we signed the contract. The first

*Here I'm with Royals GM Lou Gorman on signing day.*

thing I did was pay $30,000 worth of bills for my mom. She said it was like the whole weight of the world was lifted off her shoulders. But with the taxes, and my mother's bills there wasn't much left after that.

After we signed the deal, they wanted me to go downstairs to take batting practice with the team. The Royals were all out on the field, so nobody was in the lockerroom. I pulled on that uniform, and I walked up out into the park and, "Wow!" Everything was just brand, spanking new – the stadium, the turf. It was so big and huge and clean. I had never seen anything like it.

So, I step into the cage, and Big John (Mayberry) and AO (Amos Otis) are standing there watching. And I'm just so excited. I'm trying to hit something really hard and get the ball out of the park. It seemed like the harder I tried to hit the ball out of the park, I would hit a line drive to right field. Boom! Right field. Boom! Right field. Then I hear somebody say, "Hey, Charley he's a good student" or something like that. Charley Lau, the Royals batting coach taught everybody to go the opposite way.

*Courtesy of Kansas City Royals*

*My mother, Dorothy Lynn, was with me when I signed my first contract with the Royals. Standing (from left) Assistant GM John Schuerholz (who seems to have copied my sense of style), Summit Football coach Howie Anderson, Royals Scout Al Diez, Royals GM Lou Gorman and Wilson's agent Gill Owren.*

So, I'm supposed to take five swings, and I take 10. Then the next time I'm supposed to take six. And I take 10. So now I can hear Amos and Mayberry go, "Well, he can't count."

They were losing out on their batting practice because I was taking too many cuts. Then it was over, and everybody went inside. I couldn't stay down there and BS with any of the guys because they were going to introduce me during the game. I took my shower because I had to go up into the stands. I'm dressing back into my regular clothes, and they just started getting all over me about the batting practice.

"You're a number one?"

"You are just punching the ball to right field. You can't even pull the ball."

"What the heck are they doing signing you?"

I got so mad I turned around to Amos and said, "I'll be coming back in four years to take your job!"

Everybody looked at him like "Oooooooh." He just looked at me, and of course he dropped a couple of F-bombs on me as I left. But I said, "I'll be coming back." And I was really serious. That was a big motivating factor to get me back there. I think he remembered me saying "I'll take your job," and I think that is why he was so mean to me when I first got back to the team.

So, we're sitting right behind the Royals dugout – my mother, Gill, Howie and me. Then they introduced me. "Meet our No. 1 draft choice … " I stood up and waved. At the end of the game we started leaving, and I remember this kid came up to me and asked me for my autograph. That was my first autograph, right there.

I don't think I met Mr. K (owner Ewing Kauffman) this trip. If I did, I can't remember. It was Mr. (John) Schuerholz, he was the assistant GM. And I met the GM, Lou Gorman. But my first impression of Royals Stadium was, "Wow, this is really great. I didn't know stuff could be like this, look like this, a regular field of turf, 30,000 or 40,000 people. Everything was just so clean and brand new. I was just in awe, and I was thinking I gotta get back up here."

The other thing that was pretty funny about that trip is something that happened when we were upstairs on the fifth floor of Royals Stadium during the negotiations. I didn't know anybody on the team, not even their names. Back in Summit I followed the Pirates, the Yankees, the Mets and the Phillies when I was growing up. I hadn't even ever looked at a Royals box score, I don't think. I mean, I really didn't care before I came to Kansas City because I didn't think I was going to be there, I thought I still was going to be going to college and playing football.

But there was one guy I remembered as soon as I saw him.

For some reason John Mayberry had come upstairs before the game when we were in negotiations, and he was walking through in his uniform. As he walked by the door of the room we're in, I hear my mom go "Mmmmmm." That was the first time I had ever heard her say that, so I looked right away and see Mayberry walking by. I think to myself, "I'm going to be watching that guy. I'm keeping track of him." I mean my mother was still young, in her 30s. And I'm thinking like "Nah, that ain't gonna happen." I mean she was a good-looking lady. And I was like "Uh-oh." So I knew John before I knew anybody else.

# 7
# I NEVER PLAYED
# THE OUTFIELD

Within days after graduating from high school I was in Sarasota, Fla. playing in the Rookie League. We had a party back in Summit, and then I got on a plane and flew down to Florida. It was my first time in Florida. The Royals had two guys pick me up at the airport, Joe Gates and Darrell Parker. We were on our way back to Clark Road and the training complex, when we stopped off in this area of Sarasota called New Town. It was all black. Joe and Darrell knew a couple of girls there.

I'm just off the plane and I'm sitting in the car for about an hour or so. They just left me sitting in the car, and I'm thinking, "What the heck is going on? I don't even know these guys and already they're abandoning me."

Finally we got to the Royals Academy. It was the first year they had stopped doing the Academy, but that's where all their players in rookie ball stayed. It was like a dormitory — rooms, classes, recreational halls, a pool and a cafeteria. There were four fields. I think my first contract was for $500 a month, and by the time they took out the little bit of taxes, you needed to live on a campus (like the Academy).

The very next day I got my uniform and everything like that and I was on the field that day. I went straight into the outfield.

They had drafted me as an outfielder. Everybody knew I could run. When we would run our sprints, I would always win them. But even though I had never played outfield in my life, they had it in their brain I was going to be an outfielder. I didn't even have an outfielder's glove. You know you're supposed to use the long glove. I liked to feel the ball when I caught it. I never liked those gloves that were so long you couldn't feel anything. I just couldn't run with one of those big, tall gloves. So all my gloves through my whole career were short because my catcher's glove was short.

The first glove I had was a MacGregor, and it was made of kangaroo leather. I had that glove for a long time. I got it restrung several times, and it really looked ugly because it was restrung so many times. I think I also played with an A2000. I had so many gloves after that first one, but I could never find one that fit me like that first one I had.

I not only had to figure out what glove worked for me, I didn't have a clue what I was doing in the outfield. I barely even knew where to line up, and I sure didn't know how deep to play people. We did a lot of drills, and I was really working extra. I had two managers in the minor leagues. Billy Scripture was my rookie ball coach and my Double-A coach. John Sullivan was my A-ball coach and my Triple-A coach.

It was up to Scrip to teach me how to play the outfield. What Scrip did was that he found out what motivated me. Money motivated me. So he would put a ball bag on second base and he would say, "If you hit that bag, I'll give you a dollar every time you hit it."

That made me concentrate. I had to learn how to make my toes right, put my body in the right position and make my arm right so I could aim and throw at the bag. I'd be doing drills–ground balls, fly balls, line drives, Texas leaguers, hump back. I probably dropped three or four of the first fly balls that were hit to me. They went up in the air, and it was like "holy cow."

Balls had been coming at me from a guy's hand just 60 feet away. It wasn't like I had been watching someone swing a bat, hit it and then have to

*The Royals always kept my mom up to date on what was happening with me as I made my way to the major leagues.*

judge where it was going. I hadn't even shagged any fly balls when I was in high school. When we did our drills in high school I did them as catcher. When I went to shag balls I went to the infield, short or second. I wasn't going to walk all the way into the outfield.

---

*"I sent two other scouts to New Jersey to take a look at Wilson in competition. Both reports came back that Wilson had excellent physical skills, and he was a definite Major League prospect. The reports also indicated that Wilson had exceptional speed and should move to the outfield to utilize his speed and range for his speed would be lost behind the plate."*

*—Former Royals GM Lou Gorman in "High and Inside: My Life in the Front Offices of Baseball"*

---

I don't know if I had ever been in the outfield. When the ball went up in the air I just couldn't judge where it was going to come down, and I'd end up missing a few balls. Seemed like my first instinct would be to go one way and the ball would be somewhere else, so it was different, and it was really tough.

I missed a lot of balls out there in the outfield, and all of a sudden everybody was talking about me. That hadn't ever happened before. When people were talking about me before it was always about good things. So this was different. I felt like guys were hounding me.

"How could you be the No. 1?"

"You can't hit."

"You can't field."

"You can't throw."

Everything I was doing seemed to be hard. The hitting was hard. The catching a ball in the outfield was hard. The trying to make my arm be a long-throwing arm like an outfielder instead of a cock-it-back-at-the-ear thrower like a catcher was hard. Everything seemed to be hard.

It was the first time in my life anything was that hard. I didn't cope too well in the beginning. I was feeling sorry for myself. I was still torn up because I had mixed emotions about baseball and football. I was homesick. But feeling sorry for yourself just magnified everything. And I didn't know how to joke around. I was a football player. If you talk about somebody, you are hounding them. I know now that they were all joking. But I couldn't take it then. If you said something I was fighting mad. I was quiet, but I had a quick temper. When guys were getting on me I would withdraw even more. Then I'd get my feelings hurt, and start crying. I'm telling you, when a tear came out of my eye I was going to hit somebody. Somebody was going to get hit. I was fighting my own teammates, fighting other guys.

I finally got it and learned when people were getting on you, you can feel sorry for yourself or you can do what I did. I just got mad. I was in scuffles and arguments every day. It was like, "This is what you guys think I'm doing, I'm going to prove to you that I can play this game."

But it wasn't immediate. I not only wanted to play better to show them, I wanted to play better for me.

So we're about halfway through the season, and I was really hitting in the low 100s or something. Then I got really hot and made the all-star team for that league. But I had real trouble with pitchers for a while – and the reason is because they were so wild. It was hard to stand in and hit against them because you never knew if you were going to get hit.

Here's an example.

*"I'd like to be able to say Willie's hitting .350 with six home runs, but I can't. He's been more impressive with his running speed, and his arm has improved greatly since he's been playing centerfield. He was a catcher all through high school,"*
*—John Schuerholz during Wilson's first minor-league season.*

When you are in high school you might find one, maybe two, guys in the whole league pitching-wise that are going to even make it to Single-A or Double-A. Now, when you get to the minor leagues, you have the best players in their city or state or college. You were one of the best players in your state, but now you are competing against a bunch of guys who were also the best. You are figuring out, "I'm better than this guy and that guy, but what about the guy over there?" So with the pitching, you get the best players from all around and you put them in the rookie league. In rookie ball you might have only one guy out of that five who has control. The rest of them are just raw.

They can throw the ball hard, but they're going to throw it anywhere at any time all over the frickin' place. So for me, it was hard to stay in and hit. You have guys who can throw really hard and end up maybe throwing a no-hitter in the big leagues who were wild as hell in the minors. So it was very tough, not just for me but for everyone in the rookie league.

Billy would do crazy stuff to try and teach us to stay in the batters box with wild pitchers. If a guy was bailing out, he would turn on the machine and let the machine toss a ball into his own chest and say, "See, it won't hurt you." We're all rookies, 17, 18 years old. Our first time in professional baseball, and this is the guy we run into – a crazy man who has pitching machines throw balls into his own chest.

When you get to Single-A ball you might have two pitchers who have control. When you get to Double-A you might have three of those pitchers who have control – what I mean by that is maybe three of them who will make the majors at some point. When you get to Triple-A you might have four guys, maybe five who have control and know where the ball is going and when you get to the big leagues you are supposedly facing five out of five.

> *"Having Willie Wilson in centerfield is like having four outfielders, which says something about the range and speed right there."*
> —Rookie manager Billy Scripture in 1974

So, in that way, it's easier to hit the higher you get in the minors. That's how I did it. I would have loved to hit for a higher average in the minor leagues all the way through and hit higher in the big leagues. But the way I look at it, most of the guys who hit higher in the minor leagues don't hit higher in the big leagues. George (Brett), one of the greatest hitter of all time, never hit .300 in the minor leagues.

It might have helped my hitting if I had stayed a catcher because I would have been seeing pitchers every day from that perspective. I wouldn't have been worrying about playing a whole new position and have that occupying my mind. And when you look at a catcher who hits .250 it doesn't look that bad. But you get to the outfield … that's where you have guys hitting .320, .330 with 24 home runs and 100-some RBIs. For me it was, "OK, what do you have to do different to get in the same category with those guys?" I might have broken every record in the world if I had stayed as a catcher with speed, but I would have gotten bigger, my knees would have gotten sorer. I probably wouldn't have stolen as many bases.

So it worked out the way it worked out. I think the hitting would have been easier early in my career if I had been a catcher. But the Royals drafted me as an outfielder from the very beginning. Being a catcher was never on their mind for me.

After the season was over I went home for a few days, and then I came back down to Florida for Instructional League. Scrip was down there for that. Scrip was one of those old baseball characters. At that time we didn't have SportsCenter or MLB Network or anything like that. We only had "This Week in Baseball." They would come down and do things on Billy because he did some weird stuff, man. He would do things like take a bite and tear the cover off a baseball. So they were coming down to do films of him all the time.

Another weird thing about Billy is that he seemed to take a special interest in me. They would bring the top prospects down in the winter, the same complex where the Rookie League guys stayed. Nobody had a car down there, but there was one station wagon at the complex. Billy used to let me have the station wagon, I guess because I was always on time. If he said curfew was 11, that's when I was back. The guys knew, when I was driving, that the car was parked in a particular place. When it got to be 30 minutes before curfew, we would meet back at the car.

I'd tell them, "If you are not here, you're done because I'm leaving." So he always let me have the car … I don't know why. And he would take me places with him.

Billy was a world-class skeet shooter. He would always take me with him skeet shooting. Like on a day when we only worked half a day, the other half he would tell me to get in the car with him and we would go some place or some event where he would be skeet shooting. I saw him hit 99 out of 100 from the hip one day – not aiming – just firing from the hip.

I don't know why he did that, I don't know if it was to keep me out of trouble or for me to see and experience something different or just to keep me occupied. I respected him for that. I got to see another side of life.

# 8
# MY INTRODUCTION TO THE MIDWEST

$B$ecause it was written into my contract, I got to go to spring training with the big-league team that first year I was there. I was real nervous. I had met some of the guys on the team when I signed the summer before. But I didn't have a great deal of comfort coming into spring training.

As stupid as it sounds, I thought, if I had a great spring I could make the club. That shows you how naïve I really was.

Back in the old days at Fort Myers we had our camp at Terry Park. The clubhouse wasn't like the clubhouses of today with carpeting and big leather chairs or anything like that. It had a plank floor, and all the rookies lockers were along a back wall of the clubhouse. After a couple of weeks the number of guys on that back wall kept getting thinner and thinner because the guys were being assigned to their minor league teams.

So the guys who were staying the longest, you pretty much knew those were the guys they were looking at as far as the future. I didn't last on that wall too long that first year.

While I was there, though, I got a little taste of what it might be like in the big leagues. The players like Amos (Otis), Freddie (Patek), Big John (Mayberry), Hal McRae, Al Cowens – those were the guys who kept the clubhouse going. They were jokesters and really played a lot of games and pranks on people.

I didn't play a lot that spring, but just being around those guys you realize that they're human. I had a sense that I could compete with them. I knew I could steal bases, and everyone kept saying, "If he could just hit .240 or .250." Sometimes when you hear things like that you start getting in your head that those numbers would be good enough. But I wanted to prove to them that I could hit.

In A ball, the manager was John Sullivan. Sully was with me in the Midwest League when we were playing at Waterloo, Iowa. He was the first one who moved me up in the batting order. I don't really remember where I was batting in rookie ball, but I know it wasn't at the top of the lineup. Sully had me batting third. It was really neat to be batting in that spot. I came up with a lot of RBIs. I think I finished up with 70-something RBIs, almost double what I had at any other place in the minor leagues.

I wasn't a home-run hitter. I was more of an "if there is a man out there I was going to try and hit him in" hitter. We had a really good team. Half of us were darker skinned – Latin or black players. The other half were white. The guys all got along, played together well. Quiz (Dan Quisenberry) was on that team. Two other guys were on that team that eventually made the Royals for a little while, German Barranca and Luis Silverio. Seven guys on that team eventually made the big leagues with one club or another.

Sully was kind of like the opposite of Scrip. He was more playful, more joking with the players. Sully chewed tobacco like crazy. I always remember when Sully would get in an argument with an umpire he made sure the tobacco went toward the umpire. It was his way of getting the umpire's attention if he was going to get thrown out.

Later on, Sully ended up being a bullpen coach for the Toronto Blue Jays for several years. It was fun to see him when we would go to Toronto. He would always give me that "cross his hands" signal, saying bad luck to me that day. That was our sign. I'd put my hands across my chest to him, and he would do it for me. So that was pretty cool.

*My first introduction to the Midwest was with the Waterloo Royals in 1975.*

This is also where I first experienced real prejudice – and it could have ended my career if it weren't for my teammates.

We were up in Wisconsin, a place we used to call Whiskey Rapids. Actually it was a town called Wisconsin Rapids. I think our first four batters were black, so we would get in a little huddle before the game, wish each other luck. We would say, "Hey have a good game and yell LET'S GO!" and we would break out of it like a football huddle.

Well, there is this big fat guy sitting right behind home plate. I mean sloppy fat. He couldn't have been more than six rows up in the stands. He's drinking beers and eating popcorn and hot dogs. And he would just drop the "N" word so many times. I was going crazy.

I grew up in a city that was almost all white, and went to a school that was almost all white, and I never got called that. I mean this was cutting straight to my heart man. I don't know if we won or lost that game. My thoughts were on that guy the whole game.

That was one of those old minor league parks where you had to walk underneath the stands to get back to our locker room. The fans walk out the same way to get out of the park. So when the game is over, I just fly back there with my bat. I got it cocked, and I'm ready, man. I got my eyes on where he was. I got the bat cocked when my teammates jumped me, "Willie!"

I mean I'm going to frickin' hurt this guy. He called me the "N" word again, and I'm ready to kill him. My teammates grabbed me and hauled me out of there, coaches, everybody grabbed me.

I said to myself, "I hope I never get in that position again." I got a temper. I'll tell you what. If I was Jackie Robinson, black people would *not* be playing baseball right now. I would have ruined it for everybody. I just couldn't take it. I was 19, and it was the first time I had ever been exposed to prejudice like that. That was horrible.

The minor leagues were a little different those days. We never stayed in hotels, we were always in those one-floor motels around the minor leagues. We had to sleep two or three to a room. Some of the guys would get cots, some guys would get beds. We would flip for who would get the bed each night. And we would carry a big cooler with us. When we would get to the motel we would fill it up with ice. We'd have milk, juice, baloney, cheese, maybe beer. And that was our breakfast and lunch. You only got, like, $5 per day for meals.

For me it was my first real step into the Midwest. I had a much better season that year. I think I batted .272 (up from .252 in rookie league). And I stole 76 bases, which was the first time I really had good numbers with stolen bases.

Going from .250-something in rookie ball and up 20 points higher in A ball, I really felt good about my year. They put me in the third spot, and I had an opportunity for some RBIs. So it was a whole lot better than Rookie ball.

I felt like I had established myself and was getting noticed. After the season I went back to Florida for the second straight year for the Instructional League. I just felt like I had a really legitimate year that season and it put me in a better place going to spring training the following season.

# 9

# PLAYING IN FRONT OF MY FAMILY

In 1976, there was a lockout from March 1 to 17 when a judge upheld the ruling that Andy Messersmith and Dave McNally could be free agents. So, it disrupted spring training a little bit. I had earned my way back to the big league camp, and every time I came back down to the minor leagues I had a little different attitude.

That same year, I'm back in Florida, playing in Jacksonville. Jacksonville was in the Southern League. We were going to get to play in Montgomery, Alabama, where I was born. I was excited because I got a chance to see my aunts, my uncles and my cousins a couple of times in the summer and they could watch me play.

We also were in Savannah, Knoxville, all these places in the South where I'd never been before. True to my form, I did a couple of more stupid things that could have derailed my career before it ever got started.

I would always start the season off slow and be better toward the end. This particular year I got hurt, pulled a hammy (hamstring) a little more than halfway through the season. That's not the greatest thing to happen for a guy whose speed is one of his best assets. Then, I tried to play again, and it got worse.

Well, I didn't know you were supposed to stay and get treatment. I didn't know you had to talk to the manager and tell him if you wanted to go home. I just knew I couldn't play. So, I was going to go home, back to Summit. I went to some of the guys to borrow some money and told them I would pay them back on payday. I got on a flight and went home to Summit. The next day Mr. Schuerholz called me and told me to get back down there. I got back and had it worked on every day. Mickey Cobb was the trainer for that team. He was later with the Royals. He was the only guy who was with me every year in the Royals, from Rookie ball to the end of my time with the Royals. They let him go the same year I was let go.

So, late in the season down at Jacksonville, towards the end of August, I was supposed to come off the DL. I don't know what day exactly, but I remember we had a doubleheader the day that I could play again. So, I go to the park and my name's not in the lineup. The first game comes along, and I'm sitting there on the bench. Nothing. No pinch hitting, no pinch running. I was like, "Wow!" So, I'm not playing in the first game. Then I'm thinking I might play the second game. My mind was thinking about a lot of crap.

So, the second game comes along and I'm not in the lineup, again. Like I told you, I had a really hot temper. So, I got angry. Before the game started I went back into the locker room, I took my "uni" off and threw it in the pile, got showered and dressed and got in my car and left. I was going back to the room, the apartment. I don't know what I'm going to do when I get there. But I'm hot, making stupid decisions.

I'm listening to the game on the radio on the way home. It's a good game. The score is like tied or we're getting close to tying it or something. So, I turn the car around and drive back. When I get back to the locker room they are washing my uniform. I kind of tiptoe and peek my head out into the dugout. Scrip sees me and growls out, "Put your uniform on." I go back into the locker room, and my uniform has just come out of the wash. It's wet. But I put it on, and I go back into the dugout.

I'm sitting in the frickin' dugout in a wet uniform. But we're in Jacksonville, and it's hot so it eventually dries. Then Scrip goes, "Don't leave. Sit here. After the game I gotta talk to you."

So now all kind of stuff is going through my head. I'm going to get cut. I'm going to get fined. I'm thinking of all the things that could happen. The game finishes, and I'm sitting there. He goes, "Walk with me down the line."

He said, "I knew you would come back because you're a competitor. The reason I didn't let you play the two games is that you are going to the big leagues tomorrow." I went, "Really?" I can't imagine what would have happened if I hadn't turned around and had kept going. I don't think I would have been going to the big leagues.

I was pretty naïve about all that stuff. I was looking at it from a kid's point of view. I didn't know about 40-man rosters. I didn't know about September callups or Rule 5 Draft or any of that. It's too complicated. I just thought you play your minor league season, and once you got to the big leagues you played the big league season. Nobody had ever been called up from the Rookie or A-ball teams I was on.

It was a big surprise. I think they called me up to make me feel better for being hurt and not playing. I don't really know their reasoning, but I was happy they called me up. I got one month of the minimum Major League salary, which I think was $19,000 a year – which is a lot better than I was making. And I got meal money. That was maybe $50, $60 a day on a road trip. So your meal money was more than you made as a minor leaguer.

But you also had to buy clothes. When you are in the minor leagues, you don't care about how you look. You've got jeans and maybe some flip-flops and some sneakers. But you get to the major leagues, and you gotta have nice shirts, nice pants, good shoes. I remember those guys would just get on me about what I looked like. I would be thinking, "Hey, I'm looking pretty good," but they would just jump me about it.

When I got my first hit in the big leagues, we were playing in Minnesota. I went into the game in the sixth inning and we were behind 10-0. By the time I got to bat we were behind 17-0. There were two outs, and Rupert Jones was on first base.

Roy Smalley was playing shortstop. I think Rod Carew was at first. I think Jim Hughes was the pitcher. I hit a two-hopper to the left. He had to go into the hole, and he got in front of it. When he went to throw, he just looked at me and tossed the ball back to the pitcher. That's how fast I was running.

The main thing I remember about coming up that year was the same impression I had when I signed my contract. Everything was just bright. The clubhouse was bright. The uniforms were the powder blue uniforms. They just shined. All of a sudden you have brand new shoes. And I remember how bright the Major League lights were compared to the minor league lights. It was just bright.

It was really nerve-wracking, and I was really nervous – so nervous that I wasn't able to throw the ball from one guy to another warming up. When you're nervous it's a good and bad thing. It's good that you're excited, but you'd like to be able to throw a baseball in warm-ups.

I can't remember my first number (I think it was 19 or something). It wasn't 6. I really didn't care about numbers. You just want to be in the big leagues. I remember that fans kept calling me Mayberry. Mayberry had a 7 on his uniform. But I kept looking at these people who were calling me Mayberry. I'm thinking I know I don't look like John Mayberry. He's about 30 pounds heavier than me. He's the home run hitter. I'm skinny as a rail.

But I had a really good time. I didn't play a lot. But it was a really good experience.

# 10
# LEARNING TO SWITCH HIT

$T$he next year (in 1977) I go to spring training and the Royals have it in their mind that they are going to make me into a switch hitter. It was really kind of weird because I had never really considered it. But I was willing to try because, in my brain, if I tried hard and was doing what they wanted me to do I would have a better chance to make it to the big leagues.

They told me early in spring training that I would be going to AAA where I could learn to switch hit. But I stayed on the wall a long time that year, and I was going to try like hell to hit left-handed and do what they told me to do. Whitey took me aside and told me that even if I was hitting a dollar-and-something (in the .100s) just keep at it.

I had never hit .300 in the minor leagues, but I always had a lot of stolen bases. So, when I get there that spring they were thinking about me with the idea if I could steal that many bases hitting .250 or .270 like I had been – how many more could I get if I was hitting even .290? I don't think they ever had in their mind that I could hit .300.

I couldn't hit a slider. I could always hit a fastball. But the slider, I couldn't ever hit that consistently. When I got there they kept talking to me, talking to me about moving over to the other side and learning how to switch hit.

A slider from a right handed pitcher breaks away from a right-handed batter. It starts at you, then a really good one only breaks a few inches. It looks like a fastball when it leaves the pitcher's hand, and in the minor leagues with those wild guys I would always be a little tentative. If you were batting left-handed, then the slider from a right-handed pitcher would be breaking in toward you just a couple of inches. And you wouldn't have a tendency to bail out like you would as a right-handed batter.

Every morning at spring training Chuck Hiller and I would come out and go to the batting cage for 45 minutes while everyone else was exercising. We would be down there hitting left-handed. I had never hit left-handed, professionally … I mean, I would do it in softball games or just fooling around, but I had never done it against a pitcher. And it wasn't just me they wanted to make a switch-hitter. U.L. Washington was down there with me.

I don't know why it was Chuck Hiller who was working with me. I think Charley Lau had to work with a lot of hitters and just didn't have time to be going one-on-one with me. He had 12 other guys to take care of. And maybe Whitey thought that Chuck and I would get along a little better.

*Courtesy of Kansas City Royals*

*The Royals may have saved my career when they made me learn how to switch hit.*

I'm down there in the batting cages trying to figure out how to hit left-handed. I'm getting jammed with pitches right on my hands. I'm getting beat up. My hands are killing me because I'm in the cage so long. Trainers are wrapping my hands like a boxer's because they are just torn up. It was before everybody was wearing gloves all the time. Guys are laughing at me, joking at me, all this kind of stuff. They all knew I was hurting.

But I was actually having a pretty good

spring that year, and I actually thought I could make the team, be one of those guys who jump from AA right to the major leagues. The outfielders were AO in center, AC (Al Cowens) in right. In left field they had Pokey (Tom Poquette) and Joe Zdeb. So, I really thought I could make it.

But they had plans. Whitey (Herzog) tells me after spring training that he's going to send me to AAA because he knows I can be in the lineup every day. And he says, "No matter if you hit .100 don't quit trying to become a switch hitter." I was like, "OK, if that's what you guys want me to do."

So, for the first time in my career I didn't pay a whole lot of attention to not failing. Becoming a switch-hitter was something I was going to work on. Maybe because I was naïve about a lot of stuff, but I didn't put any pressure on myself. I was already moving up every year when I was hitting .250 or .270 something. So, maybe this could help me move up.

All the pitchers in the league knew I was hitting left-handed for the first time ever. So, they would throw the ball right at me, and I didn't know how to get out of the way. When you are not used to hitting on that side, you are not used to rolling with the pitch or how to bail out. I would just open up and it would hit me in the chest or the face or something. I would just freeze.

I don't even remember who was pitching this particular day, but he threw it right at me. I couldn't move. I didn't know which way to go, so I just yelled, "Aaaaaaaaaaaaaah!' I looked at him, and I got really mad. He threw another fastball inside, and I just swing at it as hard as I could. It shot over the third-baseman's head. It hit the line fair, popped into foul territory and went out and hugged the wall. I circled the bases and then I went:, "Hey, this thing might work."

I ended up hitting .281 I think, stole 70-some bases. It was just so much fun because I was getting on base. Even if I didn't get a hit I was getting on base because of an error or something. Guys who were fielding the ball were rushing because of my speed. Sometimes I wouldn't get credit for a hit because the scorers would make it an error, but I was getting on base, and when I got on base I was causing havoc for those guys. The catchers hated it, and we were winning.

That was a really good team in Omaha. Clint Hurdle played right field, U.L. Washington was the shortstop. Rich Gale was pitching on that team. A lot of guys on that team made a little pit stop in the Major Leagues. But those four of us came off that team and we were together quite a few years on the Royals.

AAA was the stopping point for a lot of guys who didn't make it to the Major Leagues. So, the guys you were playing against were pretty good players.

I came up at the end of the season to the Royals, again, and I hit .324 in that last month with a couple of doubles and six stolen bases. I was feeling pretty good about where I was. Then the light really came on in the off season that year when I went and played in the Dominican Republic.

You know those years when I was struggling to get even one hit I think it was mostly mental. I was confused. You have all kinds of guys telling you stuff, Chuck Hiller, Charley Lau, Whitey Herzog, other players … you're even talking to yourself. You have a lot of stuff going on. You're trying different things with your swing because people are all suggesting stuff. Then, when you start hitting the ball you ask yourself, "What are you thinking about?" The answer is nothing. When you're thinking you're hesitating to be aggressive. Once I figured out I could just react and not think everything started to take care of itself.

But I had to grow up a little. I had to get confidence. Once you get a little confidence, you go up there, see the ball, hit the ball. In the minor leagues you are trying to please everybody to get to the next level. You're trying to do all the things everyone is asking you to do. But you can only do so much and then you begin confusing yourself. You get aggravated because you aren't doing the things that you know, in your brain, you're capable of doing.

So, I came up again at the end of the year with the Royals, and I got to play quite a bit more this time. It was really exciting because it was the first time I got to play when the games meant something in clinching the playoffs. It made me concentrate. It made me want to be there even more.

I was so naïve that I thought because I was there at the end of the season I was thinking, "Crap, man, I'm going to get on their roster and go to the playoffs." As I found out, that's not how it works. But I did go to the playoff games. I bought the package of tickets.

When the season was over I had this guy drive my car back to New

Jersey, and then I got on the plane with the fellas and we flew to New York – which was really like home. I was sitting in the third deck at Yankee Stadium, just hunched down in my seat – no Royals gear, no nothing like that.

One of those games is when I see Hal McRae on first base, and he's waving his arms all over the place. I found out later he was talking to Freddie (Patek). But Hal's just swinging his arms around. What he was telling Freddie was that if the ball was hit, he was going to take the guy out at second and that Freddie should go all the way home. That's when the Hal McRae rule came into baseball. Hal would just go flying into people when he would break up a double play at second base.

That series was when Chris Chambliss hit the home run … that was bad … that wasn't a good sight. That year was the first time I really felt like I was part of the team. The next spring, I just wanted to do as much as I could to make the big league club.

I went to the Dominican at the end of the year – between the 1977 and 1978 seasons and played for Tigres de Licey, one of the teams from Santo Domingo. I was playing on a team with Manny Mota.

It was actually a great experience for me because I could be a little more relaxed. I wasn't in the big leagues. I didn't have 50,000 people watching me, or newspaper people looking at everything I was doing. And Manny was on that team. A lot of people don't know he was a .300 career batter in a 20-year career in the Major Leagues.

I took Charley Lau's methods with me to the Dominican, and Manny helped me refine it. I'm not saying Charley Lau's methods of coaching me didn't work, but I seemed to mesh with Manny a little better. He just taught a little different than Charley; that you had to be quick and relaxed. When he put his hands on your shoulders it was just a little different than the way Charley put his hands on your shoulders as he was coaching you. I had some success in AAA and success in September. Manny just made me a little more knowledgeable about what I was doing in picking out pitches and all that.

Charley's main student was George (Brett). Manny seemed to make me his main student. I wasn't ever able to talk to Charley like George talked to Charley, how to pick out pitches, how to do this or how to do that. I could do that with Manny. You know things like:

"You foul one off, do you think he's going to come back in there with the same pitch?"

"What do you look for with two strikes?"

"Does this guy like to backdoor you?"

He really kind of taught me how to study pitchers. He just happened to be there at the right time and place for me. A lot of people put in a lot of hard work and time with me. But it just seemed to click with him. It's like a boyfriend and girlfriend. One just sort of clicks. The others just don't get to the same point.

I don't know what my batting average was that winter, but I was starting to feel really comfortable. So, I had more confidence coming in to spring training in 1978 because I had just had a complete year of switch-hitting in AAA, got a taste of success in September and then worked with Manny in the Dominican League. I was really looking forward to spring training in 1978.

# 11
## INSIDE
## THE PARK

Seeing an inside-the-park home run is one of the most exciting plays for the fans, and I think the reason they are so exciting for fans is because everybody can relate to running as fast as you can. A lot of people don't know how it feels to hit a home run out of the park, but everybody runs. So, when you are coming around third, you can almost hear and feel the crowd.

"Is he going to make it?"

"Is he not going to make it?"

There was always the excitement. When I was running the bases, what I wanted to hear were the fans. I wanted to hear them screaming and all that. I remember the first one, but two others against the Yankees were the most memorable.

The first one was almost like an accident because I don't think the White Sox knew I was that fast. It was in 1979. There was a man on third, and I was just trying to hit the ball into the outfield. I think there were no outs or one out, and all I wanted to do was get the ball up in the air. I was looking for a high pitch because high pitches are the ones you're going to get up into the air.

It was a high fastball, and I just got on top of it. It went into the gap, which is also a little unusual because most inside-the-park home runs didn't come when you hit them into the gaps. It got through to the fence, and I just kept running. When I got to third, they waved me in, and I kept going.

There were two against the Yankees – the first was at Royals Stadium. We were in the 13th inning. I was leading off the 13th against

Ken Clay. That turned into a walk-off – or in my case a run-off – win for the Royals.

But the one I really remember was in Yankee Stadium against (Ron) Guidry.

First inning. First pitch.

When I went to the plate to open that game, I knew I was going to be swinging on the first pitch. I didn't care where it was. His first pitches were fastballs. He threw this one right down the middle. To me, the best pitch in the world to hit was the first one in the game. Most pitchers want to throw a strike. They want to throw it right down the middle. So, I hit it and I just took off. I had triple on my brain.

This one was also a little unusual because it was to left-center in the old Yankee Stadium where there was just so much room back there. Left-center was the deepest part of that ballpark. They just couldn't converge on it. I think it was Lou Piniella in left and Bobby Murcer in center .

The third base coach waved me in, and I just kept going. Then, the thing is when you are getting to home plate, how do I slide? You know it's going to be close, right? So, what you do is watch the catcher. This is Rick Cerone, and you just watch him to see which way he is going to move.

So, that was pretty cool.

Most of my inside-the-park home runs were down the line. Gappers usually didn't have inside-the-park potential because you had two outfielders going after the ball with the idea of holding the guy to a double or triple.

At Royals Stadium, we used to call the corners "Death Valley." There was that little lip underneath the padding where it came down to the warning track. The ball would get in there and just scoot around and hug the wall. The outfielder would try and play it like most other places and take an angle thinking it would hit and bounce out to him. Instead, it would just keep scooting. Once the ball got down into the corners I knew I had a shot.

I would usually watch where it hit as I'm running down to first, and a lot of them were to left field. The reason why is when I was batting left handed, they would play me shallow in left and back in right. Left handed, I would hit it the opposite way and when you hit the ball away

## INSIDE THE PARK HOME RUNS

| DATE | OPPONENT | PITCHER | INNING | ON BASE |
|---|---|---|---|---|
| May 13, 1979 | At Chicago | Steve Trout | 7 | 1 |
| June 9, 1979 | New York | Ken Clay | 13 | 0 |
| June 15, 1979 | At Milwaukee | Bill Castro | 9 | 2 |
| Aug. 25, 1979 | Boston | Mike Torrez | 1 | 0 |
| Sept. 16, 1979 | Seatttle | Rob Dressler | 3 | 0 |
| May 14, 1980 | At New York | Ron Guidry | 1 | 0 |
| June 19, 1980 | Cleveland | Mike Stanton | 7 | 0 |
| May 11, 1982 | Milwaukee | Dwight Bernard | 8 | 2 |
| July 21, 1982 | Toronto | Dale Murray | 8 | 1 |
| Sept. 3, 1982 | New York | Jay Howell | 3 | 0 |
| May 14, 1983 | Detroit | David Rucker | 1 | 0 |
| Aug. 9, 1983 | Milwaukee | Don Sutton | 7 | 0 |
| June 1, 1984 | At Minnesota | Mike Smithson | 3 | 0 |

from you it comes off and bounces away from the fielder. Because it was in left, I could watch the ball as I ran toward second, I could see if it had taken off. I knew exactly where the ball was.

Once I hit second, I could tell whether I was going to make it home or not. If the outfielder still had his back to me, there was no way he was going to get the ball going away, pick it up, turn and throw. I'm at full throttle coming around second. So, I never even relied on the third base coach. If you ask any of the third base coaches, they would never tell me to go. They might try to hold me up, but sometimes I just kept running through the stop sign.

For some reason I had an instinct about it that probably started in high school. We didn't have any fences at my school, so you had to run the bases to get the home run anyway.

It was really weird because it always seemed like if I needed another five yards I could go just a little bit faster. It was almost uncanny to know that you could shift into another gear. I wouldn't even be tired or winded.

That's the other thing about an inside-the-park home run. You gotta have wind and stamina to just keep going. There was one thing I liked doing. I liked running. I think there was only one time I got thrown out, and that was in the latter part of my career with the Cubbies. It was about wind and stamina. I was playing, but not full-time. The Cubs field (Wrigley Field) has a crown on it for drainage, and when you hit third base you go downhill a little bit when you round the baseline. Then you have to go back uphill a little bit to get to the plate. Boy when I was coming uphill, I was saying to myself, "I don't think I have enough strength to get there." So I tried to sneak my foot in there, and they tagged me out. I got booed. I mean the Cub fans booed the crap out of me. That's when I knew those things aren't going to happen too many times again.

What an exciting play, though. "Man!"

# 12
# FIND A DRIVER
# FOR YOUR CAR

**I** had always hoped I could be the exception, and make the club out of A ball or AA ball. I knew a few people who did like Al Cowens. But I didn't have the credentials. This time coming into spring training in 1978 I had the credentials in AAA. I had credentials in the Dominican. I was having a really good spring training. I think I stole something like 30 bases in that spring.

As spring training progressed, I knew it was the longest I had ever been on the wall. It was getting down to the last two or three days of camp and I'm still on the wall. I think it was me, U.L., Clint (Hurdle) and Rich Gale who were still back on the wall.

They were all quiet guys, so they told me I had to go in and talk with Whitey to find out whether we were going to be going up to the big leagues. A day or two before we were breaking camp I went to Whitey's office and knocked on the door.

I just said, "Whitey, can I ask you a question?"

He was like, "Yeah Will sit on down in here."

I didn't want to just ask whether I was going to make the team, so I had to figure out what I was going to ask him so I would know. I say, "Whitey, what am I supposed to do with my car."

Back then they had drivers come down and take all the cars back to Kansas City when we broke camp. So that's how I figured out what question to ask. "What was I going to do with my car?"

He kind of sat there for a second, and then he goes, "You can have it driven to K. C."

I go, "Really?"

I was so excited. I never even asked for the other three guys. In those days we didn't have cell phones, so I'm trying to find some quarters so I can go to the pay phone and call my mother. I went and dialed and went, "Mom, I made the squad!"

Then all the other guys started going into the office one at a time. But I thought that was a pretty good question I figured out to ask. Then, I found out I was going to start. That was really cool. Then, after the 18th game is when all hell broke loose.

That year we had Amos in center field, AC in right field and I think we had Joe Zdeb, Tom Poquette and me in left field. Clint Hurdle was at first in the beginning of the season. They had gotten rid of Big John Mayberry in '77, and they were trying to convert Clint into a first baseman.

This is the first time I found out about politics in the big leagues. Clint was on the cover of *Sports Illustrated* that year with the headline "This Year's Phenom." I was on the inside as one of the top prospects. Somebody came up to me and said, "You are lucky you are not on the cover." I go, "What are you talking about?" He tells me about the cover jinx – which it turns out was kind of true.

I started eight of the first nine games of the season, and we're heading into Baltimore. My mom is coming down to the game. All my friends from Summit are coming down, and Whitey tells me he is going to sit me down.

I'm thinking, "You've got to be kidding." I didn't say anything, but I'm mad now. I go out in the outfield during batting practice. I have my hands folded in front of me. Balls are going over my head, going to my left, going to my right, on the ground, line drives. I'm not moving.

Hal McRae comes over to me with some words of wisdom, and points up to the glassed-in windows where the pressbox was, where reporters, owners, front-office people all sit. He goes, "You see that glass up there. They are watching you. You know they can go down and get another (he said the "N" word) just like you to do that. You don't want to catch your ride out of here. So work hard, get your opportunity again and take advantage of it."

I tried to follow Hal's advice and keep working. I had gotten my batting average up to .291 or something after the first month of the season, and I was leading the league in stolen bases. That's when the second shoe fell.

Clint, after the first 18 games or so, had dropped a few balls at first base. I mean he was an outfielder trying to play a new position. He was batting about .200.

I guess they thought Clint had more potential as a hitter. He hit for a higher average in AAA and had a lot of RBI's. He had gotten to the big club a year faster than I did, and all I had heard was, "You can't hit. Clint can hit." When they moved him over to first it had messed him up as a hitter. too.

After going to the bench I kept working, kept working, kept working. But it seemed to me that they wanted Clint to be the one who would succeed because he had been on the cover and it would have looked bad if they sat him down early in the season. The second half of that season I think I started only six or seven games. I only had 50 at bats the second half of the season. I ended up hitting only .216. I still stole 46 bases.

It wasn't a very satisfying year for me.

*"I don't have anything against Clint Hurdle. He's a friend. But they say Clint can hit, so he's a player. I hear I'm not a player. I can't hit. Everybody knows Clint made a lot of mistakes last year in left field, but people don't mention that. Last year, I felt like I was there but not really a part of the club. I felt good when we won. I felt like they put me in there, but didn't give me a job."*
*—Willie Wilson in 1979 spring training*

The next year, in 1979, I come to camp and I didn't know if I was going to make the big league or not. In those days, I'm not trying to say anything prejudicial or anything, but in those days I was having all these guys saying to me, "If you're black, they're not going to pay you to sit on the bench."

I'm thinking I will get released or traded or whatever. Whitey has been saying all this stuff, "Willie hasn't been able to hit. Willie throws to the wrong base ... blah blah blah." He's just been talking about me all spring so bad that if I did get traded or whatever, he wouldn't look bad because of Clint.

Then AC gets hit in the head in early May against Texas. All the outfielders are hurt except me. I got my glove tucked underneath my arm. Whitey is pacing back and forth because he's been talking bad about me all spring. I was his only option.

I came in for AC and was playing left field. They moved Clint to right. Sometimes Hal McRae would play in the outfield, Jamie Quirk sometimes played. It was kind of a mix and match outfield.

The next two months I hit .354 or something. I was leading the league and having a great year. I ended up hitting .315 or something like that. That's the year I set the team record with 83 stolen bases. About two months after I first got into the lineup, I remember Whitey telling me. "You get a hit for me today and I will put you in the leadoff spot and never take you out while I'm managing." I go 2-for-3 that day, and that's when I became the leadoff hitter for good.

That was quite an interesting time.

# 13
# STEALING BASES

**I** didn't really think about trying to stretch singles into doubles because I always considered my singles were doubles. I was going to steal second. What I was trying to do was cause havoc by splitting the pitcher's brain in half between the batter and me – and mostly thinking about me. If I'm on first, your brain is thinking I don't want him to get to second. He's going to do all these throws, then, BOOM, Somebody else gets a home run or somebody gets a double.

If I'm on first, I can score on a double every time.

I never really tried to get a big lead because I didn't want guys throwing over a whole heck of a lot. If they throw over, I have to retreat to first base. If I took a big lead, I had to dive back. If you are diving, you're always diving on your chest and I didn't want to do that.

At Royals Stadium, I had one foot on the turf and one on the dirt. I knew if I was at that place I could take one giant step and be back. But pitchers knew even if I didn't have a big lead I can still steal second. So, right there you are already in their brain.

*Courtesy of Kansas City Royals*

*I always slid on my right side when I was stealing a base because if the ball got by the fielder I could see where it went.*

83

That spot was about three-and-a-half shuffles. I would never walk out to my lead, I'd take these sideways shuffles. You don't walk because if your foot is off the ground and he makes the throw, you can't get back.

I would shuffle, shuffle, shuffle. Three-and-a-half slides and I knew I was at my spot.

When I was going to steal I would take my first step with my left foot, closest to first. I had to teach myself how to get off quickly because it was always a struggle to go to my right. After my shuffle, I would drop my right foot just a little behind my left. That opened up my hips a little bit so I could just go straight across my body with my left leg.

I would take my right arm and pull it down as hard as I could and then just go. I never really worked on it, but it was like a sprinter would take off. When I did that … one step … two step … and at about the third step I peeked a glance toward the catcher. By then the ball is already there so you can see whether the catcher caught it cleanly and how quickly he might be able to get off a throw. I never really worried about the catcher because I never thought a catcher could throw me out. We had timed everything, and you knew the pitcher took two-something seconds to get the ball to home plate, the catcher took one-something getting the ball out of his glove. So, you would have about three seconds or so to steal the base.

If I had to slide I would always slide on my right side, never on the left. The reason? I don't know whether it was a conscious decision or not, but if there was an overthrow, I could see how far the ball went into the outfield and get up and go to third. If I slid on the left I was looking toward the infield, and the ball is back behind me. People could be yelling, "Go! Go! Go!" But by the time you find the ball it's too late to take another base. Another reason is I tried it once my rookie year on my left side, and I sprained my ankle.

Learning how to read the pitchers is something Amos Otis really schooled me on. When I came up we had a lot of guys who could run. Amos, Cookie Rojas, Al Cowens, Freddie (Patek), Davey Nelson. Our catcher, John Wathan, had 30 stolen bases one year. Those guys were base stealers. Amos, after he accepted me, was really good about teaching me. He was really hard on me at the beginning of my career because I think he thought I was coming in to take his spot, but it turned out he was really helpful. Besides all the center field stuff he taught me, he also taught me about stealing bases.

The best advice he gave me about stealing was, "Never sit close to the manager."

I asked, "Why? I want to learn some manager stuff."

He said, "If you are going to learn about stealing bases you sit at the end of the bench because that's the best angle to see the pitcher throwing to first. You watch that pitcher from the top, and you watch him all the way down to the end. You tell me exactly what he does different when he comes to first than when he goes home."

So, I'm sitting there one day, watching, and AO goes, "You see that?" I'm saying, "What?"

He says, "There, see that little wrinkle in his pants. When his pants do something like that he goes home every time."

I'm thinking, "Oh man, this is going to be tough." I never even saw it.

After he points it out, I can see it easy. Then he said, and I don't know if he was joking or not, but he says, "I'm going to steal a base standing up on that guy. He stole five bases, two standing up that day." That's when I really started sitting there and watching guys and watching what they would do.

*Sliding into home was one of the favorite things to do because it meant another run for the Royals.*

I had to do that because stealing bases was not something that I ever did much of before I turned pro. I stole bases in high school, but that wasn't a real focus. I was a catcher. I had a good arm, but nobody really talked about my speed in high school.

I got to the minors with the Royals rookie league team in Sarasota, and I really wasn't hitting all that well. Because I didn't hit well I felt like I had to do something else to be noticed. So, I started stealing bases. As you start stealing bases you realize that because you are stealing bases and getting in scoring position you are helping everybody else out – the No. 2 man, the No. 3 man, the No. 4 man.

The guys with the big league team knew I was fast and could steal, but they wanted me to concentrate on switch-hitting. When I got to AAA I knew I had to do something to stand out. That's what I tell the young guys now who are getting my award for base running: If the best guy is at 40 or 50, you want to be at 79 or 80. You want them to go, WOW, this guy can really run. So, that's what I tried to do.

I really wanted to learn to hit because the way to steal more bases was to get on base. The thing they kept saying to me was, "You can't steal first. You can't steal first." The reason they kept saying that was because I wasn't really hitting. When I got to AAA I was really going to give it a shot. I was getting too close.

The key to stealing bases, you have to have a short-term memory like a relief pitcher. Relievers go into the game in the ninth, two outs and they give up a run that loses the game. Just like stealing, you get thrown out, but you have to keep going. If you don't keep going that takes away part of your artillery.

Stealing is hard on your body. I mean, who likes to go out there and run as fast as you can, then jump out of a car at about 20 miles an hour on some really hard dirt? In those days you didn't have the really good pads the way they have now. We had just two pads on each side, and you had a little string and tied them up. They would roll up and get bunched up, no protection at all.

After I was up in the majors a couple of years, I didn't steal as much anymore because it actually would have hurt the team. Stealing bases, you just have to have the mentality of just go, go, go. One day, I was out there jumping around at second base, and the funniest damn thing happened.

## MILESTONE STOLEN BASES

| STOLEN BASE | DATE | OPPONENT | PITCHER |
|---|---|---|---|
| 1 | Sept. 9, 1976 | Vs. California | Mike Overy |
| 100 | Aug. 3, 1979 | At Detroit | Pat Underwood |
| 150 | May 19, 1980 | Vs. Oakland | Steve McCatty |
| 200 | Sept. 12, 1980 | At Oakland | Rick Langford |
| 250 | Sept. 29, 1981 | At Minnesota | Albert Williams |
| 300 | May 1, 1983 | Vs. Cleveland | Lary Sorenson |
| 350 | May 26, 1984 | At Boston | Roger Clemens |
| 400 | May 22, 1985 | At Texas | Dickie Noles |
| 450 | June 5, 1986 | Vs. Minnesota | Roy Lee Jackson |
| 500 | July 25, 1987 | At Baltimore | Dave Schmidt |
| 550 | July 31, 1988 | At Baltimore | Jose Bautista |
| 600 | June 13, 1990 | At California | Mike Fetters |
| 650 | July 19, 1992 | Vs. Detroit* | Kevin Ritz |
| 668 | April 8, 1994 | At Montreal** | Jeff Shaw |

* With Oakland Athletics; ** With Chicago Cubs

Hal McRae is at bat and he calls time out. He yells out to me, "Stand still!"

He's yelling at me. He's telling me to stand still. I look at him and go, "What?" He yells, "The ball's white. The uniform is white. It's getting lost in the uniform. Just stand still."

Then he goes, "I'll get you in."

The pitcher looks at him crazy, and I think, "Oh crap, he didn't just say that." The next pitch, of course, knocks him down. He just gets up and does his thing and puts the ball in right field and I score.

Another reason I didn't steal a lot was because of George (Brett). I remember we were playing at Detroit all the time and Sparky Anderson was their manager. Sparky would always say we don't want Willie and George to beat us ... but he would say, "George and Willie." That just made me angry because I tried so hard to beat them.

But if I get on base and steal second, they walk George – especially if there are two outs. So, I would sit there and say to myself, "Hit a double, George and I'll score. Hit a double."

Sometimes on lefties I would just take off. I wouldn't even know their move.

(Ron) Guidry was the easiest guy in the world to steal off. When he wanted to go home with the ball he would duck his chin. When he wanted to go to first his head would stay dead still. See, he was a power pitcher. When you are a power pitcher you want to get everything into your body so you tighten up and muscle up for the pitch. His chin would tuck down, and as soon as he does that I'm, "Whoosh!" The key against him was getting on base. That was the hard part. You had to get on, but once you got on, you could steal on him easy.

My first stolen base came when I went into the game as a pinch runner for John Mayberry in the bottom of the ninth. The pitcher was Mike Overy.

# 14
# EARNING
# MY SPOT

**W**e had a new manager in 1980, Jim Frey. I didn't think my situation was any different. I was still trying to prove myself. In 1979 I didn't play a full season. I started playing regularly a month after the season started when Al Cowens got hurt. Over the winter, they had traded AC to the Angels for Willie Aikens.

The 1980 season was really going to be my first full season, but what I was trying to do at the beginning of the year was just keep a job. I was still remembering that in 1978 I'm hitting .292 or .298 or something and Whitey came up and said I wasn't hitting high enough and he benched me.

In 1980, I'm thinking I have to do something in the first 18 games to keep a job. I didn't have a great start, I think the first 18 games I'm only hitting .250 – did I say I always get off to slow starts? The new manager wasn't like Whitey at all. If it had been Whitey, I don't know if I would

have stayed in the lineup. I didn't know what was being said in the front office or manager-wise. I just know I was worried. I'm thinking I don't know this new guy. I don't know what he thinks.

But he kept writing my name in the lineup, and after so many days I finally quit worrying and just

*Courtesy of Kansas City Royals*

*At the start of the 1980 season I received this Silver Spike award for winning the stolen base title during the 1979 season.*

91

relaxed. Then, I had something to prove. I wanted to prove to everybody that I could play, that I could hit, that I knew what I was doing. Everybody kept saying, "He can't hit." Well, you can either run away from that or try and make it a challenge and do something about it.

I started the season in left where I was really comfortable. I think they wanted to move me to center because of my speed, but Amos was reluctant to give it up. I think it was in Baltimore that we made a change, and he played a few games in left. It didn't really work out. He was mad, and I was really feeling that vibe on the field. I went into the manager's office after a series to talk to them about switching us back. I didn't want Amos mad at me. I knew I could play left field. I was judging balls a lot better. I was starting to learn how to play the corners of the outfield in Royals Stadium where the ball just hugged the wall rather than bouncing off. I was starting to really learn how to play in the outfield. Amos was more comfortable in center. I told them when they switched us around it was making him more angry and me more defensive.

We switched back. He relaxed, and I relaxed. I had a pretty good May and June, I was hitting about .325 in both those months. The team was playing really well, we were taking about two out of three games every series. Everybody was having a pretty good year. That was the year that Darrel Porter came back from his drug rehab and he hit about .290 or something. U.L. (Washington) hit .280-something. George – he hit great. Everybody who was playing was hitting great. The pitching was really solid.

We all fed off each other.

We had a mission together as a team. The Royals had been successful getting into the playoffs, but they weren't successful winning in the playoffs and going to the World Series. When I came up for the month in '76 they were in their first run to the playoffs. I got a chance in that month to feel the excitement and then to see the pain they felt in the playoffs.

In 1977, more pain and agony. That team was probably the best team the Royals had record wise. They were just ungodly. I think when I came up from AAA they had won 13 in a row, lost one and then won 10 in a row. That was kind of cool to see that.

Then, in 1978, I got a chance to play at the start of that season, and in the playoffs I got to bat against Ron Guidry and get a hit. There was a play in that series when I got thrown out at third. I swear – to this day – that I was safe. That was in the fifth inning of Game 4. Hal McRae was at bat with one out and the score tied. If I had been called safe – like I was – I would have been on third with one out and scored on his fly ball to right field. The Yankees went on to win that game 2-1. We didn't come close to scoring in the final four innings of that game.

That was the year that I first knew the kind of pain you felt when you lost a playoff because I had been with the team the whole year. Then, in 1979, we didn't get into the playoffs.

So, we were on a mission in 1980 to basically get to the World Series. I got really hot in July, hit .479. The weather was aloshot. I was feeling really good. Switch hitting was really feeling like it was normal for the first time. And I was feeling like if I needed a hit I could just make it happen. Damn near every ball I hit was to left field. And I felt like all I had to do was get the bat on the ball. I always thought if I could make the third baseman or the shortstop move two to three steps either way I could beat their throw to first. I was learning how to "jam" myself, let the ball get right in on my hands and then make an inside-out swing. Hit a high chopper and then beat out the throw.

### ROYALS RECORDS SET IN 1980 BY WILLIE WILSON

| | |
|---|---|
| *Most at bats* | *705* |
| *Most plate app.* | *745* |
| *Most hits* | *230* |
| *Most hits switchhitter* | *230* |
| *Most singles* | *184* |
| *Most multi-hit games* | *71* |

It was a really unbelievable feeling. It was just fun. We were winning. We were laughing and smiling and having a great, great time. That's what I was used to doing all through junior high and high school. Even in the minor leagues we had won. So, this was just part of me finishing up winning at the next level.

It was also a real learning year for me. It was the first time I really understood that the better you played and the better your team was the less time you had for yourself. That was a hard lesson for me.

I'm not a Terrell Owens type guy, and I'm not into that, "Rah, rah, rah, look at me I'm the man, deal." I didn't like dealing with all the stuff surrounding the game because I had to get into the right frame of mind to play well. I prepared for every game like a football player. I had to sort of work myself up into a rage. So, I didn't want anybody bothering me during batting practice. I didn't want to do any interviews. I didn't want to sign any autographs. That was my time to get prepared to play in a game. I wasn't ever really good about all the outside stuff when I was playing because I thought it was taking away from my job, which was to play baseball.

That was the year that George had that spectacular month and he went up over .400. He ended up batting .390. There was so much attention on his chase, I don't think anybody even knew I hit .326 that year. I think I broke or tied seven Major League records and nobody even frickin' knew it – which was great. I wasn't ready to be in the spotlight.

That's the year that people started putting me in another category, which sort of messed me up. You are going from a nobody to a superstar in one year. Boom! Boom! Everybody started looking at me differently: the fans, the other teams, the TV, the newspapers. Newspapers want you to say something before and after every game. Before, nobody cared what I had to say, which was fine with me. I just wanted to play. Now the TV wants an interview, the newspaper all of a sudden cares what I think. What it basically comes down to, in a nutshell, your time for yourself is eliminated.

I was a person who tried to control everything, and I had no control. If you aren't a guy who likes the publicity, you tend to shy away from it. That's where I was. I shied away – and sometimes I didn't do it very diplomatically.

Because of the year I was having, people started to put more of a spotlight on me. I think George got hurt at one point, then the light on me was even brighter for a while. It was a different kind of pressure because people are looking at me differently, more as a leader. But I'm not looking at me any differently.

In my mind, I wasn't a leader. The leaders were Amos (Otis) and Hal (McRae) and Frank (White) and George (Brett). I was part of a great team, but those guys had been the foundation of those previous playoff teams. In my brain, I was thinking I didn't want to draw attention to myself because then other teams would start noticing me more and put more attention on getting me out.

In one respect, all the attention is great because it means you have accomplished something, and you get a bigger contract and can do this and that. But in the other respect, as a player, your opponents begin focusing on you. One advantage I had in the beginning was that nobody knew me. When I was getting put in some of those other categories, I couldn't handle it.

After the game you were just supposed to turn it off as soon as it's over. Well, if I struck out four times, it's hard for me to go, "Eh, it's all right." I was 24-years old. I was cussing myself out. I wasn't a patient person. Someone would ask me a question after the game, I would go all "Jersey" on them, man. It would get nutty. Later on when I had cooled down a little bit I would feel bad about it, but by then people are gone.

I was just young. I was only 24. I was married. I had a kid. I was going from being a nobody to a somebody. All I really wanted to do was do my job and go home. That's all. But the better you do your job the less time you have. Everybody wants, wants, wants. And it's all different. Your kids are wanting stuff. Your wife is wanting stuff. Other players are wanting stuff. Fans are wanting stuff. Reporters want more of your time. The Royals want you to sign all this stuff for them.

What it basically comes down to, in a nutshell, is that your *me* time is eliminated, and I wasn't really ready for that. I think teams are a lot better at preparing their players for that now. If I had understood all that before I got to the big leagues, my mindset would have been different. Now, I'm not saying I would have liked it any better or I would have dealt with it any better, but if I had been told in the minor leagues that this was your obligation when you get to the Major Leagues it would not have been such a shock when it happened.

*Program for New Jersey Sports Writers Association 45th Anniversary Awards Banquet when I was honored as New Jersey Pro Athlete of the Year.*

95

It seemed like I was always doing something for somebody else. And every time I would think I was done, one more guy wanted to ask me for an autograph. I'm trying to get to something my kid is doing. Then the guy cusses me out and then I would get mad. I would go, "Dude, what the hell! Don't you have kids? Why are your kids more important than my kids?" And someone would hear bits and parts of the conversation and then I'm the bad guy. So, now I really go into hibernation because I just couldn't handle it.

Playing the game during those times was more relaxing to me than outside of the game because I just had to deal with the game and whether I could get a hit or steal a base.

The other thing is this was the first year I was playing this many games. I didn't know how hard you could play or if you would get tired. People were saying to me, "Willie, if you go, the Royals go." It wasn't just reporters. It was guys on my team. So, you're trying harder for them.

We finish up the season pretty strong. And now we're playing the Yankees again in the playoffs. I always loved playing the Yankees, especially in Yankee Stadium because it wasn't a road game for me. To me it was going back home. My mom was there. All my friends from Summit were there. People from my mom's church were getting buses to come over. I had a great season against the Yankees that year, statistically, because I was so comfortable there.

I knew all the Yankees guys from playing basketball over the winter with them when I was in AA. Jeff Torborg, who was a Jersey guy, got all these players to go around New Jersey, New York and parts of Pennsylvania. We would play benefit basketball games. Some of the guys I played with on those teams were Mickey Rivers, Roy White, Paul Blair, Johnny Briggs, Chris Chambliss … So, when I went to play the Yankees, I had hung out with those guys since AA. When I made it to the big leagues I wasn't intimidated by them.

That also helped me dealing with the Major League guys on the Royals, too. I had been hanging with some superstars over the winters. I wasn't as intimidated by the Royals guys who had gotten to the playoffs when I was in spring training. But I felt really at home when I played the Yankees. I had a lot of good things working for me.

The only problem for me in New York was getting tickets. We got

## The Chicago Bulls

*When I was playing those hoops games with the Yankees players in the winter, Gene Michael got me a tryout with the Chicago Bulls. They were playing in the Garden against the Knicks and had a practice session. So, I go in and dressed with them, then we did drills, took some jump shots and had a little scrimmage.*

*I was the point guard on the backup team. Artis Gilmore was the center, Jerry Sloan and Norm Van Lier were their guards. Well, I'm from Jersey, so I'm brash. We talked some stuff, and then I drove down the middle and hooked it up over Artis for a basket. Artis looks at me and goes, "Don't come back in here with that crap again."*

*But I'm cocky now. So after a little bit I'm going to go down the middle again. He smacked that ball and kind of knocked me down. When I looked up all I could see was the bottom of sneakers. I rolled out of bounds. He looked at me and said, "I told you not to come in here with that crap again."*

six tickets for every game. I would start trading with guys as soon as I got to spring training. I'd give the guys who lived in California or somewhere else as many tickets as I could so I could get their tickets for games in New York. I don't know how many tickets I needed every time, but it was a lot. My mother would say, "I need tickets for blah, blah, blah." And I would say, "You know I only get six, mom."

It was pretty cool because my mom used to come down early when we were in batting practice. She would always meet me at the same spot by the away dugout. The guards began to know her. That was pretty cool because she became somewhat of a celebrity. That made me feel good because she was getting some attention.

Well, we had lost to the Yankees in the playoffs three years in a row and had one year off to think about it coming up against them again. So, a lot of things are going through your brain.

"Are we good enough to beat the big boys from New York City?"

"Are we going to catch a break?"

They always seemed to rise to the occasion. They always got the key hit. We would hit a ball hard, but right at someone. What I remember about this year is that we were really excited to play them. We had beat the Yankees more during the season that year than any other year. So, confidence-wise we knew we could beat them.

I knew they were worried about me getting on a lot, and I knew I needed to have good games. If I got on and did what I needed to do, then George was going to do what he needed to do and everybody was doing their job.

We won the first game 7-2 at Royals Stadium, and in the second game we got one of those breaks that the Yankees always seemed to get. We're leading 3-2 in the eighth. Dennis Leonard is pitching for us, and Willie Randolph is on first with two outs. He could run pretty good. Bob Watson hit a ball down the left-field line. I had played left so long I knew it was going to hit off the wall and bounce back instead of hug the wall. So, I ran to a spot where I thought it was going to bounce. It came right to me, and I just turned and threw. I didn't even take a step, I just threw it.

The ball went over the first cutoff man's head, which was a blessing in disguise for us. That's when the Yankees third-base coach, I think it was Mike Ferraro, sent Willie home. The ball came right to George, and George turned and made a great throw to Porter and we got him at home. That helped us win game two, and then we went to Yankee Stadium.

What I remember most about this game was how quiet it became in the seventh inning when George hit that home run against Rich Gossage. We were behind 2-1, and had two outs. I hit a double off Tommy John, and then the Yankees brought Goose Gossage out of the bullpen. U.L. (Washington) hits a single to second base. Now, I'm on third and U.L. is on first. George, who's had this spectacular year, comes up against Gossage.

Boom!

The people were just stunned. It was so quiet in Yankee Stadium you could hear the trains going by on the subway. Then two innings later Quiz throws the last pitch for a strikeout, and we're all celebrating there at home plate. To be able to do that in front of my mom and all the people I knew back home was just pure joy.

# 15
# K K K K K K K K
# K K K K

In the first game of the 1980 World Series against the Philadelphia Phillies, I was the first batter in the game.

I was psyched, ready to prove to everyone that I belonged in the big leagues and that my season had not been a fluke. I knew if I could get going the team would get going. That's the way it worked all season.

I don't really remember what – I guess I don't want to remember because I think I struck out (laughter) … and again … and again … and …

I can kind of laugh about it today, but I couldn't for a long time. That World Series haunted me the rest of my career. I struck out 12 times, and we only played six games. It was the most ever in a World Series until Ryan Howard of the Phillies struck out 13 times in 2009. But it was more than just the number of times. It was when the strikeouts were coming – with men on base, at the end of the game, in the first at-bat.

We had finally made the World Series, beating our nemesis in the process. We were going into the Series with a lot of confidence, but not a lot of momentum. We beat the Yankees in three straight, and then had to wait around to see whether we would be playing the World Series against Houston or Philadelphia.

Our series was a sweep, which is normally good. The National League series went the full five games, and while we were waiting around to find out who we would be playing, I think I lost my edge. I think our whole team did a little bit.

I wanted to show the whole world why I had 100 hits from both sides of the plate, why I hit .326, why I had 32 consecutive stolen bases without getting caught, why I had 705 at bats, all of that stuff, man. I wanted to show everybody. So, I tried. I tried really hard to prove that. Then it got to the point where I was trying so hard to do it that I was trying too hard and getting tensed up. You know that saying when they tell you to, "try easy" which really just means relax and don't press. I couldn't try easy in that series.

The World Series is really different – even compared to the playoffs. Everything is different; at least that's how it felt. They give you new shoes, new uniforms, new bats, new everything. I'm looking good, but I don't feel exactly right, just a little out of sorts. I wasn't overwhelmed by being there, but I wanted so badly to do well I put a lot of pressure on myself. All season long everyone had been telling me, "Willie if you go, the Royals go." Well, that happened in the regular season.

I went four-for-26 and walked four times. I was only on base eight times in the Series. I stole two bases. After being an effective lead-off batter all season, I struck out in my first at-bat in four of the six games we played. I never really got us off to a good start. The other strikeouts came at awful times.

They were coming with men in scoring position. The last one came with the bases loaded to end the game. That was such a different feel from what had happened all season long. Stuff that was routine during the season was not routine in the World Series. I don't think I ever felt comfortable in the World Series, when I would go to the plate.

That was just the worst feeling in the world. I felt like I had let every person in Kansas City down, every guy on my team down, the owners, the people in the front office, my mom, my friends, everybody. It went from the highest high beating the Yankees in New York to the lowest low.

Looking back I think the time off between the series had an affect on us. We had swept the Yankees, and the Houston and Philly series went to five games. We stayed in New York after beating the Yankees. So, you relax a little bit. You're enjoying it. You're hanging out with your family. After three years of disappointment of losing to (New York), I think that was a little bit like our World Series.

We practiced. We had batting practice at Yankee Stadium two days, and you're doing your stuff. We were waiting for that series to get over. They not only played two more games, there was a day off for them. So, we actually had 2½ or 3 days in New York. Even when they're playing the fifth game of their series we are waiting at the airport watching the fifth game of their series on television. We have a charter plane, and we still don't know where we're going. That game ends up going into extra innings, and we're all sitting around, "OK, we're going to Houston … no, it's Philly … no Houston."

Finally, it's Philly. Then it was a quick flight to Philly from New York. We still don't play because the series didn't just start the next day. We had another day off. We were messed up.

Staying in New York wasn't a mistake necessarily because we did get our work in. But when you are playing everyday, everyday, everyday and then you have some days off you lose your rhythm, your momentum, all of that. They had played all five games against Houston, had one day off to travel back and then played six games to beat us. They were in rhythm; they kept their mental concentration and didn't have any time to relax for two or three days. When you're still playing and still mentally into it, you just go right into the series and you're still in the zone.

That's not the reason we lost. We were ready. But from hindsight, I wish we had just gone right in to it. That's what happened later, in 1985, when we won the series.

There were a couple of key plays in the series that if either one of them had gone our way I think we would have won. I was in both of them. One of them was in game five at Royals Stadium. They had beaten us twice in Philly, and we had come back tied them in game three and four. If we win, we go back to Philly with a 3-2 lead in the series.

It's the sixth inning. We're behind 2-1. Amos leads off the sixth with a home run to tie the game. Then Clint Hurdle and Darrel Porter single, and there's runners on first and third. U.L. Washington hits a sac fly to score Clint and we go ahead.

Now, I'm batting with Porter on first base and one out. I hit a ball off the right-center wall. Porter is running, but as I 'm rounding second base I know that they have a shot to throw him out at the plate. The relay guy was Manny Trillo. I see him catching the ball as I 'm rounding second base, so I start jumping up and down and waving my hands as I was going to third. I'm trying to get him to throw me out at third rather than throw to home and try to get Porter.

I can see him take a quick glance at me and think about it for a second. Then he throws a bullet to home plate and gets Porter out. What I was trying to do was get him to throw at me so Porter could score. We end up not scoring again when Frank hit a foul pop-up to Mike Schmidt at third.

Then, we get into the ninth inning and we're leading 3-2 with Quiz on the mound. Usually that season we would put Pete LaCock at first base in the seventh, eighth or ninth to replace Willie Aikens for defense. For some reason we didn't do that this game. Maybe the manager still wanted his bat in the lineup because he was coming up third in the bottom of the ninth. Anyway, Willie Aikens stayed in.

So, Mike Schmidt opens the Phillies ninth with a single. Del Unser comes in to pinch hit. Willie is holding Schmidt on at first base, and he jumps off the bag real quick when the pitch goes to the plate. Unser hit it right down the line past him into right field for a double and Schmidt scored to tie the game. Unser went to third on a sac bunt and scored when Manny Trillo singled to give the Phillies a 4-3 lead.

We had a chance in the bottom of the ninth when we loaded the bases, but Tug McGraw struck out Jose Cardenal to end the game.

We had been ahead in two of the games that we lost going into the seventh inning. In game two, in Philadelphia we were leading 4-2 going into the bottom of the eighth, and we had the best reliever in baseball there with Dan Quisenberry on the mound. They scored four in the bottom of the eighth. And we can't score when Ron Reed closes out the game for Steve Carlton. Then we were ahead in game five in the ninth.

Now we're going back to Philly for game six. Steve Carlton holds us to four hits for seven innings, and we're down 4-0 going into the eighth when Tug McGraw comes into the game. He gives up a run in the eighth and gets out of the inning when Hal McRae grounds out with the bases loaded.

In the ninth Amos struck out to lead off the inning, but Willie Aikens walked and we loaded the bases when Wathan and Cardenal both hit singles. We're behind 4-1, but are still alive with the bases loaded.

Frank comes up before me, and I'm standing there in the on-deck circle. Frank hits a semi-popup to the right side, and I'm looking and hoping it gets foul and into the stands. We get a horrible break here when their catcher Bob Boone tries to catch it. The ball pops off his glove and into Pete Rose's hands for out No. 2.

Now it's up to me with the bases loaded. Tug McGraw is pitching.

When I was a kid in Jersey watching the New York Mets, Tug McGraw was pitching for them. I have this in my brain that here is one of the guys I used to watch, but I put that out of my mind. "You can get a hit."

I was ready. I wanted to be the hero. I wanted to get that hit. I thought I could hit any fastball that anybody threw. So, I'm thinking if it's close to the plate I was going to take a hack at it. In the eighth he had walked me and had thrown everything way outside. But this time I knew he had to challenge me because the bases were loaded.

As I'm standing there getting ready to go to the plate, I could see the stadium getting ready for a celebration. Horses with policemen on them and police dogs were coming onto the field. They are coming down the right field line and left field line ready for the celebration to start. I 'm like, "Wow, man. This is crazy."

But my thoughts weren't negative. They were positive. I'm thinking I had a really good year. I can keep this going. I can be the hero.

I think I fouled off a couple of pitches, and then he threw me a high fastball – just about chest high. He had started me out low, and he kept coming up. He got to the point where he knew I was going to swing if he came close. During the season, I might have got on top of that ball. This time I went underneath it. He made a great pitch, but I felt like I was going to hit it. It wasn't like it was low and away. It was right where I could see it.

You ever have that situation where you swing at a ball, and you just can't believe you missed it. I *never* pictured that in my brain. I couldn't *believe* I missed it.

Once I struck out I was in disbelief. Everything seemed to be moving in slow motion. I saw the catcher jump up into the air, the police dogs in the dugouts, and the people in the stands. I felt like I had let every person in Kansas City down. It was like a dream that wasn't true. I was in slow motion back to the dugout thinking the season wasn't over, it was just another game. Then BOOM! It all came home to me.

I remember walking into the locker room not being able to stop crying. I put my glove in my locker ... no, I don't think I even did that.

I walked into the bathrooms in the locker room, and there was only one stall open because everybody else was in there crying. It was the saddest thing I have ever seen.

I had never failed before. Well, I had failed one other time in a playoff game that was in junior high school. But I had never failed in football. It had never happened to me and never with this kind of magnitude with everyone watching. It was just so surreal.

I really don't remember a whole lot after that. I guess I got dressed, and we're going out to the bus to go back to the hotel. The Phillies fans were rocking the bus, pushing it back and forth, back and forth. Some of the wives on the bus were screaming, and people were shouting, "Get out of here bussie!"

My wife hadn't come with me on that trip for some reason. So, I was alone and just feeling bad. They were rocking the bus. I'm listening to people scream. When we get back to the hotel I was back in my room. I was on one of the top floors, and I can just remember horns all night. Horns. Horns. Horns. Just a reminder that we had lost.

I couldn't sleep. When I got up the next day I remember being sleepy, but not really sleepy and getting on the bus going to the airport to fly home. Everything was sad, silent.

When we got to the airport in Kansas City I was really surprised because there were a bunch of people out there. Our fans were happy that we had gotten to the World Series, and it was almost like a parade going down to the stadium. People were thanking us for getting to the World Series. We had a police escort, and people at the airport yelling and screaming, but none of that made me feel good.

But then all the "12" stuff started. *Sports Illustrated* wanted to come out and do a story. Luckily, it was the swimsuit edition and maybe people didn't even read the story because Cheryl Tiegs was on the cover. There is a picture of me and my daughter back in the magazine. We were in Summit. All anybody wanted to talk about was the 12 strikeout stuff. It was a barrage of 12 strikeout stuff.

The Newark newspaper picked me as the Pro Athlete of the Year in New Jersey for 1980, but that didn't ease any of the pain I was feeling. I just wanted to hibernate that whole off season. I was embarrassed to go outside, embarrassed that people would see me in the stores. I kept replaying video tapes of me hitting during the season. I saw a batter who was relaxed, not tight, not looking up at anything. I just went up and hit.

In the World Series, I was way ahead of the ball, trying to kill it instead of just throwing my bat out. I had kept doing that even when I had my thinking straight. In fact, that last time up, I was sure I'd get a hit even with everything that had happened during the series.

The next spring, we go to Puerto Rico for a couple of games. There is this kid outside the bus, and he's putting up 10 fingers, then two. Ten fingers, then two. It was just wearing me down, man.

Coming back to Fort Myers, we're in a spring training game, and I'm trying to get ready to hit. These college kids are frickin' on the right side of home plate. They are just screaming at me. "Twelve! Twelve! Twelve!" It was negative, negative, negative. I couldn't hear anything else, and I lost it in the on-deck circle. I was going all Jimmy Piersall on them – remember Jimmy Piersall? I climbed the fence to try and get over it to get at them. José Martinez got me, and they took me out of the game because they knew I was mentally going nuts.

It was just eating me up so much inside … those 12 strikeouts … failure … and this is at spring training a year later.

All spring and summer it was eating me up. I ended up having a halfway decent year in 1981. I got hurt in spring training, pulled a hammy and I was out for six or seven weeks. I ended up hitting .303, but it wasn't, you know, good enough.

Then even when I won the batting title in 1982, that turned into something negative.

# 16
# PLAYER OF
# THE YEAR

After the 1980 World Series I felt so bad and so down for letting the team down, the city down, myself down, my family down. So all through 1981 I was trying to make up for it.

For the first two months of the season we weren't doing such a hot job of it. We were 10 games under .500 and we were 12 games behind the Oakland A's when the players went on strike on June 9. As bad as that was for baseball it probably was the only thing that saved our season. That was the year that baseball had first-half and second-half champions. And they met in the playoffs.

We caught fire the second half that summer, winning the AL West. We were one of only two teams in the AL West to have a winning record

*Photo courtesy of the Kansas City Royals*

*Rounding third and heading home was when I needed the fans to help me through that last 90 feet. Late in my career I would end up playing with the A's.*

the second half of the season. We made the five-game playoff against the A's, who had won the first half.

For me the season was another step in trying to be consistent. That was my whole focus in '79, '80 and '81. I was just trying to have consistent years. It was really gratifying for the Royals to give me Player of the Year in 1981, but I think they were just thinking, "Maybe we should give it to him to make him feel better." (Laughter.)

A lot of stuff went on that year with the strike. I wanted to go out there and do the best I could and then maybe the fans wouldn't be quite as mad at us. You know we were never a really good early-season team. We were always a late-season team. It was almost like we would play the first half, then figure out how far you were away and know how much you had to put it in gear.

Standings mean a lot to the fans, and they do to players, too. But with us we were a veteran enough team that we knew it wasn't what you did at the start of the season but  what you did toward the end, where you finished.

When we came back from the strike I think I hit .331 and helped lead us through the second half of the season. At the start of September we won 12 of 16 games to put us in position to win the second-half championship.

I might have been in the best shape of my life then because of what I did during the strike. We didn't really know when it was going to end because it would look like the strike was about to be over, and then some player would say something that made the owners mad, and then an owner would say something about breaking the union. So it went on.

During the strike I started doing tae kwon do with Larry Gura and Willie Aikens. I think that was something that the Guru did all the time, so I was doing it with him. So, I was working every day, stretching every day – and if you have ever done tae kwon do, you know what kind of shape you have to be in to do it.

Some of that depends on the teacher you have. We had Ri Kon Ko. He was really a good guy, but he was intimidating as far as a teacher goes. He would walk up to you and say something in broken English, look at you, and you would go, "OK, I'll do it" and bow down and do something, so I really kept myself in shape.

*Courtesy of Kansas City Royals*

*George Brett knocked me in for an RBI more than 300 times in my career, but this time I got home before he could get to the plate.*

The other thing we did during the strike was we would drive to KU to take batting practice. We were locked out of the cages at Royals Stadium because of the strike. At the time that was the closest place we could go to, so we'd make arrangements to have an hour or two and go in and use their batting cages up there.

I guess it worked for me because I hit pretty well after the season resumed. You know it's harder for hitters to be ready after a break than pitchers because a pitcher can keep his arm in shape just by throwing. He can go out and simulate pitching, then, do his running to keep his legs in shape.

But for the hitters, you aren't doing all the stopping and starting, the swinging the bat every single day. So you have to get your hands back in shape, your eyes have to get back in shape. When you start spring training – and none of us really wore batting gloves back then like they do now – your hands would get blisters, then they would break, and they are going to heal and form into calluses. When you first come back that's what you deal with if you haven't been picking up a bat.

The A's really had the best team in the AL West that year. They won the first half championship with a 37-23 record and finished second in the second half with a 27-22 mark. We got into the playoffs even though we had the fourth best record overall that summer. We were 11 games behind the A's.

And the playoffs weren't very competitive. The A's were really good – even though the guys on those A's teams weren't as well known as the '70, '71 and '72 teams or the late '80s teams with (Mark) McGwire and (Jose) Canseco. But that was the start of Billy Ball out there, and we all know how good they were. Oakland had a really good pitching staff.

Getting to the playoffs was really good, but you know losing 3-0 in the five-game series was another disappointment.

# 17
# I SHOULDN'T HAVE SAT OUT

*"I don't know what my lineup will be, but I'll probably sit Willie down ... He's my guy, and I want to take care of him. Robin Yount will win everything else this year. I want Willie to win it. It's something he will remember the rest of his life."*

—*Dick Howser, the night before the Royals*
*final game of the 1982 season.*

If I had known how much grief I was going to get about sitting out the final game of the 1982 season, I would have played and tried to get as many at-bats as Robin Yount just to say I had won the batting championship.

I was leading the race with a .332 average. He was at .328 going into the final day of the season. He was having a great season, and Milwaukee was on its way to the World Series. But I was leading the batting race.

Even before I went to the locker room, Dick (Howser) and John Schuerholz were waiting for me as I walked in the front door. They said, "Come into the office." In my brain, I'm ready to play. I'm not thinking about Robin Yount. So I'm not even thinking about what the heck they are talking about. I didn't even think anything about it. I was just trying to play. What they said to me was Robin Yount had to go five for five to win the batting title if I didn't play.

That was the first time I had heard of that. They said, "What we think you should do is sit out. He has to go 5-for-5 to beat you."

I said to them, "You guys think I can't get a hit? Why are you doing this? I mean, even if I go 1-for-3, I still beat him." But finally I just caved in.

We were out of the pennant race, but the Brewers were still in it. Even though they were playing in Baltimore, their game started a half hour after ours did because it was on television. So I'm sitting there, sitting there. Meanwhile, Robin hits a home run in the first, then another in the fourth. He flied out in the fifth, and then hit a triple leading off in the eighth.

Now we're sitting at .3316 for me and .3307 for him. Since he batted in the eighth, we're pretty sure he won't get another at-bat.

We get to the ninth, and I'm not thinking anything about it. I think it was Mark Ryal at bat with two outs in the ninth for us. Meanwhile, the Brewers and Orioles are also heading into the ninth, and Yount would be the fifth batter in the inning. Two guys get on, so now he's going to come up again in the ninth. A hit would have put him one-thousandth of a point in front of me.

The next thing I know Dick is telling me to get up and get loose. So I'm down there getting loose, and now I'm thinking, "Man, this is a lot of pressure. I have to go 1-for-1." If I had started the game I had a chance to go 2-for-3, 1-for-3, whatever, but not 1-for-1. That's pressure.

So Dick has Ryal come over to the dugout to do something with his bat to stall for time, and Dick is on the phone to the pressbox to see how Yount's at-bat is going. Ryal walks back out toward the plate, and the dugout phone rings again. It's Billy Martin, the A's manager. For some reason he knew what was going on. He says, "You want me to delay the game until you find out?"

I think the only reason he did that was because he knew Dick through the Yankees. But what manager does that? You don't get too many managers who go, "Let's delay the game so this guy from another team can win the batting championship." To me that's the ultimate respect you can give someone.

Then we get the call. Yount got hit by Dennis Martinez and didn't get the hit, so I can sit down. We whistle out to Billy. He's out there just BS-ing with his pitcher. The pitcher is probably going, what the hell are you out here for? Then Billy walks off the mound. I look over and I tipped my hat down, and he tipped his hat down. It was like I was saying, "thank you."

Ryal makes an out and the game is over. I won the batting title .3316 to .3307.

Now we go into the locker room after the game, and all the reporters are asking Dick about the delaying tactics. And they're asking me. Everybody (reporters) is telling me, "I would have done this" or "I would have done that."

I'm saying to myself, does it make a difference if you sit out the first game of the year, or a game in the middle of the year? Does it matter? I mean,

> *"Two, three years from now, nobody's going to remember he sat out."*
>
> —Dick Howser, following the final game of the 1982 season.

you miss a game, you miss a game. Why is the last game so important? That's the stuff I didn't get. I already had missed a bunch of games at the start of the year when I pulled a hammy in spring training. So why was this one so frickin' important?

I didn't know the politics of baseball. As a young kid I'm listening to the front office. George had won a batting title a couple of years before, and they were saying how good it would be for the team for a Royals player to win another one. Man ... if I had known.

One thing that was strange that season is I didn't have to overcome my usual slow start. I missed almost a month of the season because of a pulled hamstring I suffered in spring training – trying to do something special for one of my former high school football coaches.

Coach Tremblay, one of the assistant coaches at Summit High School, had moved to Florida and was living in Dunedin where the Blue Jays had their spring training. Dunedin was a long bus ride from Fort Myers, where the Royals trained. By 1982, I had been a starter for most of three seasons, and I had established myself a little bit. I saw how the veteran guys worked in spring training, how they would start off and try to get themselves slowly into shape and work their way to the last week of spring training to really get hot.

So, we're playing the Blue Jays. I'd leave tickets for my coach, and he and I would always talk before the game. We'd talk about Summit. I'd always try to do something a little special for him – steal a base or stretch a single to a double, something like that. This time I had been feeling a little tightness in my legs on the bus ride up and I probably talked to him a little bit too long before I started warming up. But I'm only 22, 23 years old and you don't really think about warming up –

especially back then. So, I do my warm-up really quick, and I don't ever get my hammies real loose.

I get on base, and I'm trying to do my thing and show off in front of coach. So, I take off for second and I get about two steps when, POW! It was like somebody shot me in the right leg. I go down instantly. I get taken out of the game. I'm icing down, and then I find out later that I got a pulled hammy. It's not going to be ready for six weeks. I mean I pulled it bad.

So, I'm not doing too good after that. I'm going through all the rehab stuff, and I'm working out and doing all that. Six weeks come, and I might have played one or two games early. I think I played one game in early April and another in the middle of April, but it just wasn't right. I think I kept trying to come back too early, and they would put me back on the DL. Me and Mickey Cobb were always out in the outfield, stretching, running, putting that heating stuff on the back of your leg. I was getting really frustrated. I really wanted to play so bad, and you don't know what is going to happen. They weren't giving out the big guaranteed contracts then, and I'm trying to get going so I can make some money.

The guys are also saying, "You have to come back so we can win."

Finally, about the middle of May I got healthy and came back. I was hot right away, and I stayed hot most of the year. When the weather got hot, I got better. Instead of having to go through that cold spell at the start of the season, I wasn't even playing until it was getting pretty warm. I bet if you look at my batting average in April over my whole career, compared to the rest of the months, I probably only hit .240 or .250. I didn't really function too well in cold.

So, I missed that cold month at the start of the season, and I stayed hot the rest of the year. It was also the first year I made the All-Star team. That was pretty cool. I was just in awe of everybody there at the game. I didn't start, but I replaced Fred Lynn in the bottom of the fourth. I struck out twice in the game – I remember it like it was yesterday – and I didn't really care because I was just so happy to be there.

The game was in Montreal. What a great city. Me and George (Brett) went out to a couple of clubs while we were up there. That squad, we had five guys on it: Frank (White), Quiz (Dan Quisenberry), Hal (McRae),

George and me. Dick Howser was one of the coaches and Mickey Cobb was the assistant trainer. That made it pretty cool because it was like the Royals. We might have had more representatives in that game than any other team in the league.

We lost the game, but I was just in awe of being there with all those other players.

The All-Star game is a little weird because it comes at a time of the season when you would like to have a couple of days off. You're tired. But you want to be there. As a young kid, that's part of your check-off list. I had a list. I wanted to be Rookie of the Year when I was a rookie. I wanted to win a batting championship. I wanted to win a stolen base championship. I wanted to win the World Series. I wanted to go to an All-Star game. And the biggest thing I wanted to do was hit a home run *outside* of the ballpark.

After the All-Star game I stayed hot. I think I hit something like .370 in August, and my average was way up there. I can't even explain it. When I was getting jammed in on my fists, I would get a hit. I was getting regular hits. It seemed like everything was falling in.

Well, I didn't really check a lot of stuff in the paper when I was playing. I would check our standings and figure out what our magic number was toward the end of the season. Then all of a sudden everyone was telling me about the batting championship, and how I could win it.

You know that saying "try easy." Here's a perfect example of that. After hitting almost .340 the whole season, I started trying to do a little more to win the batting championship; trying to get more hits, trying to make sure I had enough trips to the plate to qualify because I was only going to play about 135 games. So, I was putting a lot of pressure on myself to win the championship and I just kept going down and down.

We come into the final week of the season and I'm neck and neck with Robin. Going into the final day of the season I was leading him .331624 to .32805. That's when all the drama happened on that final day.

Like I said, I still get grief about that. When I'm down in spring training with the other batting champions and doing those autograph appearances at the ballparks down there, it never fails. Some guy wearing a Milwaukee cap will come up and sort of growl at me, "Hey

Willie! Robin should have won your title." They all know – and they don't ever forget.

And that next year, they beat me up bad in Milwaukee.

"You sat down!"

"You suck! Robin should have won!"

It's that negative stuff all over again. I can't even win the batting championship without criticism. I have a little fun with it now, but after those guys who tease me about it leave I lean back with the guy sitting next to me at the autograph thing and say, "You sit out one game (laughter) and they never let you forget."

It's not like I backed my way in there. I frickin' hit .332. C'mon, man.

I can laugh about it now, but it still feels bad. Just once, I would like for them to say, "Hey, you won a batting championship" and leave it at that, but somebody has always got to say something. And I missed a bunch of games that year. I don't know what the big deal about the last one is.

# 18
## PEER
## PRESSURE

**N**egative. **Negative. Negative.**

For nearly three years almost everything around me had been negative, starting with the 1980 World Series when I struck out 12 times. I felt like I hadn't had a good enough year in 1981 to make people forget about the 12 strikeouts in the 1980 World Series, even though I won the Royals Player of the Year Award.

It was a strike season, and I batted .303 and was second again only to George Brett. I played more games than anyone else on the roster, and I had a 15-game hitting streak and finished with 133 hits and 34 stolen bases – in a strike-shortened season, but I still felt like people were thinking about the World Series.

So, in 1982 I win the batting championship, but when I didn't play that final game that's all anyone was talking about. I don't know how many games I missed that year (26), but all anyone was talking about was the last one.

I'm feeling like no matter what I do, no matter how good I am, there is still harping on the negative, the negative, the negative. That may not have been what everyone was saying, but it's all I was hearing. No matter what I did, it was never good enough for a reporter, for a TV guy.

Never good enough.

Never good enough.

That's what I felt like I had been hearing from the Royals, too. Whitey Herzog always said I could never hit good enough. It was always something. Even that final game in 1982. It was like they didn't think I could get a hit and win it outright.

That winter, after I won the batting title, is when I first tried cocaine.

I was a shy kid growing up. I didn't even have a date until the 11th grade. I had a little clique, and I just hung around with them when I was growing up. So, I was not as outgoing as everybody thought. Getting on drugs made me more outgoing. It made me feel better. It made me forget about all the negativity. It came at a time when it was almost a savior to me.

It was wrong. I knew it was wrong. And even when I was doing it, I knew it was hurting me. By late that year, before Christmas, I finally figured, "You know what? This isn't right. It isn't going to help you." But it sure made me feel good at the time.

The feeling cocaine gives you is it makes it seem like you are invincible. You feel more positive. I wasn't sitting there doing cocaine a whole evening or anything like that. You would do a couple of lines, and then you would go to a party, go and have a drink, hang out or go to a place and dance.

This was causing a few problems at home because I was going out partying. I had never done that much before because I had young kids. So, my first two or three years in the league I didn't hang out or go out with the guys after the game. Now I wasn't going home. It wasn't my wife's fault or anything. It was the drugs and the partying. It wasn't a good combination.

I was introduced to the drug by Vida Blue. He had come on the team in the 1982 season, and he's the one who introduced me to the gentleman who had the cocaine (Mark Liebl). Mark was just a regular guy. He was a fan, and he was just a guy that we knew. We would see him every now and then and go to his house or meet him at a bar somewhere. It was all in fun. It wasn't to do anything to hurt anybody. It was just us having fun and trying to be like everyday people.

I can't remember the very first experience, but I'm sure it was at his house. That's how we all got caught because there were all these expensive cars showing up at this guy's house in Overland Park all the time. I think his neighbors started noticing it.

I didn't even know how to do cocaine. I just followed what everyone else did. They would have a straw or roll money up and snort it that way.

I really didn't think much about it being against the law. I just never thought of that. I didn't worry about anyone telling on me because I always thought that whoever else is doing it is going to get in trouble too, if they are going to tell on me. And the people I'm doing it with have a lot to lose just like I do. Some of the guys who were doing it were high-powered people. Some were doctors. Some were everyday people.

You have to remember in the '80s, cocaine was for people who had money. It's not like it is today. You weren't a scumbag if you were doing cocaine in the '80s. It was the drug of the rich. It wasn't stuff you get in the ghettos. I wasn't getting it from some guy on the street. I went to a guy's nice house. Nice town, good job and everything. I never really thought anything about it.

And the other thing that people don't realize. I never did much with Willie Aikens or with Jerry Martin, two of the other guys on the team who got in trouble at the same time. We sometimes saw each other coming to get something and leaving. But that's how we got caught, all the cars coming and going.

Actually using the drug didn't last very long for me. It wasn't going to do anything for my game. So I did it for a little while, then said, "OK, that's it" and I quit.

I'm not even doing drugs anymore by the time spring training comes around in 1983. I'm clean. The drug thing is not even on my radar screen. For a change I got off to a pretty good start. I was hitting over .300 the first month of the season, and by June – when I would normally start to really warm up – I was at almost .290 in June.

Then a guy on another team who I knew was in town and asked me if I could get him anything. It was the late Al Cowens. (I hate to say his name now.) I sort of felt like I was obligated to him because I got the chance to play when he got hit in the jaw in 1979. I know that seems crazy now, but that's how I felt. I got a chance to play in '79, and the year after that he was traded away from the Royals.

So, now it's at least six months since I have bought any cocaine, and he is in town with Seattle and asks if I know anybody. I said, "I really don't do it now, but I know somebody who does. I can make a call for you."

This was before cell phones, so we would make all our calls right from the locker room. So, I made the call. Liebl answered.

"Hey Mark, this is Willie."

"Which Willie."

"Wilson"

Then I told him what I wanted, and he said, "I'd like to help you, but I got nothing." So I said, "Thanks, I didn't want to be involved anyway."

I hung up and went out and told AC that I "ain't got nuthin'" and then I never thought about it again. I actually felt guilty when I was telling him I couldn't get anything because he was asking me for something, and I couldn't help him. And here I was the guy who took his job after he got hurt.

Later on I learned that they were only tapping Liebl's phone for about a month. I was on the phone tap for a 20-second phone call when nothing was bought or passed from one person to another.

I never even really thought about it again until about a month later when that 20-second phone call would come back to bite me.

# 19
# THE DAY MY
# LIFE CHANGED

Most people remember the defining moment of the 1983 season because of the Pine Tar game. That was when George Brett homered against the Yankees, then went ballistic when the umpire called him out because pine tar extended too far up on his bat.

To me the Pine Tar Game holds an entirely different meaning. I injured my left shoulder that afternoon when I tried to make a diving catch in the outfield. I was in the clubhouse getting treatment when George hit the home run. It was the final game of a series against the Yankees and we were going home. I had an appointment with Dr. Steven Joyce the following day to have him look at my shoulder.

I'm driving in to his office down on the Plaza from my home in Blue Springs, (Mo.) and I'm having a nice little conversation with myself as I'm driving.

"You're a young kid."

"You'll be all right."

"Maybe it's not so bad."

"Maybe I can get in the game tonight."

I was listening to music, driving the freeway through downtown and I got off at the Southwest Trafficway exit to head up the hill on toward St. Luke's Hospital. I came up to a light and gunned the motor to get through on a yellow. This dark-colored car followed me through on the red, and I'm thinking, "That's good because if the police are going to stop anybody it will be that guy."

The next light was red, so I stopped. This dark-colored sedan pulled up beside me at the stoplight. I glanced to my left at the two guys sitting in the front seat, probably nodded at them or something because that's what I usually did. Then, the one closest to me reached into his coat, pulled out a badge, tapped it on his window and pointed over to the side of the road for me to pull over.

I didn't know what's going on, but I was nervous and started to sweat. My mind was just racing. It's funny how much you can think about in such a short time. I know it's serious. The KBI (Kansas Bureau of Investigation) – which is really just the FBI of the state – doesn't pull you over for going through a yellow.

My mind immediately raced back eight months in time. I had experimented a few times with cocaine after the 1982 season, but I had quit by December. I realized cocaine made me feel better for a little while, but it wasn't going to make me a better baseball player. When you've done something like that you always have it in the back of your mind that something bad could happen. So, I think subconsciously I kind of knew what it was about.

So, that was going through my mind, but I hadn't used in about eight months. Surely it couldn't be that. I didn't even think about the phone call I had made to Mark Liebl just a month earlier. Why would I? Nothing had ever come of that phone call.

I pulled over, and one of the guys asked me to get out of my car and into theirs. They introduced themselves as agents from the KBI. I don't remember if there were flashing lights or anything, but I know I felt like everyone who was driving by us would recognize me and know the police were talking to me. Then these guys started asking me questions about Mark Liebl, the guy who I had bought cocaine from back in November.

"Do you know this person?"

"Do you know that person?"

They're playing "good cop, bad cop" with me. One guy would be real nice and then the guy in the backseat would jump on me real hard trying to confuse me. After the questions, they tell me that they know I had tried to buy $20,000 worth of stuff. Hell, I didn't have $20,000 to give away, let alone to buy drugs.

This went on for a while, and I was starting to get angry. They're telling me they know I have done this and done that – stuff I had never done. Finally, I look at the one guy and say, "Well, if you know so damn much and you think I have done this, then arrest me right now. You are telling me stuff that I never did. I don't even know this guy or that guy you named."

Finally they let me go, but they said, "We're going to stay in touch."

So, I'm just in a fog. What's going to happen to me? Who knows about this? Has everybody who drove down the street seen me? What am I going to tell my family? I still haven't seen the doctor, and now I'm late for my appointment to get my shoulder checked out.

I'm just absolutely done, mentally. I'm really down in the dumps.

I got to the hospital, and I was walking into this public place with all these people around. They're talking to me, asking for my autograph, how the shoulder is … I'm trying to be civil, and I sign stuff, but I'm also wondering whether anybody knows what's going on.

I saw the doctor, but honestly, I can't even remember what the diagnosis was. I don't have any idea what he said. I finished there, and then I had to go to the ballpark because we were playing the Cleveland Indians that night.

I usually never listen to the sports shows on the radio because someone was always criticizing the Royals or me or something, and I had stopped listening pretty early in my career. But this day I turned it on because I was curious now about whether anything has leaked out or what. And I heard that there are Royals involved in this drug thing and a "Royals superstar" was involved.

As silly as it sounds now, in my brain I was thinking, "Who is the superstar?"

When I got to the stadium I parked behind right field and walked in through the tunnel. As soon as I got to my locker there was a message that I needed to go upstairs to see John Schuerholz, the general manager. I was still in kind of a fog. I can't remember my conversation with him, but I know it wasn't a very good conversation.

When I got back to the locker room I remember the players sort of whispering to each other and looking over at me. I was sitting in the corner at my locker, and I was wondering who else might have gotten stopped that day.

I don't remember whether I played that day or not, but I felt like everybody at the whole stadium was staring at me the whole time and that everybody hated me. I don't have any recollection of the fans or how they reacted that day, but I was as low as you could go, and I wanted everyone to know the truth.

"I was clean."

"Yeah, I might have done something, but I had stopped doing it for months by then – damn near eight months."

I kept wondering, "Why was this happening now, why not when I was doing it?" I was trying to think through everything in my brain. Everything I had worked so hard for might be gone. All the things I wanted to do as a young player and a young man might be over. Would I still be allowed to play baseball? Would I have to go to jail? Would my teammates ever talk to me again? How would this affect the rest of my life?

Worst of all … I had to tell my mother.

That was harder than dealing with the police, harder than getting stopped by the side of the road, harder than having fans yell at you every day. She was the one who took care of me, who raised me, who put clothes on my back. My mother always wanted the best for us, and she worked hard to get it. So, the disappointment for everyone else was secondary to disappointing my mother and my grandmother. That was a really hard phone call to make … I mean, really hard.

And you know the only thing she wanted to know.

She told me just one thing, "Tell me the truth, and we'll get through this."

I'm telling you, man, that was a rough day.

From that day, all the rest of the 1983 season it was coming out a little bit at a time. It was me then Vida, then Aikens, then Jerry Martin. I am sure the KBI had other people they thought were involved. They were going through the whole team, but I wasn't really worried about anybody else but me.

What I found out later, which upset me for a long, long time, was that the reason we got caught was because Vida got caught. Vida got caught with the stuff. And to save himself, he told on us. That's how they started tapping the phone – through Vida.

What upset me most is that he was still on our team when this was happening. I'm thinking, "You couldn't even tell me something?"

You know what I'm saying? "You couldn't say, 'Hey, they're tapping his phone' or 'Hey … something.'" But I guess he couldn't because it would have messed up his deal.

For a long time I was angry at Vida. Later on when I was with the A's in 1991 and '92, he would sometimes come into the locker room, and he just couldn't look at me. I wouldn't look at him, and he couldn't look at me. One day, he walked over and said, "Man, I'm sorry." When he said that, I forgave him. I finally let it go.

The whole situation was on my mind for the next month of the season after I was stopped, "What would happen to me?" I knew something bad was going to happen, but the uncertainty of it was just eating at me.

If I got a hit, I didn't care. If I got two hits, I didn't care. I just didn't care.

I mean, I knew something was going to happen. You just know something is going to happen to you when an FBI guy talks to you – or KBI. But it seemed like the investigation was being dragged out and dragged out.

What I could never get my brain around is that nothing got passed to me the day I made the phone call. Nothing got bought. That's like if you talked about robbing a bank, then somebody robs the bank and they put you in jail for talking about it. That's what I felt like I was being investigated for.

Finally, they charge me. I think I was in Seattle on a Royals road trip when my lawyer calls and said I had a choice of a felony for alleged distribution of cocaine or pleading guilty to a misdemeanor for attempting to buy cocaine.

My lawyer and I wanted to challenge it, go to trial because I didn't get anything. I was just talking. I thought I could beat the trafficking charge. My lawyer thought I could beat it. But my agent goes, "If we do that, it will be a long drawn-out trial and probably take over a year."

We checked with the DA and what they were saying was, "Well, if you cop to this, then we are sure you can get probation." So, my attorney did the research. He talked to the police. He talked to the DA. He looked up all the cases in the books and no one had ever gotten jail time. One case was a fine; the other was a year probation for what I had done.

I trusted my attorney and I trusted my agent, but they weren't the ones in trouble. I was the one in trouble.

We had put together a petition and had 10,000 names on it from fans that didn't want me to go to jail. We had announced a youth drug prevention program with Mr. K. We did whatever we thought we could to help make the sentence a little less.

We go to court, and the judge asks everybody what they thought. So the DA recommends probation. The judge asks if we agree with that, and my lawyer and I said we did. And all the time everyone is talking, the judge was just sitting up there and pouring himself a glass of water like, "I'm not even listening to what you guys are saying."

I'm sitting there watching him. The courtroom is filled. The buzz is going through. There were TV cameras. It was crazy.

Then the judge looks over and says, "I'll tell you what I'm going to do. I have people downstairs who don't get this much attention. They have committed murder and other things. I'm going to give you a year in jail ... "

That ... is ... all ... I ... hear.

I jump up and say "For what! I didn't do anything. I didn't get anything." I was so stunned and shocked. The lawyer grabbed me and pulled me back down. I never heard the judge say "nine months suspended."

Then, the judge hits the gavel and says, "Order. Order." He started talking and I was just in a blur thinking I got to go to jail for something I didn't even get. I thought if the prosecutors recommended a sentence that was what the judge was going to do.

I learned later that what the judge was saying afterwards is that he sentenced me that way because I was "a national hero who occupied a special place in our society. There are responsibilities you must live up to."

That's a responsibility I never asked for. The people might have asked for it. Baseball asked for it. But all I did was sign a contract to play baseball, and that's my job. I didn't sign a contract to take care of anybody else's kids or be a role model for anybody else. I didn't have athletes for my role models. Well, I did for how they played on the field, but not their private lives. Those are two different things. How can you put those two things together as one?

Even the police were stunned at the sentence. They were shocked. I got apologies as they walked me downstairs to fingerprint me. They were saying, "Willie, we're really sorry. We didn't know this was going to happen. We didn't know it was going to turn out like this."

The judge had his own agenda. I found out later that he was a third-string jock in some sport and he had to let it go and ended up being a judge. Who the hell knows what his reason was? What I found out later is that they were cracking down so hard on drugs because it was (President Ronald) Reagan's "Just Say No" campaign. They were giving people time for stuff they were just on probation for before.

But I know my life changed from the day that KBI guy stopped me on the street.

From that point on everything that day was foggy for me, and my life changed forever in ways I didn't even understand at the time. It changed for me, for my family, for the Royals, for every baseball fan who ever heard my name. By the end of the day, I would be embarrassed, have to make the hardest phone call of my life and I was worried that I might never be allowed to step on a baseball field again.

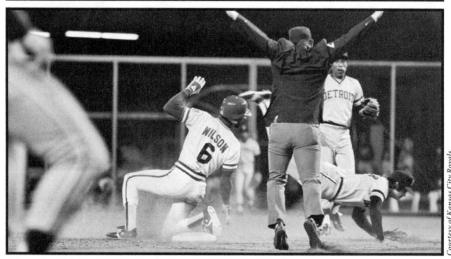

*They created the Hal McRae rule to limit hard slides into second base. But I learned the technique pretty well too.*

*Wilson family photo*

*We won the Suburban Conference championship during my sophomore year. I'm third from right on the front row.*

*Wilson family photo*

*This is my sophomore baseball team at Summit High School. I'm in the middle on the back row.*

*L-R I'm standing with my high school coach Art Cottrell and teammate George Gross. Gross threw a no-hitter while at Summit and later was drafted by the Houston Astros in 1977.*

Wilson family photo

Courtesy of Kansas City Royals

*SAFE!*

*Wilson family photo*

*This is my buddy and roommate U.L. Washington. We were teammates in AA, AAA and the major leagues.*

*Wilson family photo*

*My mother would often travel from New Jersey when we were playing the Orioles.*

This is one of the early pictures of me with the big league team in spring training.

*Wilson family photo*

WILLIE WILSON
Royals Hall of Fame - July 1, 2000

*Art illustrated by John Boyd Martin*

Portrait montage painting for Kansas City Royals Hall of Fame.

132

*Courtesy of Kansas City Royals*

*Sliding into the base was a thrill for me and the crowd.*

*Courtesy of Kansas City Royals*

*I was not a natural left-handed batter. But once I embraced hitting from that side of the plate my career really took off.*

*Courtesy of Kansas City Royals*

*Frank White and I were among a group of seven who were at the 1982 Major League All-Star Game in Montreal*

*Wilson family photo*

*Bill Cosby was one of the many celebrities who sang "Take Me Out to the Ball Game" when I was playing with the Cubs.*

*My grandmother, Annie Mae Timothy, "Madear" to the family, raised me until I was 7 years old.*

Wilson family photo

*My aunts, Martha Ann Gardner and Lula Mae Gibbs and my mother, Dorothy Lynn, (L-R) at a family reunion in 2010.*

Wilson family photo

*Wilson family photo*

*This is my daughter, Shanice.*

*Wilson family photo*

*My younger brother, Anthony Lynn.*

*Wilson family photo*

*Here is my oldest son DJ.*

*Wilson family photo*

*Trevor's son Trey Shawn is my youngest grandchild.*

*Wilson family photo*

*My son, Max, attended a Royals game with me.*

*My son Trevor and I at the All Star game in K.C.*

*Wilson family photo*

*Wilson family photo*

*I love having my children around me (from left) son Trevor, daughter Shanice, granddaughter Anisa, grandson Kayden and son Max.*

*Wilson family photo*

*My granddaughter, Anisa and grandson, KJ (Kayden).*

*Wilson family photo*

*When I was with Oakland, my oldest son would travel to spring training with me. Loved hanging out with him!*

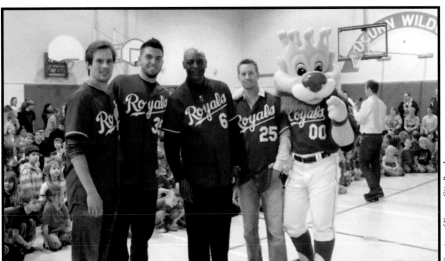

*Courtesy of Kansas City Royals*

*Great getting to hang out with some of the current players. Aaron Crow, Eric Hosmer, Everett Teaford and Sluggerrr on a Royals Caravan outing at Crow's elementary school in Topeka.*

*Willie Wilson Baseball Foundation*

*2007 Willie Wilson Legends game at CommunityAmerica Ball Park.*

*Negro Leagues Baseball Museum*

*I worked with the Negro Leagues Baseball Museum to conduct this clinic for players from RBI.*

*Explaining the highs and lows of being a Major Leaguer to youth from RBI.*

*Don Motley of the Negro Leagues Baseball Museum and former Royal Amos Otis at a RBI clinic.*

*Negro Leagues Baseball Museum*

*I'm becoming more comfortable as a speaker with events like this for the Legacy Awards banquet at the Negro Leagues Baseball Museum.*

*Negro Leagues Baseball Museum*

*I'm here with (from left) Fred Patek, Al Fitzmorris and Frank White at a State Farm Luncheon benefiting the Negro Leagues Baseball Museum.*

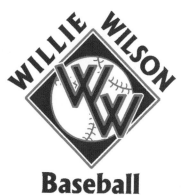

Here I'm talking with former pitcher Bert Blyleven. I can tell you it's a lot easier facing him here than in the batter's box.

*Negro Leagues Baseball Museum*

*Negro Leagues Baseball Museum*

Jim "Mudcat" Grant (left) can be really entertaining for guys like me and former player Brian McRae.

*Negro Leagues Baseball Museum*

*Wilson family photo*

It was an honor to be among the VIPs at the screening of the movie "42: The Jackie Robinson Story" at its Kansas City premiere in the spring of 2013.

With my baseball career in the background, my sport is now golf.

*Negro Leagues Baseball Museum*

Being around Buck O'neil was always an honor. Here we're at a Negro Leagues Museum event with Buck's biographer Joe Posnanski and DeMorris Smith, son of former KC Monarchs player Hilton Smith.

# 20
# JAIL TIME

**I**'m going to jail.

Whatever anybody was talking to me about being sorry or they didn't think it was going to happen or this and that after the court verdict, the bottom line, in my brain, was that I was still going to jail. None of those little things meant a lot to me because I was going to jail and not anybody else. Now, everybody is going to look at me in a whole different way.

What I was trying to accomplish as a young sports guy was going to be different. What I was trying to accomplish as a man was going to be looked at differently. There were a lot of things going bad.

I found out later that part of the reason the judge had given me the sentence was because he said I was a role model for kids, and maybe he needed to make an example of me. One of the things he said in court was, "An athlete does hold a special place in our society. The court realizes the life of a professional athlete is not a bed of roses. But all the court can do is take the totality of the circumstances and impose a sentence the court feels can meet the objectives of the case."

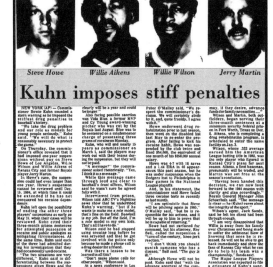

*Steve Howe   Willie Aikens   Willie Wilson   Jerry Martin*

**Kuhn imposes stiff penalties**

So now it's pretty clear to me that I got jail time because I was an athlete. I got singled out for more severe punishment because I was an athlete.

Let me tell you, long before Charles Barkley said he shouldn't be a role model for your children, I was saying it. I got vilified for it. Your parents should be your role model. They're the ones who make you brush your teeth, comb your hair. They make you go to school.

I know the judge said all that, but that's a responsibility I never asked for. I didn't really think I had a special place (in society) or whatever the situation the judge said I have in it. If he wants to make me a role model, that's fine – on the field. Baseball is my job. But off the field I'm a role model to my own kids. That's all I have to do.

But I'm still going to jail.

I had to turn myself in at the prison in Texas. Unlike what you might normally expect, I bought my own plane ticket to Dallas where the prison was located. I jump in a taxi and they drive me to the penitentiary, and I turned myself in. I didn't even get my change back from the driver. Once you walk through the doors you can't go back out. My luggage was outside, and the taxi driver brings it in and sets it down. All I had was a $50, and he ain't got change. He probably got the biggest tip of his life. Hell, I probably wouldn't have had change either. So, that was quite an experience.

This was one of those "country club" prisons. But don't be fooled. No prison is a country club. It's a jail. Yeah, we got to wear our own clothes and everything and didn't have to wear prison clothes. But it's *jail*. You can't go anywhere for three months. It's over Christmas and New Year's. Your family can't depend on you. I had two little children. So, it's tough.

If I hadn't played baseball, the jail time might not have happened, but it did.

All the guys in the prison knew we (the players) were coming down there because all the newspapers and television stations had gone down to do reports on the prison, what the room would look like, what the facility would look like, all that stuff. I was sitting at home thinking, "That is where I'm going."

I was down. I had never been in jail before. All kind of things are going through your head about jail, the people in jail. What's it going to be like? How am I going to deal with it? What's going to happen when I get out? Just all kinds of stuff.

When I finally got there it was almost like, "OK, I can hide for a while. Maybe they will forget about me for a month or two months." I need to relax and use this as an opportunity to stay in shape.

They had a track. They had handball courts, a basketball court. I would take a 9-iron and the couple of golf balls they would give me, and I would hit the golf ball between places when I had free time. I would run on the track. I mean, you better think of something to do in there or you would go crazy. So, I did everything to keep moving, to not think, to stay out of trouble.

My job in there was to wax and wash the floors. All depending on how good the floors were waxed or washed determined whether you were going to lunch first, second, third or fourth. My deal was that I wanted to go to lunch first. So, I tried to do a really good job on the floors.

I didn't really try to get to know anybody in there because I didn't want to know anybody in there. But there was this one guy, who was about 20 years older than me, who sort of kept me from getting in trouble. This guy was from some place out in Kansas – I can't remember where exactly, but for some reason he latched on me.

I don't know how he knew when something was going to go down in the prison, but he would always look out for me. He would tell me if there were drugs near me – because I found out that drugs came through that prison all the time. He let me know if there was going to be a raid on somebody so I could not be close to that guy. I remember one time he came over to me and said, "C'mon! Let's go!" I started to question him, and he just grabbed me and pulled me away. Then the guards came in and got this other guy.

When that happened, this older guy just looked at me, and said, "Now, when I say move, you move. Don't question me, just move." I don't even know his name. At the time, I didn't want to know his name, didn't want to be friends, but he latched on to me for that part and made sure I got out in time and kept myself out of trouble. I kind of owe that guy a lot. It made me realize that there are good people everywhere and there are horseshit people everywhere. Here I was in jail, and for some reason God gave me a guy to trust like that.

The only thing that was a positive in any way was that for those three months, I was sheltered. I had a chance to look at my life without any outside interference. The prison thing is something that I don't wish on anybody. But it was something I had to do to do some reflection. It made me a harder person, less trusting, colder.

In the drug section we would have to go in at the end of the day and have talks, counseling. I told my stories, and got a lot of stuff off my mind. It was almost like therapy, man. I learned a lot of things. I learned you don't have to be a bad person to be on drugs. You don't have to be an angry person to be on drugs. Drugs don't discriminate.

I also learned that I needed to accept that I wasn't a victim. I was the one doing it. I needed to take responsibility for my own actions and not blame other people. That was a hard lesson to learn – and really one that I would have to re-learn again about 15 years later.

# 21
# SUSPENDED

I got out nine days early for good behavior and then I went home for just a little bit. Then I had to go to spring training.

For the first time since I made the team, I was really nervous about going to spring training this year. I had been suspended for a year, but Commissioner Bowie Kuhn said he was going to review the suspension on May 15. So, they let me go to camp, but I couldn't play in any games in the spring.

I didn't know what was going to happen when I got there. I was worried about everything. I hadn't been involved with the world for about three months. I wondered if I was going to start, whether I would even make the team after the stigma of the drug conviction. I was worried about what people were going to be saying about me. I knew I had to have a press conference when I first got to camp.

But after that, I just basically put my head down and started going to work and blocking people out. I didn't really have a good spring training because I couldn't play in games. So, I would practice and go home. Practice and go home. I always felt like if I was just a "Joe Blow Player" I would have been out of the league. I had to be a pretty good player to still be in the league. So, that's how I had to think about it. That was my mentality coming back.

I was getting crucified by people in the stands, yelling at me, shouting stuff like, "Don't snort up the lines" and all kind of stuff like that.

I got great support from Mr. Kauffman, what a great man. He called me up to his office before spring training began. He said, "bring your family." I knew this wasn't going to be a good meeting as far as my brain was concerned.

He got me in there and he scolded me like a little kid. I just felt as low as I could be in front of my wife and my child. But then he looked at me and in the same breath goes, "Here is what I'm going to do. I'm going to give you a new contract. But ... if ... you ... ever ... do ... that ... again ... you will feel the wrath of Mr. K."

I just went, "Yes, sir."

Me and my wife kind of looked at each other. I was surprised. I thought he was calling me up there to release me and get on me and tell me he was sending me somewhere else. He scolded me, but then I felt like that was it as far as he was concerned.

I started getting ready to go, and he told me I was the only one coming back to the team. The others were all being let go. I just thought, "Wow."

Mr. K was really a good man. He was the kind of guy I knew back in my days in Summit when I had some really great role models around me. I knew he could have sent me anywhere else.

I didn't want to go anywhere else. I didn't want to go to Minnesota or New York or Chicago or L.A. I just liked it here.

*Courtesy of Kansas City Royals*

*Mr. K was one of the best owners in the game. It was an honor to know him and to play for his team.*

# 22
# COMEBACK
# STORY

**I** **had been suspended for the year, but I think we all sort of** knew that when the commissioner reviewed the suspension in May, I would be reinstated. Otherwise they wouldn't have let me go through spring training. They let me be with the team in the first part of the season.

I would make all the trips with the team when we went on the road. I would work out, take batting practice, take infield and do my running before the games. Then, when they were all getting ready to play, I would get showered, get dressed and go upstairs to the press box or in the stands to watch the game. When the game was over I would go back down and get on the bus and go with the team.

I can truly say that my teammates were very good to me. Back in those days you had the same core group of players for several years, and we were all sort of like family. I remember one game down in Texas, they were really getting on me – yelling at me and throwing stuff. The guys in the dugout all stood up and looked back into the stands.

You were family. When you were hurting one of us, you were hurting everybody. If you were yelling at one of us, you were yelling at all of us. Those guys were there for me

The first day I came back, I think I was in Chicago. It was really funny. The first plate appearance I got a walk. Floyd Bannister was pitching, and Carlton Fisk was behind the plate. After Darryl Motley struck out, I stole second when Frank White was at the plate. Fisk overthrew the ball, and I scored from second on the overthrow. That's when I knew I was really ready to play.

People looked at me a little differently. I got called more names in 1984 … people were just beating me up. They were crucifying me. You know, they talk about how bad it is in New York with the fans. It was bad everywhere. No place was worse than the other. Everybody was saying the same thing. After a while I just got immune to it.

At Royals Stadium, it was usually OK because we were winning. I was doing good, so they were cool with me most of the time. But even that was a surprise to me because anything that was good that happened to me was a surprise. I didn't expect anything good to happen.

I also felt like I had to prove myself to everybody all over again and I had to hit .300. I just had to be a really good baseball player. I also thought the people in the Royals' front office looked at me differently then, didn't quit trust me. John Schuerholz would look at me, and would be looking AT me trying to see if I'm high. He wouldn't be looking me in the eyes. He would be looking everywhere else.

That year was also the beginning of my divorce proceedings. There was just so much attention on us all the time. She was starting to question herself. She always used to tell me that she had a first name. She wasn't just "Willie's wife" or "Mrs. Wilson." I think she felt like she was losing her identity, and she was hearing what people in the stands were saying.

I think it probably hurt her more than it hurt me. It kind of made her crazy. When people were writing stuff, they didn't think about how they may be messing with people who weren't even involved.

I also lost a lot of money – not only during the suspension when I didn't get my salary for 45 days. I also got fined. I lost a contract with New Balance shoes. I also came to the realization that I was never going to get any awards anymore or get voted to any All-Star games or anything like that no matter what I did. It was like people made a decision that they were not going to put me on TV or show any of my highlights. That seemed to last the rest of my career.

I hit .301 that season, second on the team behind Hal McRae who batted .303. We went to the playoffs, but we lost in three straight games to the Detroit Tigers. Nobody on the team had a good series. We only scored four runs in three games. Getting to the playoffs and having that year started letting me put stuff behind me.

I won Player of the Year for the second time that season, and actually that was a surprise to me that the Royals would honor me that way. When you've gone through what I went through and what I put the team through I thought nothing good was ever going to happen.

But people like a good comeback story, and I know that's what I was that year. I was very surprised they gave it to me – happy, but very surprised. It's always good to be Player of the Year because you got to hang with Mr. and Mrs. K. At the banquets, they would introduce them, and then introduce the Player of the Year. So, that was very cool.

But I knew I had to do something special that year to make up for what I had put the team through. It didn't cover everything up because people are still going to talk, but it was a good way to come back that year.

I knew I was clean, and the Royals knew I was clean because I had to go through being tested for drugs on every road trip. It was quite an ordeal to know what people were putting you out to be. You have to live with it. How am I going to live with it? I'm going to be as cold to them as they are to me. So, I became cold.

# 23

# I COULDN'T HANDLE BEING A CELEBRITY

**I** was an ass.

I'll be the first to tell you, I was an ass about being popular when I was a player. I didn't want to do any autographs. I didn't want people hanging around me clamoring for something. I didn't want any of that stuff. I just wanted to play baseball.

But there are two sides to this celebrity stuff and all that happens when you're a celebrity.

As I look back on it now, being popular is about a 70-30 proposition. The 70 is the good part, The 30 is the bad part, but the 30 can be really tough. I enjoy being recognized more now because I don't have to play the game. I can concentrate on fans instead of thinking about going out and trying to stand in the batter's box with Ron Guidry throwing sliders at me.

The thing that probably set the pattern for the rest of my baseball career happened very early, right after I had my first child, Shanice.

It was after a game at Royals Stadium in 1979. In those days we walked out the front door of the stadium because all the players parked between the two stadiums. I was walking out of the ballpark with my daughter and my wife. I think Shanice was 2 to 3 months old, so this would have been in 1979, my second full year in the big leagues. The fans would all wait outside that front gate, and the Royals were really popular then so we were just surrounded by fans. I'm trying to sign all the way while I'm walking to my car.

I get to the car door, and this guy comes running over through the crowd and he wants an autograph so bad he hits my wife – bumps into her – and she's starting to fall down with our baby. I had to catch her and the baby.

I just went off on the guy.

"A frickin' autograph is not worth someone's life! What the hell, man! What the hell!"

I didn't say anything else. I got in the car, and we drove off.

But people only heard what I said. They didn't see what happened before, and they made a judgment about me as a person without understanding what was behind it. I decided that if an autograph was more important than a human life, then I wouldn't sign anymore. That was the reason I quit signing for years.

The way I prepared myself to play games made it really difficult to do anything before games when I was down on the field. I used to prepare myself to go play a game like a football player would prepare himself. I worked myself up the whole day. So, when I started toward the ballpark I wasn't in autograph mode. I wasn't into being Mr. Nice and all of that. I was in game mode.

On the road that meant I wanted to walk from my room straight to the bus, get on and go to the park and play. During warm-ups and batting practice I didn't hang around and chat up any of the other players. I didn't smile. I didn't want to hang around the dugout and talk with the fans.

My days were the same every day. I would stay in my room until it was time to go to the bus. I would eat breakfast in there. I would eat lunch in there. I would watch General Hospital in there. Then, I would come downstairs and try to figure out how I could get around all the fans just to get to the bus.

That's how I got up for games. I even invented things about an opposing player in my brain. I held a grudge against the pitcher I was facing that night – he made too much money or he threw this kind of pitch or something else. I had to have something to be mad at him or I didn't think I could hit him. I didn't want him to be my friend because then when I got a hit off him I would feel bad.

In football, I thought you had to be angry and tough instead of having a carefree attitude. That's all I knew. I couldn't go to work liking the guy in front of me. I couldn't like you and get a hit off you. But if I hated you, it made me feel better when I got a hit.

Even in 19 years in baseball I never got to the point when I could relax playing the game. I had to have something for me to get motivated. Ask any camera guy or any fan who tried to get my autograph just before the game.

One time Dean Vogelaar, the team's PR guy, asked me why I didn't smile. I said, "I smile, but how many people smile when they are getting ready to go to work?" I was getting ready to go to work. I was like, "Dude, I'm not here to smile. I'm not here for that. I'm here to play baseball. I'm going to work, and this is how I prepare to go to work. I can't prepare by being nice, 'Hey how you doing? Oh, I gotta play a game. Excuse me.'"

As I got better and a little more recognized, the team even started asking me to do more things for them. If you talk to some of the Royals clubhouse guys from the old days you would hear some stories about me going off in the locker room on autographs. Sometimes guys would come downstairs from the front office with dozens of balls: "Willie sign this, sign that." I'm like 40 minutes from the game, and they want me to sign stuff. I feel bad about how I reacted now. But then I felt like it was taking away from my preparation for the games – and that was my most important job.

I would see other guys doing autographs. I don't know how George (Brett) could do it. He had the most demand of anybody on the team. I could see sometimes in his face that he wasn't into it, but he didn't say anything and just kept signing and walking, signing and walking. I wish I could not react and just sign, but I couldn't do it that way.

I didn't really get what was so important about a signature on a piece of paper. I wanted a reason to sign. I mean what is so important about my name. That boggles my mind. And as a player you have to write your name again, again, again. Sometimes I looked at it as sort of a punishment. You know when you get in trouble in school and you have to write something on the blackboard 100 times. That's what you were doing signing autographs.

Part of the other guys dealing with it better than me was they had been in the big leagues longer than me, and they knew the ins and outs. But I was young and brash, and we weren't taught in the minor leagues how to deal with people. Coming up through the minor leagues we were taught to play baseball. I think they do a better job of that now in preparing guys as they come up to the major leagues.

The thing was after all these guys would go through the crowd signing, I would hear all the bitching about it in the locker room. So, you knew that they didn't want to do it, but they didn't let that show so much as they were walking through a group of fans or before the games.

The other thing that just stuns me is how strident some of these people are. My grandmother taught me manners. My grandmother used to say if you want something you should ask nicely. You don't just go and say, "Sign this!" When I'm in a bad mood and you just say "Sign this!" I'm like, "What the hell, man, can't you ask me any nicer than that?"

Then there was the guy who would say, "You know, I pay your salary."

I would go, "Wow, I didn't know your name was Kauffman."

Then he would say, "Well, indirectly, I pay to get into the ballpark so that money is going to Mr. Kauffman and he's paying you." Wow, all this over an autograph. That was mind boggling to me. I mean wouldn't you rather me sit down and talk to you. Isn't that better than a piece of paper where I don't say a word to you and just sign it.

To me, that was just way out of whack with what should be important. I just didn't get that whole hero-worship kind of thing. I always thought that fans put hero worship onto the wrong people. That should be reserved for doctors, teachers, policemen, firemen. But sports guys? I mean, we're just playing a sport.

And I was vilified when I said anything like that. You know what Charles Barkley said about athletes shouldn't be role models? I was saying that years ago. Charles got put in a commercial, and people thought I was just being a jerk.

But athletes shouldn't be idolized as role models – maybe for how they play the game and how hard they worked to become as good as they did. That's something you can point to with a young kid and say you should work as hard as that. But it should be your parents or your teachers or somebody like that who should be your role model for life.

But there also were the good parts. In one respect it was great to be recognized. It got me status in the big leagues from other big-league players. It got me a great contract. When I went in to a bank for a loan on my house, the banker knew I had a contract for a certain amount of money over the next four years, things like that.

And it was cool to be recognized some of the time. After we won the World Series, I went over to Hawaii. We were on Kona. I was in a little store in a village and this car goes by and I hear some guy go, "Willie! Willie!" I'm thinking, Hawaii? And they know who I am here. It was crazy, man. So, that was kind of neat and that was kind of fun.

But even now if I'm in a place like a hotel or a restaurant I'm a little uncomfortable. One guy recognizes me. Then another, and heads start to turn. Then, I want to hide because I know what is coming next. I'm trying to be better about it and go with it instead of being negative. I try to say, "Great, you want me to sign something." But that's still hard. And if you ever don't react exactly the way somebody wants you to, then you are still criticized for it.

So, I'm trying to do things a little different now because it's more like a business for me. And I'm starting to really like being a celebrity because I don't have to play. I don't have to worry about umpires, or people drinking beer and screaming at me from the stands.

I have become a little older and a little wiser. It's kind of nice to be recognized and kind of nice for people to want my autograph. I wish I had been a little more in tune to that when I was coming up and all that kind of stuff, but you can't cry over spilled milk.

Now when I go out, I know, in my brain, that I'm going to try and be nice. I'm just going to enjoy it, take it in and do it that way instead of having a bad attitude about it. It's all about how you think about it now, and my thinking these days is a lot better than it was before. Holy cow, it's a lot better.

Another good part of being a celebrity is that I can lend my name to help some small organization or help raise money for them. We do a lot of events where if you want an autograph a $20 donation goes to the charity.

And if the autographs are for kids, that's way better. When there are adults there, a lot of time they are just getting the autograph to sell. Sometimes I look on my computer and the next day there is something I signed selling on e-Bay. When that happens I just want to jump through the computer screen.

## CRAZY LADY IN THE HALL

After that 1980 season I got a commercial from Kentucky Fried Chicken, and it was getting some play around the country. People were coming up to me more. When we were on the road, more and more people were noticing me after games.

So, we're in Milwaukee after a game and in the bar at the hotel. I have a few drinks, and I go up to my room. My roommate in the adjoining room is U.L. (Washington). All of a sudden there is this banging on the door. Boom! Boom! Boom!

I look through the peephole, and I see this really good looking girl, who I have never seen before. I go, "Who is it?" and she just starts screaming, "Open up this door!"

I have U.L. come into the room and look through the peephole to see if he knows her. And I call security and tell them someone is banging on my door. Five minutes go by, eight minutes, no security and Boom! Boom! Boom!

I'm thinking that security isn't coming, so I'm just going to open the door and when I do WHAP! she just slaps me across the face. I slap her back and say, "You don't even frickin' know me."

She says, "This won't be the last time you hear from me" and she gets in the elevator and goes straight to a doctor, like the emergency room. The doctor tells her there is nothing wrong with her. Then she goes to a lawyer, and this guy thinks he's got cash walking into his office.

The next day it's all over the radio in Milwaukee that I hit this girl. Of course, if it's news in Milwaukee, it becomes news in Kansas City. I'm talking to fellas on the bus as we're going to the stadium and telling them what happened.

Hal McRae, in his wisdom, says, "You know, she can sue you."

I say, "It's self defense, man."

But he goes, "I'm just telling you … "

Sure enough, after the game – I had a horrible game – I'm walking down underneath the stadium to get to the locker room, and I see two policemen waiting there.

"Are you Willie Wilson?"

"Yeah."

"Do you know so and so."

"No."

"She claims … ."

I'm talking to the manager. He's telling me it's all over the news; it's on the radio back home. Anyway, all the way back to Kansas City on the airplane I'm thinking about it. When I get off the plane in Kansas City my wife is at the airport. She never picks me up at the airport, but she's at the airport.

You can imagine that conversation. How do you explain that you don't even know this person? My wife is telling me that this is not the life she wanted to live.

Anyway, the woman who slapped me ended up going to four different lawyers – four. Every time they dug deeper they found more crap on her. She had a baby by a guy who she didn't even know his last name, she never went to college, she never finished high school. She was just doing this to try and get money from people.

After a month or so, the D.A. calls me from Milwaukee, and he goes, "Willie, we'd like to apologize … ."

I go, "REALLY? For weeks you guys have just been pummeling me and now you're apologizing." Then they tell me if I pay $250 they will drop the case. She couldn't pay her lawyer, so I end up paying her lawyer $250 so I can get out of trouble.

This is all for a girl who smacked the crap out of me. She hit me so hard if I had false teeth they would have come out. And this is all because of a commercial and because I'm becoming a little more known and people think I have money.

When the case was dropped, there wasn't the same kind of headline or anything like that.

I guess she must have been in the bar the day before or the night before and picked me out. I'm telling you, that was crazy. After that one I started inviting my wife on every trip to Milwaukee. That was never going to happen again.

So, what I'm saying is that there are two sides to all those celebrity stories you hear – and I wasn't even that big of a celebrity.

# 24
# A LIFETIME DEAL
# LASTS TWO YEARS

*"**D**o you know you're going to be rich the rest of your life?"*
*—Willie Wilson to Alysia Quisenberry when*
*Wilson and Dan Quisenberry signed their lifetime*
*contracts with the Royals on April 10, 1985.*

That was a very happy time for me. They were good numbers. I was going to get paid for the next 40 years. But just as important for me I was going to be a Royal for life. To have a steady job in the same place where your kids were being brought up and where you were a part of the community was important to me. It was a great deal. I didn't want to go anywhere else. I didn't want to be anywhere else.

I was a Royal. I was drafted as a Royal. I played in the minor leagues as a Royal. If you count up all the years, I had more than 15 years as a Royal. That contract, for me, meant that I was a Royal. That was the first and second thing I thought about.

The funny thing. My *lifetime deal* only lasted about two years.

The deal was entirely Mr. (Avron) Fogelman's deal. He had bought about 49 percent of the Royals in 1983. He negotiated the whole deal with Dan Quisenberry, George Brett and me. They wanted to do one with Frank (White) also, but for some reason Frank didn't want to do it. I remember hearing by word of mouth that Mr. K pretty much didn't like the deal at all.

The way the deal was going to work was that for the next four years I would get $1.25 million a year. Of that, $250,000 was going to be invested in one of Mr. Fogelman's real estate deals, and I would get $1 million in salary. The real estate investment would provide the money for the lifetime deal.

I would be getting guaranteed payments every year until 2005. Then in 2005 I could continue with guaranteed payments of about a million a year for the next 20 years or I could take $16 million in a buyout. It could have been more depending on the value of the real estate.

But two things were going on.

I was going through a divorce, and I didn't think I wanted to be paying half of everything for the next 40 years to my ex-wife. We were talking to Mr. K since he didn't like the deal anyway. We negotiated out of the lifetime deal, I think in 1987. I got a $5 million buyout of the lifetime deal. My ex-wife got $2 million in the divorce settlement, and I had to pay $800,000 in taxes for her.

We never talked about changing the terms of the contract. I had a four-year contract making $1.25 million a year that ended in 1990. After that, the team had four years of options – their options – that they could keep me another four years when I was going to make $1.7 or something that would eventually rise to about $2.3 million or something like that.

It never got to that because they didn't exercise their options. That's when (then general manager) Herk Robinson and (then manager) John Wathan were deciding to get rid of the whole heart of the team – Frank, Quiz, me and Bob Boone. They just decided we couldn't play anymore, which I didn't understand at all. I had hit .290 that year. The only guy who had a higher batting average on the team was George. They'd give a lot to have guys who could hit .290 today.

Sometimes, I think about that contract now and just go, "Wow, what would it be like?" It was going to be a million bucks a year. If I was smart, or my ex wife was smart we would have done something else. But we were in our mid-20s, and we weren't thinking straight. You don't think about when you are going to be 40 or 50. You are right in the moment.

It was a great deal. I was very pleased and happy that they thought enough of me after what I had gone through in 1983 and 1984 to give me a lifetime deal. I didn't think it was a deal that could be turned down.

I don't know if I could have made more money by becoming a free agent, I probably could have because the money was really out there at that time. (George) Steinbrenner (of the New York Yankees) was giving people money that weren't even top-notch players. He was just giving money away. I don't know if the drug thing would have made it less likely for me to get a big contract. I thought about not signing the deal and becoming a free agent – though it was a short thought.

I also remembered how the Royals had treated me. The Kauffman's were great owners, great people -- both Mr. and Mrs. K. I felt indebted for how they stood by me. I wanted to be around when we won things. We had gone to the World Series (1980), we had lost three years in a row to the Yankees, we lost a one-game playoff with the A's, and we lost in '84 to the Detroit Tigers.

I just wanted to stay there and win at that place for those people and that owner and the players I had been with for those years. I respected everybody in that organization. Sometimes it was hard for me to express that because I had outbursts (laughter), outbursts here and there. But in between the outbursts, I thought I was a really good guy.

I didn't like a lot of attention, and I was getting it there - for the wrong reasons as well as the right reasons, but I just felt this was the best place for me as far as having an understanding owner with a great heart and wanting to win a championship. This was a team that took a chance on me more than once.

# 25
# GETTING BACK TO THE SERIES

There's a turning point in every season. I'd like to say it's when I went on a tear and led the team during the stretch run. Actually, it was when I got hurt (laughter).

We could have folded, but we got better. We had a lot of guys really step up. Omar Moreno was playing good. Lynn Jones was getting key hits. Pat Sheridan ... Darryl Motley. Everybody pulled their pants up and went a little harder.

We were two-and-a-half games out of first place when I received an injection from the Texas Rangers team doctor near the end of August. I was out of the lineup for the next month-and-a-half. They Royals won 13 of the next 15 games, while I was in the hospital. After I got out of the hospital and was getting close to being back to full speed, I'm thinking that  the team is going so good, would you be messing it up if you try and put me back in the lineup. But the thing about us is that it always came down to the last week, or so, of a season. It was almost like that every year. I knew I could help at the end of the year.

What made my season was – after I had the allergic reaction to the penicillin shot – we get to the second-to-last day of the season and we had clinched a tie for the American League West pennant. We were playing the Oakland A's, and I got the game-winning hit in extra innings to put us in the playoffs. That made my season.

It was in the 10th inning. Sheridan had hit a one-out single. Then, Greg Pryor singled, and Sheridan went to third. Lonnie Smith had a ground out. I come up with two outs and a runner in scoring position. In the bottom of the ninth, Jay Howell got me on a ground ball to second leading off the inning. I knew he was a fastball pitcher, so that's what I was looking for in the 10th. I got the single that sent us to the playoffs.

That ended what was a really scary time for me because when I got hurt I didn't know if I was ever going to be able to play again or run the way I could before. It was such a freaky thing.

I had a bad cold or the flu or something in August, and I was just hacking around and not having much energy. We're in Texas. It's about 100 degrees like it always was. I'm talking to our trainer, Mickey Cobb, and saying, "Holy Cow, Mick. We gotta do something." So Mick says after the game we're going to get you a shot. The doctor is going to come in and see you.

It's the Texas Rangers doctor because we were on the road. I didn't know it at the time, but he's the same doc that punctured Billy Martin's lung one time when he gave him a shot. I'm seeing him in the training room, and I'm feeling pretty good as far as us being in the race. But I have no energy. I see the doc, and he says he's going to give me a shot. He's going to mix these two penicillins together, one for quick results in 48 hours and a longer lasting one that works for seven days. He's mixing them up, and I thought he said take your clothes off and get up on the table.

I took my shorts off, and I'm getting ready to climb up on the training table. I feel a pinch in my butt and I just go, "Yeow!" I jerked back and it just ... I bent the needle. I was like, "Wow. I thought you said get on the table."

I get up on the table and I'm lying down, and within two, three, four minutes I know something is wrong. I can't get off the table. I'm frickin' sweating and just can't move. I say "Mick, something is wrong."

I knew my body, and I knew immediately something was wrong. But Mick says to lay there for a few minutes and see how I feel. I mean I just can't move. By now everybody has left the locker room. I need to get a shower and get back to the hotel, but I can't move. They help me into the shower and sit me in a chair. That's how I take my shower, sitting in a chair like I'm drugged up and just "blah." What I don't know is that my left buttock is moving backward, swelling up and getting bigger, bigger, bigger, little by little. What I feel is that it's like somebody has taken a sledgehammer behind my left leg and just hit it. Boom! Boom! It's just driving me up the wall.

I finally get dressed, but now I have to go through the crowd outside the gate to the hotel about 200 yards away. I can hardly walk. I'm groggy. People are lined up all the way to the hotel, just hounding me for autographs. I'm just, "Please, please, let me get to my room."

"You suck!"

I'm dying, basically. They are yelling and screaming at me. I'm just trying to make my way to my room. When I get there, I can't go to sleep. I'm just hurting. Mick always said he was a 24-hour trainer, so I call him at 1 or 2 a.m. or whatever time it was. He gets in a taxi with me, and we go to the hospital.

We see another doctor there, and he goes, "I'm going to give you a shot."

I say, "You give me a frickin' shot, I will kill you. There is no way you are going to give me a shot, man." So he goes, "OK, I will give you these pain pills. Take one every 45 minutes or whenever you need them to get rid of the pain."

He has no idea what is going on. Nobody does.

I go back to the hotel and pop a pill. Fifteen minutes later, I pop another one. Then 45 minutes later, I pop a pill. It is not making a dent in the pain. I don't get a lick of sleep all night long.

We have an afternoon game the next day. I'm trying to get over there, but I can't bend down to put my pants on. I have to sit on the bed, put my pants on the floor, step into them and try to pull them up that way. Then, I notice I can't button my pants. My butt is getting bigger, and bigger, and I don't know it. When I sit, it hurts. Everything hurts.

I walk into the locker room. I'm half dressed, and half awake. I haven't gotten any sleep. I walk into the locker room and Mickey says, "You gotta go home now to see Dr. Myers and Dr. Joyce." So, he gets me on a plane and I'm flying home. I'm sitting in first class, and every time the plane hits a bump, I'm going, "Ooooooooooh." The stewardess is going, "Poor baby."

I'm going through a divorce and not living at home, but I ask my wife at the time, to pick me up at the airport. I had just bought her a 'Vette – we were going through all that "I don't want to be a minivan mom" stuff. Well you know, in a 'Vette you can feel every bump in the road, and I swear she was finding them on purpose – no, I'm just kidding about that. But I am banging around in the 'Vette just screaming.

I get home, all I want to do is sleep. I haven't slept since Friday, this is Saturday night. I can't go to sleep. Sunday she just looks at me, and I must look like I'm dying I guess because she goes, "I'm going to take you to the hospital."

Dr. Joyce is waiting on me there. He takes one look, touches my butt and I just scream, and he goes, "Emergency room, NOW!"

The next thing I remember is that I'm lying on my stomach. I look over and I see Dr. Joyce has this puzzled look on his face like I had never seen before. He is holding some kind of ruler, and he's putting it in the cut he has made on my butt. He says, "If this doesn't go down another centimeter, we have to go back in and re-operate."

I'm laying there, grogged up and I'm trying to put this in my head. What is going on? He's already operated once? The next thing I know, they take me up to a room in the hospital – not the operating room, thankfully.

He came in the next day and told me what was going on. I had an allergic reaction to the penicillin. I don't think I had ever had a shot before. I didn't break out in hives or anything like the normal reaction. My muscles were just tearing themselves apart. He even asked me if they could put my symptoms in a medical book because it was so weird.

The biggest thing I can remember was the look on his face. That scared me. He looked like he was puzzled about what was going on. I had never seen that look on his face. It was a look that really freaked me out. Then he told me, "If you had waited one more day, you would have died." That is some scary stuff. I was being poisoned by the penicillin.

I'm in the hospital for a couple of weeks, and that's the time the Royals were winning 13 of 15 games or something like that. I would follow the standings while I was in the hospital. I was so out of it that sometimes I would try and listen to the games and I would think they had lost when I went to sleep and found out the next morning that they had won. Man, that was really hard. To be in that hospital listening to it every night. I got more nervous listening than I did performing. Every day I'm trying to figure out, "Did we win?"

Now, when I'm getting ready to come back, I'm thinking my muscles have been ripped apart. I have to work myself back in shape, and I'm wondering if I take a big stride whether the muscles would rip and I would never play again. I was kind of hesitant. I mean I got a big old scar on my butt, and all that scar tissue was really tight in my buttocks. I didn't know if I could ever run again like I used to. I was worried if I went too hard I would hurt it again. The team had been doing so well. I came back in the middle of September, and we were playing about .500 ball during that little stretch. I felt like I was hurting everything.

Then one day I'm out in the outfield. We had lost three straight or four straight, something like that. There was a ball that I knew I had to get to. My instincts just kicked in. I had to go get the ball, and I was just playing the game again – not thinking about it. I took off, and I could almost feel everything breaking up in there, all that scar tissue. I was running again, and that made me feel good. That's when I knew I was all right.

This team was really different than the 1980 team when everyone was having a great year on offense. This was a pretty disappointing year for me offensively. I think I only hit .278. We didn't have anybody hitting over .300 except George. But we were a winning team. You know a lot of people look at offense. Offense doesn't win a majority of baseball games. Defense does, defense and great pitching – and timely hitting. Not just hitting, timely hitting.

I know guys who go 3-for-4 and when you come up with a runner on third and two outs, they go 0-for-1. It's not about how many hits you get, it's when you get them. A lot of guys on that team were getting timely hits. We had three young pitchers on that club who really developed.

I don't know that we had a feeling at the beginning of the year that this was going to be the special year, but we felt pretty good about our team. I had come back in 1984 and hit .301, and we had lost to the eventual World Series champs in the playoffs. In 1985, we lost three of our first four or something. We were under .500 in the middle of May, and didn't reach .500 for good until the middle of June. We had a lot of veterans who knew it was going to be a long season. We just keep playing and didn't panic. If we went through a bad spell, we knew that other teams were going to go through it too, so nobody panicked.

The three young pitchers had some success in 1984 and felt like they still had something to prove: Bret Saberhagen, Mark Gubicza and Danny Jackson. Sabes pretty much became our No. 1, at least it turned out that way that he was kind of matched up against the other team's No. 1.

Sabes was a young, I won't say cocky guy, I'll say very confident. There's a difference between cocky and confident. He was confident about his ability and what he could do. I think that rubbed off on Danny Jackson, and it rubbed off on Gubicza. The other guys? Charlie Leibrandt was somewhat of a veteran and Buddy Black was there. We could have had some controversy with the older guys and Saberhagen because those guys were here before the young guys.

They could have bitched and moaned about not being No. 1, but it was more so that everybody wanted to win. Gooby had a great fastball. He was tall, long, and an intimidating kind of guy. He wasn't smooth. Neither was DJ. He had tenacity. DJ was a grinder.

It wasn't just the starting guys. Quiz was a great reliever. Don't forget about Steve Farr, Joe Beckwith and Mike Jones. I think we had nine or 10 guys on the staff. All the guys got along. It was really kind of crazy how it all happened. Everybody blended in.

That's one thing I can say about Kansas City Royals players. They blend in together. I was with the A's and Cubbies at the end of my career. With the Royals, we never had a Jose Canseco type of guy who set himself apart. Even our superstar guys blended together. Our teams were always pretty much like the city itself. Mr. K was that kind of guy. Mr. Schuerholz was that kind of guy. The guys on the team – everybody worked. Everybody did their job. We didn't complain.

Don't get me wrong, it wasn't like that every day. Some guys complained. I complained – I know that's hard to believe (laughter) – but all in all we got along. That was pretty cool about all our Royals teams.

One thing was a little disappointing for me was that I hated to see the Guru (Larry Gura) not be a part of it. He meant so much to me the year before when I came back from the suspension. He really looked out for me. I always felt a little close to him because people don't remember that my number when I came up to the team in 1977 was 32. When I finally made the team, 32 was the Guru's number. That's how I ended up being No. 6.

# 26
# DON'T COUNT
# US OUT

Toronto was hot. They had a good team. We open the playoff series up there and we're hoping to split. You don't really think that you could sweep a hot team at home. We went up there to split and get them back to our place.

They beat us 6-1 in the first game, but we were right there in the second game. We're tied 4-4 going into extra innings. I lead off the 10th inning with a single. Then George (Brett) strikes out. I steal second with Hal (McRae) at bat, but he strikes out too. Then Frank (White) singles me home, and we're going to the bottom of the 10th with the best reliever in baseball.

Tony Fernandez opens the bottom of the 10th with a single for Toronto, and he moves to second on a groundout by Damaso Garcia. Lloyd Moseby hits a single, and that gets Fernandez home and we're tied again. Then bad break No. 1. Quiz picks Moseby off first. But Steve (Balboni) doesn't handle the throw, and Moseby ends up on second. The next batter flies out, and if we had the putout on the pickoff play we would have been out of the inning. Instead, Toronto wins when George Bell hits a single that scores Moseby.

We're down 0-2 in the series, but we're going home. We're really upset about losing. Our team has stuck together all season. We didn't blame anybody. Nobody was pointing fingers. If this had been a year earlier, we would have been in real trouble because 1985 was the first year that the ALCS was a seven-game series. We have three games at home and two back at their place. We were hot at home. We had our own crowd.

Game 3 at home is pretty much a must-win game, and we're trailing 5-3 as we head into our half of the sixth. Sabes (Bret Saberhagen) had to leave the game after he was hit by a batted ball in the fifth. Doyle Alexander is pitching for the Blue Jays, and he's doing a pretty good job. We only have four hits in the first five innings. If they hang on, they have a 3-0 lead, and that would be really tough to come back from.

I opened the sixth with a single, and their manager, Bobby Cox, comes out to talk with Alexander. The manager has his back to home plate and he's telling Alexander to walk George. George has already homered and doubled in the game. So they're talking, and I can read Alexander's lips. He's saying, "I can get him out." The manager is telling him to walk George because George was the hottest guy on the team. When Alexander said "I can get him out" the manager said, "Well, OK, get him out" and he goes walking off the mound.

I'm screaming at George, "C'mon!" I was just hoping he would hit a double. I didn't even think about him hitting it out. But when he hit it, I just jumped up in the air because I know that this is out of the park. I'm thinking in my brain, "Yeah, you can get him out all right." Then Hal hits a double, and Alexander is out of the game.

To cap off his game, George opens the ninth with a single and scores the winning run of the game when Balboni drives him in with a single. George had one of those games you never forget.

The Blue Jays win game four of the series 3-1. This is another example of the breaks going against us because Charlie Liebrandt has pitched a really nice game, taking a four-hitter into the ninth when the Blue Jays score three in the ninth.

We still had our backs to the wall because we had to win the fifth game or the series was over. We did not want them to beat us at home. It was one thing to lose, but don't lose at home.

Everybody talks about the fifth game being the most pivotal. For us it was do or die, and Danny Jackson was going for us. It seemed like DJ always pitched the fifth game for us. I remember DJ just shutting them down. His slider was working. For a lefty, DJ could really shut down right-handed batters. If we don't win this game, we're done. DJ really pitched a great game. We score one in the first and one in the second, and DJ just shuts them down.

What I remember most about the end of this game is that there is a big message on the scoreboard afterwards that said: "Bring us the championship back."

We're going back to Toronto for the final two games. We're down three games to two.

We get on the busses in Toronto, there are some newspapers there. So, I grab one of them, and the big old headline in the Canadian papers was "Me for MVP – George Bell." George Bell had a great year, alright. He ended up having an MVP year. What I remember is that everyone on the bus was reading the paper. And without anybody saying a word, people just got mad. It was like the Blue Jays were saying, "we're going to take care of business right here and whup up on the Royals."

I remember everybody on the bus thinking, "Oh yeah? They think they are going to do this! We'll see." After the Blue Jays messed around and started talking like it was over, it was almost like everybody on our team knew we weren't going to go down without a fight.

I don't know how a team thinks when it has a 3-2 lead and is heading home because we were never in that situation. I don't know whether you subconsciously think all we have to do is win one game. We are at home. But when things start to go differently, you can feel the momentum change.

Mark Gubicza starts Game 6, and he pitches great. I scored in the first. George hits another home run in the fifth – his third off Alexander in the series. We win! And now we're tied 3-3 going into Game 7.

I think because most of us had been in the Series in 1980, we knew how to handle the pressure of a seventh game a little better than them. This was their first time in a series like this.

Sabes gets the start for us, but he gets hit by another batted ball and Liebrandt, who usually was a starter, came in and pitched great in long relief. I'm telling you it is a nail biter. We're ahead 2-1 as we come to bat in the sixth. Then, Jim Sundberg blasts a triple off the left-field wall with two outs and the bases loaded. When he did that, you could just see the air come out of (the Blue Jays).

We win the series. It was really funny because the Canadians didn't know how to react, like they didn't know what happened. It was new to them. You could hear the Royals people, the front office and the few scattered fans screaming. Everyone else was in shock because they had lost.

This was like most of our season. We had played great defense. We got key hits.

But for me, it was the "Me for MVP" headline in the paper that got us started. That's what pumped me up. I thought, "OK, Man. You're going to get the MVP, but talk about that later. Don't talk about that now because you ain't finished this season."

We get on the plane, and we were pretty happy, man, just celebrating. We're going home to start the World Series at our place.

# 27

# "WELCOME HOME WORLD SERIES CHAMPS"

**W**e get to start the World Series at home, and then of course we lose the first two games to the Cardinals.

I had been hitting No. 2 in the lineup behind Lonnie Smith since I missed that time in August, and to be truthful it was kind of nice to bat second and be able to see how a guy was pitching instead of being the first guy to face him in the game. Lonnie was a great leadoff hitter, and Lonnie was a better clutch hitter than me. That year everybody had been playing me to the left side so I was trying to pull, pull, pull. That was probably another reason my batting average was a little lower because I was trying to pull.

We get in the first game, and I'm thinking positive. I was out the first two times I was up. Then, I got a single. At least in this World Series I haven't struck out yet (laughter). So, we get to the seventh and we're down 2-1 and the bases are loaded with me coming to bat. I fly out to left. A hit would have tied the game or put us in the lead. We only get one runner on base in the final two innings and lose 3-1.

In the second game, Charlie Liebrandt was pitching a great game. He took a two-hitter into the ninth, and we were leading 2-0. The Cardinals score four in the ninth, and now we're behind 2-0 in the Series. This time we're heading to their place not ours.

The next thing that happens is just like Toronto. It was the exact same scenario as it was with George Bell. Something fired us up, only it wasn't a headline. What they had was on the top of the control tower of the airport.

You know teams don't go through the terminal. We'd get off the plane out on the tarmac and get on a bus and drive out of the airport. As we're walking down the steps to get to the tarmac, you looked off to the right and there was a sign that said, "Welcome Home 1985 World Series Champions."

We're all going, "I can't believe this. They ain't played but two games." And they are saying we are going to lose four straight. It was like collectively, again, it just irked everybody.

In the third game Sabes pitched great. He was hit by batted balls in his two starts in the ALCS, but this time he comes out and throws a complete game. He gives up six hits, but nobody is on base after the sixth inning.

In the fourth game John Tudor throws a shutout at us, and we fall behind 3-1 in the Series.

Again, it's something that really irritates me before the fifth game. I can remember coming into the stadium, and all the TV people are there and setting everything up for a team to win the Series. They're doing it in our locker room, too, for reaction from the losing team. I just said, "Y'all can take that away and get that out of here because we ain't losing today. Not here. Not today." I was dead serious.

It's little things like that. People don't think that something as little as TV cameras getting set up is going to motivate you, but it does. We're not even playing the game yet, and I know you gotta set your stuff up, but at least wait until we get out of the locker room. So, I'm thinking, "Y'all better take that down because they ain't going to win today. They're going to have to come to us."

In my brain, I'm thinking, "If we ever get back home, they ain't winning there, either." That's how I felt.

I talked a lot of crap in the locker room. I said it out loud and I hoped that everyone in that locker room heard me. "We ain't losing today!" That's how I felt, and it turned out that we didn't lose.

I didn't want to feel the way I felt in 1980 all over again. That's the worst, worst, worst feeling you could ever have ... besides going to jail. What I'm saying is that in sports it's the worst feeling you can have. When you have dreams about what you can accomplish, your dreams aren't losing. You're putting your heart and soul into this. When you do that and lose, it's like your whole body aches. For that instant, everything is not right in the world. I didn't want to feel that way again.

It's DJ (Danny Jackson) again in the fifth game. He gives up a run in the first on two hits, and he only gives up three hits the rest of the game. They don't even come close.

Back home in Game 6, we have runners on base almost every inning, and we just can't get a timely hit for, like, the first time all season. The Cardinals score one in the eighth, and we can't answer. I get on base after Lonnie Smith struck out, but George strikes out behind me and Frank hits a fly ball to center field.

We're down to our last three outs to get something done. Jorge Orta pinch hits for Darryl Motley to lead off the inning. Orta hits a grounder to first, and Todd Worrell is coming over to cover the base. I was sitting down at the end of the bench by first base, where I always sit. When umpire Don Denkinger called him safe, I jumped up and starting pacing up and down the bench. I knew he missed the call. We *all* knew he missed the call. We were standing right there. We couldn't believe he missed it, but we were glad that he did.

What it did for me is it made me know we could win. It might be just the break we needed because I had seen us come back so many times that year. Everybody felt like it was new life for us. That first out is the most important out of the inning. If you get that first out, things start looking like they are going to go down from there. But when you get a break on the first out – who knows why you get that first break – you start thinking, "Is it our time now? You got a break, let's take advantage of it."

Of course the Cardinals are hot. That's all the Cardinals and their fans want to talk about. But it wasn't the only thing that happened in that inning. They had some screw-ups that nobody talks about. Bones (Steve Balboni) was up next, and he hit a popup foul down the first base line. Jack Clark comes over to make the play. The dugouts at Royals Stadium didn't have railings, and during the season we would stand there and hold the guy up in case he fell into the dugout. This time we were all sitting down and just looking at the ball.

You could see Clark look at the ball … look at the dugout … look at the ball … look at the dugout knowing no one was going to be there to grab him. He took his eye off the ball, then boom, he dropped it. Bones hit a single on the next pitch.

Then, with one out and runners on first and second Jim Sundberg tries to bunt them over. Orta was forced out at third base. Then Hal McRae gets called to pinch hit. Darrel Porter, who was playing for the Cardinals by then, supposedly called a fastball, and Worrell threw a slider. The pitch went (past the catcher) to the wall. That's how each runner moved up to second and third. Then he walked McRae.

That right there is another reason the Cardinals thought they were going to win because the DH (designated hitter) was null and void, and Hal was the best DH in baseball. You could use the DH in the ALCS, and later on you would be able to use the DH in the American League ballpark in the World Series. But this year you couldn't use the DH. So that took Hal out of our lineup as a regular batter – he only went to bat three times the whole World Series.

By this time I don't know what the Cardinals were thinking. I imagine they were panicking a little bit after that first call because they had been in a spot where all they had to do was win one game out of three when they were up 3-1 and in their brains it's probably feeling like things are going a little bit worse, a little bit worse, a little bit worse. They don't want to play a Game 7 in the other team's ballpark. They wanted to get it over right now because they got the champagne in their locker room, they got this all set up. All of a sudden now the bases are loaded in the bottom of the ninth with one out.

It's funny how guys get a sense of what is happening. There is a bad luck feeling for them and a good luck feeling for us. We have been down this road before. After not getting any breaks and being down 3-1 (in the Series), now we're getting them. You can feel the momentum change. They weren't getting the timely hits. They'd get hits, but we would back ours up with a second or third hit. That's how we were starting to beat them. Our pitching staff just started pounding the ball in, pounding them every at bat. DJ was working the slider. Sabes was working the fastball, just running it in there. Gooby (Mark Gubicza) would come in with the slide ball and Charlie would make sure they would be off pace because he would change-up them to death.

After McRae walks, Dane Iorg comes up. He pinch hits for Quiz. We had gotten both Dane and Lonnie Smith from the Cardinals. Dane came in 1984.

His liner to right scored Onix Concepcion and Jim Sundberg.

I ran straight toward Dane when he made the hit. He was between second and third. I hit him like a football player, I just smoked him with my shoulder. I was sprinting at about 9.2, I went past everybody else who was running out there and just, BOOM! I was hugging him, and then I noticed his nose was bleeding. I went "oooooooh" like that. And everybody stopped and looked at him, and he just went "Yaaaaaaaaaaaaaah!" and we were all screaming and jumping on him again.

Then we went inside and just started chanting "Tudor! Tudor! Tudor!" We knew who was pitching the next game. Throughout the whole locker room "Tudor! Tudor!" He had beat us twice, but we just ... we knew we could beat him in Game 7. I mean momentum is a mother, man. It does something to your psyche. You feel invincible, like you can't lose. That's how we felt. We didn't want to go home. We would have played Game 7 right then, right there. That's how jacked up we were. We felt like we had fought all the way back in two frickin' series. There ain't no way we are losing this thing now.

The next day seemed like it lasted forever before the game would get started. You know you have all this stuff going on. Big corporate people, movie stars, business people, TV people, armies. I'm just sitting there, "Wow ... now get this out of the way and let's go." You could see guys just tapping their feet like, "C'mon let's play."

Here's another thing that was cool about that team. We all shared stuff with each other. I don't know if they do that in the big leagues anymore. I was batting second, and so Lonnie (Smith) would tell me stuff about his at bat, and I would say something to the guys after me. We had played Tudor twice in the Series, and he always goes fastball, change, change. This time he went fastball, fastball. I hit it hard, but straight to the second baseman. I came back to the dugout and said, "Hey, he's doubling up fastballs."

I don't know if they listen or not, but in the second inning Balboni walked. Darryl Motley comes up and hits a home run foul. Usually

Tudor would do something, take something off it, move it around, but he changed his pattern. Next pitch, fastball, "Mot" kept it fair.

Most people remember Joaquin Andujar losing it in the fifth inning, but Tudor lost it first. He went over and hit his hand up against a fan at the end of the dugout when he came out of the game in the third. Then when Andujar gave up a walk to Sundberg … he lost it after a walk, started pointing at the umpire and telling him it was a strike. It wasn't even about the pitch. It was just about him having a breakdown.

We all understood what was happening, but it was hard to watch it. He was feeling the same way about it that we would have. You put your heart and soul into it and … I don't know any good losers. I don't know anybody who plays this game or any sport who's a good loser. A good loser is just a loser. If you don't fight, you're just a loser, man. I wouldn't expect anything different from him because of how much he put into it.

We win  and it's just the greatest feeling ever. We are in the locker room, excited, throwing champagne around. I was so elated. I felt like I had redeemed myself, and I felt like I had paid the people back for going to jail. I know that's stupid, but that's how I felt. Being there and having that experience, that's something that lives with you forever. It was so exciting.

For me it was also a little disappointing because … I was going through a divorce. So we won, but it was like I don't have anybody to celebrate it with. So, me and a couple of my buddies, we drove down to the Plaza – at least as close as we could get to it that night. We had some beer, and we just sat on the front of the car, just sat there and watched all the people pouring into the Plaza that night. Nobody recognized me. There were soooooo many people. I remember lying back on my windshield, looking up and just watching everything.

After that, there was the parade. It was a great parade. We were in these old classic cars coming down Grand Boulevard and then to that park across the street from Crown Center. Well, like always, I was near the back of the parade because I'm a "W." My wife had decided to come to the parade and celebrate for this part. So, we're driving down the street, and there is all this confetti coming down.

Right by the newspaper building my car caught on fire, not just mine but a couple of them. There was so much confetti. The confetti was piled up. These old cars are getting hot, and all of a sudden I start smelling smoke. We were sitting up on the back of a convertible, and I look over and the fire is coming up the back. So we jump out, the guy shuts his car off. I got my daughter out of the car, my wife has my son. She had a fur coat, and I can remember her going "My coat! My coat!" So I gotta go back, hop through the fire and get the coat. Then, we decided she was going to take the baby home.

My daughter and I walked from that point all the way up the street to the park. We didn't know what else to do because everybody else had taken off. When we got there we could see the stage they had set up, but we couldn't get around all the people there to get to in. So, we walked around the back and we climbed up the back of the stage. I can remember that we got on the stage at almost the exact time they go, "Willie Wilson."

I go up and say, "We shocked the world!" That whole day was pretty funny. We got a ride back to where I had parked my car, and I took my daughter back to the house.

Then we got to fly out and see the president – then it was (Ronald) Reagan and (George HW) Bush. We had a plane come get us, flew to DC, got off and had a police escort to the Senate and the House. Then, we went to the White House and had to go through all the metal detectors and everything.

We were out on the lawn. I think the President took George and somebody else into his office. Then, we all got to talk to them. It was really cool to hear the President talk about the game, you know in his voice (imitating Reagan) "George Brett, Willie Wilson … " He's mentioning your name, I mean, wow, the President is mentioning your name. We give him a jacket.

I got this picture somewhere of me waving at Reagan and Bush to turn around. I'm standing there and I'm going "Hey, what's up?" The camera has me just waving to them. That was pretty cool. I got the Prez over there waving at me. It was a really good day.

Then reality sets in.

The season is over and I gotta go through a divorce.

# 28
# BEGINNING OF
# THE END

**W**e thought we could do it again when we came to spring training in 1986. It took us five years to get from our first trip to the World Series to our second. So we knew it wouldn't be easy, but we knew it was possible.

Spring training was great. I don't really know what our record was, but any time you come off a championship or have been in the playoffs, everybody in the world is watching your games. You're a little more popular. More fans come to the ballpark in spring training.

One thing we did notice that spring is that Dick (Howser) started to change. He would go inside and take naps, and some other coach would run the drills. So, there were a few whispers in the clubhouse about Dick's health.

But the day I really knew *something* was up was after we broke from spring training and we were coming up north. Dick called me "Hal" one day. It was going through the tunnel in right field. Dick was coming down or I was going up – whichever way it was. I said, "What's up, Skip?" He says: "Nothing, Hal."

I looked at him, and then I just kept going. I don't remember for sure, but I think I said to Hal: "You know, Dick just called me Hal."

Little by little we started hearing rumors. He was taking longer naps. What I noticed is that he was just not there as often. When someone is not there, of course you are going to ask what is going on? You would get evasive answers. The front office people, the coaches … they were all trying to keep it low key, trying not to let players know anything.

At the All-Star game we noticed he was pronouncing the lineup wrong. He said a couple of things wrong, which was really unusual for Dick because he was really sharp – I mean really sharp. So, that's when we really started hearing he had brain cancer. The All-Star game turned out to be the last game he really coached.

That was a weird time, man. Now your leader is down. You were just hoping you got enough veterans and hoping you have enough talent. But we were all feeling for Dick. Mike Ferraro, "Mikey Mike," became our manager. It was weird.

We had been looking forward to repeating a great season. You look forward to getting your World Series ring. That was something you treasured. You are going through all the "patting on the back" and hoping you can do it again. But we weren't really winning, losing a little bit more than usual. It was a really trying time.

I think we were right around a couple of games over .500 right at about the end of June, then we lost 11 straight games. We never got over .500 again the rest of the season. That happened right about the time when Dick left us. There was a lot of chaos going on around our club. You know, our leader was down. There was a little different philosophy as far as the manager was concerned. There were some personality conflicts.

I know I had a little bit of a conflict that year with Dick and with Ferraro. I was pretty good friends with one of the reporters who was covering the Royals. We would sit and talk every day, not just about the game, but about everything that was going on in our lives. One day, just before a home game, Dick had sent Mike Ferraro down to talk to me and tell me I couldn't have any conversations with this reporter unless it was news. This was right before the National Anthem. I thought about it for a second, and just before the anthem started I was so upset I said, "You tell that little SOB he can't tell me who I can talk to. And if he needs to tell me that you tell him to get down here and tell me and not send you."

I loved Dick as a manager, as a guy you played for. I respected Dick immensely. But that incident right there kind of angry me off. I mean what is going on here? Who is he to tell me who I can talk to? A healthy Dick, I don't know if he would have said that because he had never said it before, but I don't know. I do know that really irked me.

I thought my job was to play baseball as hard as I could for the organization and the leadership of the team. Then, after the game was over, it was my life. I wouldn't think of going over to your place and tell you who to talk to. So, why would you tell me who I could talk to, like I was a little kid.

It was just a little chaotic the way Dick went down and the way things happened earlier with me and Dick and Ferraro – and then feeling bad for it afterwards. You don't ever wish that on anybody.

There wasn't a lot of turmoil between the players. We always thought we could maybe pull it back together, but it didn't happen. We went from winning the World Series to not being able to win a game. We finished 16 games behind the Angels or something like that.

All the guys were having bad years. I think the best batting average on the team was .290. That seems like a lot, but that was George Brett. He doesn't hit .290. Everything was just bad. You were wanting to get it over with, and when it was over, it was a relief. You could just go home and think about next year and start over.

I can tell you, everybody was glad when that season was over – at least I was. It was a tough, tough year for everybody. To lose our leader, who had gone through the pain with us and the blood, sweat and tears and to have won a world championship with him and then have him go down like that really hurt. I don't think anyone was mentally prepared for that.

This was also the first year that any of us got a glimpse of Bo Jackson. He had been drafted No. 1 in the NFL draft by the Tampa Bay Buccaneers in April. The Royals drafted him in the fourth round. He signed to play baseball with us. He came up in September with a couple of other guys – Kevin Seitzer for one.

Seitzer was a more polished baseball player than Bo, a better fielder, a better hitter. We knew Seitzer was going to make the squad no matter what the next year because they were already trying to move George over to first.

Bo … Bo was different. He was a high-powered, well-talked-about Heisman Trophy winner, but he was naïve about things in baseball. And he was cocky – not confident in baseball just yet. He was cocky because he was trying to impress. It would have been different in football because he had won the Heisman Trophy and he had a reputation as a football player, but he didn't have a reputation as a professional baseball player. There also were things you had to do in the Major Leagues just to survive. When Bo first got here, we couldn't joke with him because he couldn't take it. He would want to fight you all the time.

I didn't know how to joke with people when I became a pro baseball player, either. But he was different than I was. I learned how to take a joke in the minor leagues. Bo never really had a bunch of minor leaguers joking with him. Now, he has Major League players joking with him. If you can't take a joke in the big leagues, you will drive yourself crazy.

I mean, we had a champion with the needle, just poking at Bo – Hal McRae. The first time Bo came up he was handing out his Heisman pictures, putting them on our chairs around the locker room. About five or six chairs behind him, Hal was picking them up. When Bo finally figured it out, he looked back at Hal kind of angry off, and Hal said, "We don't care about your Heisman. You ain't done nuthin' up here, yet." He was joking with him, just being Hal.

Bo was so mad he started stuttering, like F … F … F … you. I mean you know what Hal was like. Then at the very end, Hal stuck the needle in again and said, "Hey, if you ever get any tickets for the football games at Tampa Bay, I live in Bradenton over the winter. Can I have a couple?"

Bo would get so frickin' angry because everybody is laughing now. You could see he just wanted to choke McRae to death. But Hal did that to everybody. That's just the way he was. And if you couldn't take it, he would do it even more. Hal took everything to the limit.

But man … Bo was the biggest, strongest, fastest dude I had ever played with. I mean he was really fast and strong. When he threw a baseball, it was so effortless. I mean, the ball just went, "Bweeeek!" and it was just there. I had never seen that. I had heard stories about people who could throw it like that, but I had never seen it before.

I saw Dwight Evans throw. I saw Ellis Valentine throw. I saw Andre Dawson throw. I saw Dave Parker make a great throw in the All-Star game. But I had never seen anybody who just flipped the ball. It wasn't like he reared back and threw up. He just flipped it, and it was like a BB – like it was shot out of a rifle.

He was just so much of a raw talent. You knew that if he ever learned to play the game the way you were supposed to do it, he would be a superstar. He was so raw, he was hitting home runs and he didn't even know where the ball was going. I saw him hit one in Yankee Stadium. He got jammed on the pitch and connected with the ball. He stood at home plate and looked at left field. Then he looked at center field. When he finally looked at right, the ball was going over the fence. He was just so freaking strong.

I mean, who breaks bats over their head or over their thighs? You would break your leg or your kneecap if you try that. He hit the longest home run I ever saw, up around the flags in left-center, using my bat. Then he wanted to take the bat. It was a little short dog, like a 32 (inch), 30 (ounces). He just goes up there and, "Whap!" The crowd all goes, "Ooooooh." He comes back to the dugout and he goes, "Who ... who bat is this." I go, "You see the 6 on the handle. It's my bat." He says he's going to take it. "No, you ain't. That's my bat. You can't just take my bat."

Bo used to not ask anybody, he would just go up there and take whatever bat he wanted. One bat was everybody's bat. He didn't know everybody had their own model, their own bat and you put your numbers on the bat so when you would go to the bat rack, you would know it.

Bo was just a different dude, man. But damn, I wasn't going to just let him take my bat. That's just how he was, but once he got to know you he was the best friend you could have. The next year me and him and Danny Tartabull became really good friends.

The Royals always had really good talent coming up in September. What we tried to do as players – at least I did – was try and teach them about playing in the Major Leagues. As much as I talked about Amos (Otis) in those first few years, he was my mentor. I learned later that he treated me bad to learn about my character or to see how my drive was. But he also did the greatest thing he ever could have, and that was to teach me how to play center field.

Bo was playing left field most of the time. But toward the end of my career with the Royals some days I would play left and he would play center. You could see the greatness there, but it was raw. About the time he really started to know how to play baseball, he got hurt (playing football).

He was just doing stuff and having so much fun doing it.

# 29
# FINAL FOUR YEARS WITH THE ROYALS

**B**y the end of 1986 it was clear the Royals were going toward being young. They were already trying to move George (Brett) over to first base. In September of 1986, they called up Kevin Seitzer and Bo Jackson, who would both be with the club the next year. In the winter they traded for Danny Tartabull. I think we had Angel Salazar at shortstop.

In spring training of 1987, Dick Howser tried to come back as manager, but he wasn't able to. So, we had another new manager, Billy Gardner. And we actually got off to a pretty good start. I think we were like 10 games over .500 at the start of July. But there were a lot of things going on that made it really hard to keep that going.

Dick died on June 17, and that took a lot out of the guys who had played for him on the World Series team. By the middle of July, the Royals released Hal McRae and I think that took away a big piece of the heart of that team.

Hal only played in 18 games because they moved George to first and made Steve Balboni the DH. So, Hal hadn't been able to contribute like he had in the past. That changed a lot of things he

*Courtesy of Kansas City Royals*

*My final four years with the Royals were full of ups and downs.*

191

could do for the team. When you aren't playing, you can't *show* people how to play, you just have to talk. With the younger guys they aren't thinking about what he has done for the Royals in the past, they're thinking, "What are you doing right now?" For me, and Frank and George and some of the older guys, Hal was the same kind of leader. But not the young guys, and more of the leadership role fell to us.

George was an action leader, by example, of how he worked at the game. Frank was more quiet. I was vocal, the angry guy. I wasn't actively trying to be aggressive or anything, but I think just the way I played showed. I was vocal on the bench. I was vocal in the locker room. You saw every emotion I had out on the field because I let you know it. If I was happy, you knew it. If I was angry ... frustrated ... you knew it. If I got called out, I would show all kinds of emotion coming back to the bench.

But none of us really filled that same Hal McRae role. All those successful Royals teams had several leaders. But Hal was the *one* guy who everybody looked up to. He was vocal, but he always backed up what he said. If he told you that you had to hustle more, he was hustling more. He had this fire inside of him.

The successful Royals teams had been built by those kind of players, the ones who knew how to win. Amos Otis came over from the Mets right after they won the World Series. Hal came to the Royals right after the Reds were world champions. Steve Balboni, Jim Sundberg, Cookie Rojas, Freddie Patek – they were all veterans with winning experience. When we would bring in younger guys like Frank and George in the '70s – and me a little later on – there was still this big group of veteran leaders.

Those were guys who put high expectations on you. Hal used to have this thing where he would hide in one of the laundry carts in the locker room with a sergeant's shirt on and they would cover him up with laundry. If you were even debating whether you would play that day – whether you were sore or tired or whatever – he would have someone push the laundry cart in front of your locker room and jump and shoot you with the bat, "Brrrrrrrrrrrrrrp!"

Then he'd shout, "Why don't you go somewhere else? We don't need you if you can't play! Get out of here!" Meanwhile, everyone in the locker room was watching as he is getting pushed up in front of your locker. So, now they all knew. He would get underneath your skin to the point where you wanted to play so bad just to prove him wrong. At least that's how it worked with me.

He'd use psychology on you, and he would do that a lot to goad you into performing. He'd be pushing it to the point where sometimes you would just want to punch him out. And then he would cackle, "I'm not going to fight you," and he would walk away.

On the field, you could see the fire and the desire to play a certain way. You could see the hustle. He would say things to you on the bench, too – quietly sometimes and not so quietly sometimes. His main deal was to win ballgames, and he wasn't afraid to let his opinion be known.

When we went into that slump after Dick died, Billy Gardner didn't last real long. Then they brought in John Wathan, who a lot of us had played with as a teammate and who had just retired two years before. So, you had four managers in less than two years. With me it became more of a psychological game because now the manager was a guy who didn't want me to live in his neighborhood and signed a petition against me back in 1984. I never said anything until he became the manager. I asked him about it and whether he could treat me fairly.

He told me he had not signed the petition – that his wife signed it. I always thought that was a pretty weak explanation of why he tried to keep me out of his neighborhood. He wouldn't even tell me about it at the time. When I would go to the ballpark I was mentally looking at the manager in a whole different way – and that carried over to 1988, 1989 and 1990.

When John got the job, I remember a meeting when he called all the veterans in – me, Frank, George, Quiz – the guys he had played with a long time. It was like, "I need you guys to help me out and this and blah, blah, blah." Then, the next few days he wasn't putting me in the lineup. So, I'm thinking, "How do I help you out if I don't play?"

Over those few years they were getting rid of the veterans who had been leaders on our team. A year after they let Hal go in the middle of the season, they cut Quiz in the middle of the season.

That was the other thing that was frustrating for some of us was that we were finding out this is the way the organization treated some of their important veterans. I know you get older, and you maybe aren't as productive, but it was frustrating to know that this is how they treat you at the very end, not with dignity or pride. That's when you really know it's a business, and they pick and choose who they want to continue with.

For some of us black players, we were looking at it a whole different way. What we see, in our brain, is that the white guy is getting treated one way and the black guy is getting treated another way.

And I'm not talking about George. We all accepted that George was going to be the man. George was no problem with us because of what he had accomplished. What we couldn't accept as easily were the people who weren't as good for the team who went farther in the organization. That's where we would look at it in a different way.

The way they had released Amos after 1983, flat-out telling him he wasn't going to be a part of the team while the season was going on. I mean how do you do that to a guy who has been that important to your team? Then you see how they release Hal in the middle of the year, Quiz in the middle of a year. And Bonesy (Balboni), he was our first baseman. You take him out of the mix and put George at first and Seitzer at third. You are messing up continuity – not because you think they can't play but because you start looking strictly at the numbers instead of the heart of the person. They start to push you off to the side.

The Royals, at one time, had all these dudes who were giving knowledge to young players. Hal McRae, Amos Otis, George gave me knowledge, Cookie Rojas gave me knowledge. Vada Pinson, Davey Nelson, Paul Splittorff, Dennis Leonard – they all taught me things. When I was coming up it was all those dudes giving you stuff, and you saw how they reacted to a loss or a victory and what they did the next time. How they prepared, what was going through their heads.

It was disheartening to see what was happening with the team. When I came up, it was like 21 older dudes and four young dudes, and we were a winning team. Now it's four older dudes and 21 young dudes, and we weren't a winning team anymore. We're not in second or first. We are in last or second-to-last.

For me, when they are letting guys go who I know, I'm losing friends, losing buddies. It's going to my emotions.

What they were really lucky with were the pitchers. The young guys were coming through at that point. Sabes won the Cy Young Award in 1985 when we won the World Series. He had another good year in 1987 and won the Cy Young again in 1989. They also added Tom Gordon in 1988, another young pitcher who made his mark. In 1989, Kevin Appier came in, and we finished second in the AL West.

In 1989, I could see the beginning of the end coming for me. Bo had been playing more and more center field, and I was in left. Then they brought in (Jim) Eisenreich and he was getting more playing time with Bo and Danny Tartabull. By 1990, Brian McRae had been added to the mix. At second base, Terry Shumpert was getting more and more time as they were moving Frank out.

We could see the writing on the wall from all the moves they started making from 1987 on. They got rid of Hal in the middle of the 1987 season. They also got rid of David Cone and Jim Sundberg that year. They got rid of Quiz in the middle of the 1988 season. That same year they traded Danny Jackson and let Lonnie Smith and Balboni go.

They didn't give Hal or Quiz any kind of a big send-off. Quiz is one of the guys who put your team on the map, winning a Fireman of the Year Award. We're looking at it and thinking, "That's the way you take care of your great superstars? What are you going to do with me and Frank?"

We are trying not to say stuff because we are thinking – hoping – in the back of our minds that maybe we will be different. At least I was thinking that maybe they will treat me a little different.

So, in that last year when they are sort of weaning us out of the lineup, Frank and I would be sitting on the bench. We were getting less and less playing time, but when the game was on the line they would put me in or Frank in. It used to just piss us off – at least I know it used to piss me off. I used to say to Frank, "If they had put me in the game in the first place it wouldn't be this damn close. Now, I gotta go up there, get a frickin' hit, steal a base. I could have won that in the first six or seven, not the ninth. Now you are really putting pressure on me." It was hard.

And I remember one day they were having a "Frank White Day." I think it was some group outside the Royals out in the community who arranged it. Wathan didn't have Frank in the starting lineup. All of a sudden, during the game the phone rings in the dugout downstairs and they're like, "Do you know it's Frank White Day?"

That cut to the core of me in a lot of ways. How can you not start him?

When we did get to start games, they might take us out. Instead of walking down the steps and up to the locker room, we tried to be a part of the team and sit on the bench and root for the team – trying to be professional. But it hurt like hell.

I was just a little dummy, but I was thinking that they might want players who could pass along experience and knowledge on to the team, but for some reason that regime of Royals people decided they were going to go young. They didn't think that an eight-time Gold Glover had anything to give. They didn't think I could pass along knowledge to the young guys they had coming up in the outfield.

That final year with the Royals, 1990, I played in 115 games. The regular outfield was Jim Eisenreich, Bo Jackson and Danny Tartabull. I had the highest batting average of any of the other outfielders, and only George had a higher batting average on the team, but I was expendable. I'll never quite understand that except that the guy who was the manager just wanted to get rid of me and they didn't want to pay my salary.

# 30
# MY WALKING PAPERS

They released Frank (White) and me right after the 1990 season. They actually released Frank over the phone. Frank called me, and I knew right then they were gonna call me.

The next day, I get a call from Herk Robinson. He wants to come out to my house. There was so much flak about just calling Frank and releasing him on the phone that he called me to come to my house. I said, "No, just tell me on the phone like you told Frank." He said no, he wanted to come to the house.

I said, "All you're going to do is come to my house and tell me I'm released." But he wanted to make himself look better and the Royals look better because of what happened with Frank.

I think I had four more years on my contract that were the team's option. They could renew the contract for four years at a salary that already was negotiated. I thought they would just hit the option. I hit .290 as a utility guy. After the season, I just thought they would pick up the option.

But when Frank was released, I knew what was coming.

Herk comes all the way over to my house and tells me that I'm released. It was a short conversation. I didn't really know Herk all that well. I didn't know anybody in the front office all that well except John Schuerholz. I really respected him. He was there when I signed my first contract. I have had this relationship with him through all my minor league and major league career. He had just left to go to the Atlanta Braves. Herk always had been around, but I didn't really know him.

There wasn't really any conversation after he told me. I mean, why? What am I going to do, beg for them to keep me? I'm not begging, I'm betting. I'm betting that I'm going to get on with somebody else.

I did ask him why, and he said that the team didn't think I had five more years in me to play. Well, he was right about that. I only played four more years (laughter). I think they just didn't want to give me the money. I think the option year went up to like $1.5 million or something. Then, he told me they wanted a leader. It was really weird the way he put it. They wanted a different kind of leader … basically, I was too controversial.

There are some things that people in the organization just won't let go of. You know that old saying, "Sometimes you are a prospect, sometimes you are a suspect?" I felt the Kansas City Royals looked at me a completely different way after 1983 and 1984. I don't think Mr. K looked at me any different. I wasn't treated like a prospect. I was getting treated like a suspect.

You know, after 1984, I never wore sunglasses when I wasn't in the outfield. I always thought that people were looking at me a little different, and I didn't want any of them to think I was hiding anything. When I would talk with John Schuerholz or somebody else with the team, I would look right at them so they could see my eyes and know I wasn't on anything.

I never really had a conversation with Mr. K. I wasn't the kind of guy who would go talk to him. He was a great man, and I'm thankful for the way he treated me after 1984. After he allowed me to stay with the team and signed me to a new contract, I didn't ever want to leave him. If the boss said he didn't want you, I wasn't going to fight it.

I wasn't mad at Mr. K. I was mad at the whole organization, but never at Mr. K – and he might have been the one who made the final decision. I don't think so, but he might have. After what he did for me, I would never be mad at him.

What I'm disappointed about is that even now, people think I wanted to leave the Royals. Now if a guy leaves a team, he has a press conference and all that. I still run into people who come up to me and say, "Why did you choose to go to Oakland?" I didn't choose to go to Oakland. The Royals released me.

So, after Herk tells me that they released me, I sort of say, "OK, you can go now. I know you only came here to make you look good. I don't care how you look."

I know Herk told Frank that the decision was made by Schuerholz before he left for Atlanta. I don't believe that. I feel like if Schuerholz had done that he would have called us himself.

I just think it was Herk's first job as a general manager to release us, and it was probably a real tough thing for him. He becomes GM and the first thing he has to do is get rid of me and Frank, as his first priority?

That's just my version of how it happened.

# 31
# PLAYING THE
# GAME

There are a lot of little things that go on during a game that the casual fan maybe doesn't really know about – things learned from guys like Amos Otis, Hall McRae, Frank White. I'd like to share a few of them.

\* \* \*

In our day, we played together so long and spent so much time with each other, all the information you could share with the guys coming up behind us would help out. So, we gave up that information. I don't know if they give that information up to the other guy because they might be on a different team tomorrow, but we gave it up.

Hal McRae, when he hit second behind me, always used to ask me, "What's he look like? How's his fastball?"

I would say, "Hey, you better tune it up because he's throwing hard" or "He's not throwing as hard today, but his changeup is working." I would give him a picture of what he had to look for when he went up there. When he saw me strike out, he knew the guy was throwing hard fastballs and say something like, "He's throwing it hard, ain't he?" I'd say, "Yes, he is because you know I don't miss no fastballs."

That was a factor in winning Game 7 of the 1985 World Series. St. Louis pitcher John Tudor would usually go fastball, change, change. My first at-bat he went fastball, fastball. I came back to the dugout and said, "He's doubling up fastballs." The next inning Darryl Motley homers on a second-pitch fastball.

\* \* \*

Being in the infield is a lot different than the outfield, but one thing Frank White told me really stuck with me over the time, and when I do the clinics now, I tell it to all the kids. Frank said never let the runner get in between you and the ball. What he meant by that is when you're covering second base against a steal, always set up in front of the bag. If the guy is sliding in, then you are in front of him and in position to catch the ball and tag him out.

\* \* \*

I was on the caravan this past spring (2013), and I was talking to Eric Hosmer. A fan at one of our stops gave us a copy of a video of the 1985 season, I think it's called, "The Thrill of It All." And we're watching it on the bus. Hosmer says, "You know, what I noticed at the start of this film. Everybody pitched in. Everybody pitched in."

I go, "You noticed that?"

He says, "Yeah, I noticed that."

I said, "I wanted you guys to watch this so when you win, you will learn how to react and how to deal with all of that stuff."

Then, we started talking about the game itself. I said, "Hos, all you gotta do is look at the scoreboard. The scoreboard will tell you what to do every time you come to bat." He says, "Really?"

It's true. You only have to look at the scoreboard. One out, man on first and second. It's telling you what you need to do everytime you come up there. If you need a single, it tells you.

Man on first and third one out. You need a single. You don't need a three-run homer. You just need a single. It's telling you what to do.

So, you play the game. You don't worry about your stats or money or any of that. Just look at the scoreboard. After you end your career, it adds up. But don't start thinking about where the stats will get you. That's where trouble comes. Let it happen.

You don't need your manager telling you what to do. The scoreboard will tell you.

He looked at me like, "That's so simple."

Yeah. That's the game.

* * *

Amos Otis was great for me. He taught me how to play center field. He told me one thing I always remember.

He goes, "Always keep the double play in order."

I didn't understand that. But he said take your ego out of the throw. If you have a runner going from first to third and you are, "I think I can get him" you aren't going to get him. If it's a "think I can" and you throw the ball to third, the guy who makes the hit is going to go to second. Now the double play isn't in order.

You are hurting the team. You are hurting the pitcher. But if I make the throw to second, we hold the runner to first and keep the double play in order. Now, we might get a ground ball and a double play and get out of the inning. So, he says always keep the double play in order.

When you're going after the ball, you should know, in your brain, if the ball is hit a certain way I have a chance. If it goes that way, make the throw. If it isn't hit exactly where you know you have a chance, go to second.

When he played, he had already thought about it before it happened. You see guys in the big leagues now go, "Oh, I can go there … I missed that one." And then you are hurting your team by making a bad decision. So, play it out in your head before it happens on the field.

* * *

Amos was hard on me in the beginning because I think he knew I would eventually take his position. But he is also the one who told me how to watch a pitcher and learn his move. He also told me to keep a book on every hitter

He didn't have to teach me what he knew, but he did because he didn't want the next person to embarrass center field. I wanted to do that with the next Royals center fielder after me, but I didn't have the chance because they released me.

* * *

When I was in the minor leagues, I couldn't hit a slider consistently as a right-handed batter. That was the main reason they asked me to move over to the other side. A slider from a right-handed pitcher breaks away from a right-handed batter. It will come at you, then a really good one breaks away.

A curve is like a clock. Think about a mental clock from 12 to 6. That's what they call a good curve ball, 12-6. A curve ball will start off high, then it will drop down. A slider will come off like a fastball and at the last second move away from you. But with a good pitcher, everything they throw is from the same arm motion so you don't know what is coming.

What we were taught is that if the guy throws with the same motion for every pitch, then you look at a little square above where his hand comes out. That way instead of looking at his whole body, you are concentrating on the ball coming out of his fingers. So, you don't look at anything else but that little square.

That's one of the things I didn't know as a young hitter. What separates the good hitters from bad hitters is that you know what's coming faster than anybody else. Hall of Famers might recognize the pitch just a mini-second before you see it.

For example, George (Brett) always said he could recognize the pitch as soon as it left the pitcher's hand. I might see it an inch or two after he did. But the guys who don't recognize the pitch until it's halfway to the plate – they have no chance.

# 32
## TWO YEARS WITH THE A'S

"*What did you do to them? You know they had you on a black list. I knew you could play, so I wanted you anyway.*"
— Tony LaRussa to Willie Wilson spring training of 1991.

I never wanted to leave the Royals. That's a big misunderstanding with many of the Royals fans. I wanted to play my whole career here. I wanted to retire a Royals player, but that didn't work out.

After the 1990 season, I became one of the expendable Royals, joining Frank White, Hal McRae, Amos Otis, Jorge Orta, Dan Quisenberry-all guys who had been key players in the World Series win just five years before.

It was hurtful. I didn't understand why they were releasing me after hitting .290 that season. I mean, who releases a guy who is hitting .290. That was a higher average than any other player on the team except for George Brett.

So, now I'm hoping that somebody else wants me. I don't know how many teams got in touch with my agent. It wasn't a lot, but when he mentioned the A's, I stopped

*Courtesy of the Fergie Jenkins Foundation*

*My two years with the A's were enjoyable after getting over the disappointment of being released by the Royals.*

him right there and decided that was the team I was going to play with. When I was a younger man, I just loved the Oakland A's uniforms. When I was watching baseball in high school, they were kicking booty. In 1990, they had just been in the World Series, so they were kicking booty again.

Shoot, Oakland wants me. I'm going to Oakland. I knew Tony LaRussa was a good manager. I didn't really know him as a man or a person, but I knew he got the best out of his players. I kind of figured my role was going to be a utility player.

I go to spring training, and it was really different. I had never been to Arizona before to have spring training. I didn't know where to go, where to stay, anything. I knew Tony LaRussa a little bit. I knew the players, but I didn't really know them, if you understand what I mean. I had been in Royals blue all my life and had never tried on another uniform or never did anything except the Royals for 15 years.

When I get over there, I'm wearing yellow socks, green stirrups, white shoes, white pants (great pants), a green and yellow top. It was just different stuff, and I felt awkward. I felt like a fish out of water. The only guy I really knew on the A's was Jamie Quirk, who had been let go by the Royals a couple of years before me. He was wearing my No. 6 on his uniform.

His number when he was with the Royals was No. 9, and when he had gotten to the A's Mike Gallego was wearing No. 9. I guess he chose No. 6 because it was just the 9 upside down. I ask him if I can have the number, and he tells me he wants $5,000 for it. I just said, "You know what, I'm just going to put a 1 on the side of my number because this is my first year with the A's, and I'm going to try and do something different." So that first year I was wearing No. 16.

Everything was different about the A's camp than the Royals. The first thing was the weather, the humidity. In Florida you are sweating, sweating, sweating. You get in shape really quickly. Out in Arizona you sweat, and in two or three minutes you are cool again. So, in some ways it was better because there wasn't the humidity. If you wanted to lose some weight, it wasn't going to happen.

There wasn't as much rain, not as many rainouts. The skies were so high, just brighter and higher up. I misjudged a lot of balls out there when I was first coming to spring training like the first time I was an outfielder when I was a rookie.

We started camp at this college for two weeks for spring training. After two weeks, they broke everything down and took a certain number of people down to Phoenix Municipal Ballpark for the rest of spring training. I had never had to pack up my stuff together and then move to another spot. The other thing that was really different about Arizona is that the spring training trips were 20 to 30 minutes to another team. You might go to Yuma, and that would be a long trip or Palm Springs, Calif., But the rest of the time you were going 20 minutes instead of 3 and a half hours in the morning and 3 and a half hours back in the afternoon.

I had never been on a team with so many superstars. We had George (Brett), we had Hal (McRae), we had Quiz (Dan Quisenberry) and Frank (White). They were all nice guys, and I don't think they thought of themselves as superstars. But with the A's you've got Jose Canseco and Mark McGwire – the Bash Brothers – Rickey Henderson, Dave Stewart, Dennis Eckersley ... superstars everywhere. That was the first time I had been around that many people who thought of themselves that way. I had never been around a team that could hit home runs like they could. It was just really different for me, and I felt like a fish out of water.

I'm not having a great spring. I felt like nobody knew me. Here I was a Punch and Judy hitter, and they were all bashing home runs all over the place. How am I going to fit into this team? I really had a bad spring as I'm going through the mental process of coming to another team and having the fans look at me differently than the Royals fans looked at me. A lot of things were going bad. To make it worse, I have a number on my back that is unfamiliar. I can't even get my own number. It was really bad.

That's when I really found out what a good guy Tony LaRussa was. One day in spring training he said, "Walk with me down the line."

He says, "You gotta relax. You're going to make this team. I know you can play. That's why I brought you in here. Just be yourself."

That's when he asked me what I had done to the Royals. I go, "What are you talking about?" He said there was a list and I was on the list. I don't know what the list is. I'm not in a front office. But the way I understand a black list is that it's something they have and they make it clear that they don't want anybody else to sign you or pick you up. It's like collusion, but they can't prove it.

That really made me mad. Maybe Tony was lying to me to get me motivated, but I don't think he would. When I got to know him more and more, I understood that he didn't lie to his players. He told it like it was. He told you the truth. That's why I respect him to this day. He was a good people person. That's why he would get the best out of his players. He would tell me this is what he was going to do, and he never lied to me. That was pretty cool because I got lied to a lot in Kansas City. That sounds like that organization at the time. I wouldn't put it past them – not the new regime that is there now, but the old regime.

At Oakland, it was a whole different ball game. The GM, Sandy Alderson, was a cool dude. He didn't walk around with a tie on all the time. He was wearing shorts and a nice shirt, just like we were. I'm like, "This is the GM." I mean you know. Wow. And even he would say stuff … "I heard this about you Willie" but "you're a nice guy." I guess that's what the Royals did to me, they put it out there that I was a bad guy.

That really angry me off. Nobody in the Royals organization – I'm not talking about the players – took the time to really get to know me. So, when I got to Oakland, it was like a breath of fresh air. They treated me like a man. They were a little more free spirited out there. It was probably the perfect situation for me.

I wasn't starting out there, so I didn't have the pressure of starting every day the first year I was there. It was different than Kansas City the year before when they didn't tell me anything. I never knew if I was going to be in the lineup or not. It was kind of neat at the A's to be able to sit on the bench and have somebody hit a 2- or 3-run home run to win the game. The only bad thing was they had won the AL West the year before, and when we didn't win it in 1991 I felt like I was the reason they lost.

I know that's silly. But they won in 1990, now they aren't winning and I'm the new guy coming in. Is it my fault? Is it this? Is it that?

The dynamic on that team was really different than the Royals, too. Rickey was easy to know. Jose was difficult. Jose thought I had just come up from AAA (laughter). Really. At least this is what I understood from (shortstop) Walt Weiss. Jose thought baseball couldn't survive without him. We're in Cleveland a little ways into the season. I come downstairs with Walt, and Walt says, "Jose asked who you were the other day. He thinks you just came in from A A A."

I don't know if Walt is joking or not, and I'm going, "Are you kidding me?" Walt says, "Hey man, that's just how Jose is." Jose and Walt were like bosom buddies. They would eat breakfast and lunch together almost every day. They wouldn't go out in the evening together because Walt was married … well, Jose was married too, but … you know the superstar thing.

Rickey was really good to know, and Dave Henderson was a pleasure. He was just fun, fun, fun, fun, fun, fun. If you saw him on the field, he was having fun. He taught me a little different way of playing the game – have fun at it. When he got hurt in 1992, the second year I was there – I had to play every day.

I only played 110 games or so (113), and I only started about half the time (64) that first year in 1991. I do think I started every game that we played at Royals Stadium that year. Tony set up a regular rotation that I would play for Rickey every Tuesday, Dave every Wednesday, Jose every Thursday and pinch run or pinch hit the rest of the time. That would give those guys a regular day off. But every time we were coming into Kansas City Tony arranged it so those were the days I would be in the lineup.

He knew I was angry off. Nothing was said, but he knew. If you had played for this team or that team, Tony knew you had some fire left. One time in there I made this really nice catch in left center. I got hit a couple of times and had a little flare up. I think it was Mike Boddicker who hit me. He hadn't even been a Royal, but I knew he was doing it on orders. So, after the second time I get hit, I'm really angry. So, I come to bat again and Mike MacFarlane was catching.

I looked at Mac, and I said, "You tell Boddicker the first time he comes to Oakland, I'm going to kick his butt. And if I get hit again, I'm going to kick *your* butt because *you* called the play. You called the pitch that hit me. Really, what I was trying to do is show them that they got rid of me too early. I had an attitude against them … it's even vivid to me right now as I'm talking about this.

The fans were kind of mixed when I would come back to Royals Stadium. A lot of them were yelling at me like I had left the Royals.

They had it in their minds that I didn't want to play for the Royals anymore and I went to Oakland. But it wasn't like that at all. The Royals released me. So, the fans would boo me some, but that was OK. It was like that everywhere the A's went. It was kind of funny. You play 15 years with a team, go to two World Series with them, go to four or five playoffs with them, rank in the top five of almost all their records, and they boo you.

One plus of coming to Kansas City is that I did get to sleep in my own bed and stay at my own house. I really wanted to beat them. I didn't like them at that time. I didn't like what they were doing. When you go to a different organization and you see how different that was compared to the tight-ass Kansas City Royals at the time. I just wanted to beat them every day.

I was still friends with the players, and I remember one game in Oakland when I came in to pinch hit. Luis Aquino was pitching for the Royals. Louie and I hung out a lot when he first got up to Kansas City. So, we were pretty good friends. He had already asked me if I could give him a ride back to the hotel after the game. That's how friendly we were.

When I get up there, he throws a fastball, and I don't swing at it. He throws me a curve, and I hit it right back up the middle. He yells, "Conjo. You say you no like curve ball!" I yelled back, "I don't like it, but I didn't say I couldn't hit it." He had heard me yelling in the dugout after I had struck out while I'm in Kansas City. I'd get struck out by a curve ball or a changeup or something. I'd yell, "I hate that pitch." So he's heard this and remembered it. Now that I'm an older guy I'm a little smarter, so I'm thinking, "OK, he's going to throw the curve ball."

## THE JUICE

With Jose and Mark McGwire everybody found out later on that they were doing stuff. Jose kind of blew the lid off all that with his book. I never saw anyone do anything at the park. As far as I knew, they were just bigger guys. I had seen them as younger guys, and they weren't as big. I never lifted weights … never went in the weight room. So, I didn't know if you could just get bigger by pumping the weights.

If I didn't see anything, I wasn't going to make up any rumors about it. Besides I'm just trying to keep my head down out here.

This is just my opinion, but I do think the GMs knew it was going on. I think the writers knew. I think they all knew. But nobody was going to say anything because nobody wanted to be the first guy to open up that can of worms. When Jose opened up the can of worms, then everybody started going, going, going.

I didn't know that certain guys were on it. I thought they were just big. I had played with Bo Jackson, and he was big. Imagine if Bo had come up in the '90s, everybody would have associated Bo with that and it would have been false.

It was none of my business. I never saw it. I never thought about it. It was none of my business. I wasn't going to come over here to the Oakland A's and start any kind of crap.

## 1992 SEASON

The second year in Oakland, I'm back in my regular number again – and I didn't have to pay Jaime for it. The A's had gotten rid of Mike Gallego in '92 and Jamie could get his old number. So, I was back in my No. 6.

This year was different from the beginning. I was playing a lot in spring training, and I was wondering what the heck was going on. I'm playing every day, and I'm wondering if they are showing me off to trade me, or something … I don't know. So, Tony pulls me off to the side again.

"You're going to be happy that I'm playing you all spring," he says.

I say why. Then he tells me I'm going to start every game until the first half of the season is over because Dave Henderson is hurt. Hindu had pulled something and wasn't going to be back until the All-Star break. Tony was telling me I had to be mentally prepared to play every day. It was pretty cool to be a part of that lineup. I was really happy I got a chance to play every day again, but I hadn't played every day for two years and I was like, "Wow, man, this is tiring." Hindu came back for a little bit after the All-Star break, but re-injured himself again.

Rickey and Jose were going through some little tantrum stuff, too. Jose had migraine headaches, and I don't know what was going on with Rickey. So, a lot of the time it was this makeshift outfield of me and Eric

Fox or Randy Ready or Harold Baines. Then, from what I remember, Rickey and Jose said they wanted to play more. Tony said all right I'm going to go to you guys after the All-Star break, but I don't want to hear any complaints about migraines or this and that.

The All-Star break comes and they were in the lineup again, right and left of me. One Saturday Jose comes in to the park right after we had finished batting practice. Everybody is just looking at each other like, "What the hell?" He had another migraine. So, August comes along and it's close to the trade deadline. Jose was playing in a game – actually in the on-deck circle – and the phone rings in the dugout. Tony answers it, then yells, "Jose, come here." Then he yells, "Blankenship!"

Lance Blankenship was funny. He thought he was getting released. Then Tony says, "Go in for Jose" and Blankenship is going, "thank you, thank you, thank you." He grabs a bat and goes up there, and Jose sat down next to Tony. I don't know what Tony said to him, but Jose just rips his shirt off, all the buttons come flying off his shirt everywhere. He grabs up all his bats and walks upstairs out of the dugout.

He goes up into the locker room and locks all the doors because he doesn't want any reporters in there. Hindu is hurt, and I don't think I'm playing that day. We follow him up. Dave Henderson, in his wisdom knew the trade deadline was getting close and he says, "Where'd you go?" Jose goes, "They traded me to blankety-blank Texas." Henderson pauses, and he's sort of smiling at me, then says, "OK, now the important question. Who did we get?" I'm laughing my ass off. Jose goes "Ruben effing Sierra!" Hindu goes, "OK, good luck." Me and Hindu run back downstairs.

Jose was in shock. But Tony had said, "If you come in here with a migraine one more time I'm getting rid of you because you are already messing up my lineup." It seemed like every Saturday just about, he would come in with a migraine and we would have to rearrange the lineup. I think Tony just got tired of it and got rid of him. I don't know if the migraines were real or not. I wasn't inside Jose's body.

That second year was pretty fun, though. It was cool just to be associated with those guys. I wasn't batting around the top of the lineup – I think I was sometimes. Rickey was leading off. Then probably Carney Lansford or Walt Weiss, then you have Mark McGwire, Jose,

Terry Steinback, Harold Baines was the DH, Dave Henderson. When you're hitting at the bottom of that lineup, that ain't bad.

We win the division, but we had been ahead by a lot of games, and toward the end we were slipping and almost losing our lead in the standings. I tried to go all Hal McRae psychological on them one afternoon, I think we were playing in Milwaukee. I'm shouting, "We don't deserve to win this crap!" That was a Hal McRae move right there. Everybody looked at me and said, "Don't say that crap. We're going to win this thing."

At the end of the year, we had to wait and see if some other team won, and the whole team went to this restaurant in Oakland. The other team lost, and we won the championship and we all celebrated in this restaurant. That was pretty cool, everybody shaking hands and stuff like that.

## 1992 ALCS

We should have beaten Toronto in the ALCS. We went up there and split, won the first game, and Toronto won the second. So we're tied as we head back to Oakland for the third game.

In the second game at Oakland, we're leading 6-4 in the ninth inning when there's a ball hit to left. Rickey goes over, and he's going to get there and he decides he's going to catch it the "cool" way, you know just sort of flip your glove at it and snatch it – be cool. He flipped it all the way down the left-field line. It hit his glove and looked like it was jai alai sending the ball down the left field line. I'm now chasing the ball and screaming at Rickey, "Why can't you just catch the damn thing. Why do you have to be so fancy?" I mean, what the hell? They score two runs in that inning and we end up losing the game in extra innings.

We had a pretty good pitching staff out there, Ron Darling, Dave Stewart, Mike Moore. Bobby Welsh, Goose Gossage, Dennis Eckersley. But you get that one game. You don't know how important that one game or that one out could be. That happened in the fourth game of the series. If we win that game, we beat them. That would have tied the series. We won the fifth game and would have gone back to Toronto with a 3-2 lead. Instead, they go back home with the 3-2 lead in the series and win it in the first game back in Toronto.

I really wanted to get the Series again because I hadn't been there since 1985. I was really happy to be a part of a team that could get me there.

A little time after the season, Tony talked to me again. I had signed a two-year deal with the A's. I didn't know if I was going to get another contract with them. I didn't know if anyone else wanted me. We had been talking with the A's, but that's when Tony told me that they would like to have me back, but I should probably take another offer. The A's couldn't pay me what another team would offer.

I love him for that. How can you not play for a guy like that who tells you the truth? If more people in this fair game of ours would just tell the truth and stop playing games with people they would get more out of their players. That's why LaRussa won all the damn time. He told the truth.

# 33
# THE CUBBIES

I really liked it with the A's, and I probably would have stayed there. Tony LaRussa was, for me personally, the best manager I ever had. He treated me like a man. Nothing against anybody else (laughter), but he treated me like a man. He told me what was going to happen, and he never lied.

After the '92 season, the A's were figuring out what they were going to do. Some of the guys were starting to go elsewhere. That's when Tony called me up and said he'd love to have me back, but ...

So, I decided on the Chicago Cubs. The reason I went with Oakland was because when I was younger I liked the "unis" and they had a good team. The reason I went with the Cubbies is that I had always wanted to experience the National League. I had always heard about it, and at the time I was starting to watch afternoon baseball I saw them all the time on WGN.

I don't know if there was another team out there trying to get me. The Cubs wanted to give me the same amount of money I was making with Oakland. So, I went with them.

Just like two years before when I went to the A's, this was different. The Cubs trained in Arizona. Just like the A's, but the Cubbies were a little different.

When I first got there and walked into the locker room, Randy Myers was there and had one of those electricity guns – bzzzzzt, bzzzzt. He was wearing a bandanna and army fatigues and chasing this young guy around the locker room with one of those taser things. He's joking, but that's the first image I saw in the clubhouse. Then he stops, and he yells at me, "Hey, Idol!" Randy turned out to be a really good friend on the Cubs. They were kind of a young team. He bought me a leather chair. Everybody else in the clubhouse had regular chairs, and Randy bought me this big leather chair. That was kind of cool.

The first spring training, Jimmy Piersall was there as an instructor and coach. We were doing some infield practice, and he told me, "You're smooth out there when you are doing stuff." That was kind of neat to have Jimmy Piersall say that. I remember watching the movie the "Jimmy Piersall Story." So, it was quite an experience and I could relate to him in a lot of ways.

What would happen is that he would say that to me, and in the next breath he would jump on this young guy kind of yelling at him. He would say, "You think I'm crazy ... I got the papers to prove it."

I'm like, "Wow."

There was a bunch of good guys. I really got along with Mark Grace, the first baseman. I thought he was a gamer. Ryne Sandberg was a quiet leader. I had never been around a leader who was that quiet. He did it all by example. I think I kind of helped get Ryno out of his shell. We went out a couple of times in spring training, and I got to know him a little better. I had this saying, "That's a beautiful thing ... when it's working." I'd say it when sitting in the dugout as a sarcastic joke.

He would look at me, and I would say it at an opportune time, and he would start laughing. That was pretty cool. Ryno was a good dude. Mike Morgan, I got a really good chance to hang out with him. Steve Lake was about my age. They were good people. They also had a bunch of younger guys like Shawon Dunston, Derrick May, Dwight Smith. They were good kids, but really into being in the big leagues. Dwight Smith could really sing, and I thought that was great because I liked singing, too.

It was good to be in the National League. I was going through the same thing I had with the A's, being with new guys and trying to fit in and all that kind of stuff. I wasn't trying to impress anybody.

The Cubs fans didn't take to me right away. I signed with them and they got Candy Maldanado from the Blue Jays. The Jays had just won the World Series, and I had just lost to their team in the playoffs. I thought they were getting a couple of pretty good players.

What I didn't know is that the Cubs had gotten rid of Andre Dawson. He goes to Boston. But down in spring training, you don't read the paper or really hear from the fans at that time. Unbeknownst to us, we were getting pummeled in the papers because everybody thought we were the reason they traded Andre Dawson, their beloved Andre Dawson.

When we opened the season in Chicago, boy, there were some boo birds. We were getting booed when we stepped on the field, and we couldn't understand why. Then, later on, we found out it was because they blamed us for Andre Dawson getting traded.

It was really cool to play at Wrigley – really cool to see the vines come in. When you first get there at the start of the season, the vines are all bare and brown with just a few leaves. Then you go on a road trip, and it gets a little warmer. The leaves just pop out. And the Wrigley people out there are fanatical. They love their team. I wanted to try and win them a championship. But there were a lot of things going against that.

It wasn't too hard to make the transition to the National League as far as the pitchers were concerned. Everybody was starting to switch from one league to the other, and I ran into a lot of guys who had been in the American League. One funny thing did happen. You know the National League always considered itself the "senior circuit" and in the American League we were the "junior circuit." They played real baseball the regular way in the National League, and in the American League we had the DH. So, the first time I get a hit in the opening game of the year I'm standing at first base and the umpire, I think it was Bob Davidson, says to me, "Welcome to the *National* League."

I got to see different cities. San Diego was beautiful. I got to go back to Philadelphia – where

*Getting to play in Wrigley Field as a Cub finished off my career.*

Courtesy of the Fergie Jenkins Foundation

they jumped on me like crazy because of 1980. Man, they were jumping on me so bad. I got back at them late in the season, though. We were playing in Philly in September of that year. Steve Buechelle homered to left in the sixth inning. I was up next and homered to right, and then Steve Lake completed the trifecta with a home run to left field – back-to-back-to-back. That was pretty cool and it made me feel good because I silenced some of the Phillies fans. Boy, they were getting on me.

The Cubbies had a new manager that year, Jim LeFebvre, the father of Royals broadcaster Ryan Lefebvre. He was an extraordinarily good batting coach. It was only his second managing job, and we heard the reason he got rid of Andre Dawson is that he didn't like veteran players. He wanted young guys that he could mold.

We started off against Atlanta that year so I got a chance to face (Tom) Glavine and (John) Smoltz and those guys. I was hitting almost .500 against the Braves, then had a rough series against the Phillies. I think I started nine of the first 10 games. We didn't win every game, but we were in the games. Then we went to Philly, and Lefevbre said he was going to give me a day off. He had Dwight Smith play. Dwight hit a home run. So, I knew my starting days were over (laughter). He (Lefevbre) liked that. He wanted home run hitters. That's what he was teaching as a hitting coach.

I didn't balk because I thought I would get to play plenty. It turned out that it was kind of true that he didn't like veteran players. He sat me down and sat Candy down. He couldn't sit Ryno down because he was sort of a Chicago legend. The hard part for me was that I really wanted to continue the trend of having at least 20 stolen bases every year. I had 11 years with 30 or more stolen bases. Then my final two years with the Royals and the two with the A's I had at least 20. So, I really wanted to keep that going. I wasn't in the games enough to really keep that going. Subsequently, every now and then I would bitch and moan.

It wasn't pleasurable, but I dealt with it. The upsetting thing for me was the standard that the manager set for the team. He said, and this is a quote, "Our goal this year is to be a .500 team." I had no idea what that was about. I had never been around a manager who would say that. I don't know what he was thinking about.

Tony LaRussa wanted to be the last team standing. Every manager I had before that wanted to be the last team standing. I just didn't understand that you were making our goal to be just a mediocre team.

The Cubbies had not been .500 in 18 of the previous 20 years, and I think we ended up finishing four or five games over .500 (84-78). I guess it wasn't that bad. But we didn't *win* anything.

Part of that first year with the Cubs, baseball was secondary on my brain. My grandmother died in 1993. She was my love. She's the one who raised me when I was a little child. I learned of it when my cousin Michael called me early in the morning on a day when we were traveling to Houston with the Cubbies. I answered the phone like you do in the morning when you've been woken up. He told me my grandmother died. I was so sleepy, I hung up. I laid my head back down on the pillow, then immediately opened my eyes and realized what he said and called him right back.

We sat there on the phone and cried like babies. I … I'm still feeling it a little bit when I talk about it right now … that really hurt. I flew to Houston with the team on April 28, then went to Montgomery where we were making funeral arrangements. I was going in and seeing her and just really missing her. Having to go back to the ball club really didn't sit well.

The next year we come back and there is a new manager and a new coaching staff. That was Tom Trebelhorn. As soon as I had gotten used to Lefebvre, I gotta go through months of getting used to another manager. Trebelhorn wasn't a bad guy, but I'm going through a long learning period. I really didn't get a chance to learn from him that long because I was released in May.

I wasn't playing too much in 1994. I think I played only 17 of our 35 or so games before I was released in May. I was mostly being used as a pinch runner or defensive replacement late in the game. I only had five hits and 23 plate appearances.

I knew I was not long for the Cubbies world when about a month into the season the GM came down and started talking to me in the locker room. I had been in the league for 19 years, and whenever the owner or the general manager or somebody from the front office would come down into the locker room and talk to players they would be gone in a day or two.

In early May the GM came down and started talking to me in the locker room, saying I was doing this and that, and they liked what they were getting out of me. When he left, I turned to Mark Grace in the locker next to mine, and I said, "I'm going to be leaving in a few days."

He goes, "What are you talking about."

I said, "Man, I have been here too long."

This being my 19th year in the league, I knew what was going on.

My final game was May 16, 1994. The Cubbies were playing the San Diego Padres. I wasn't starting, but I was getting in quite a few games as a pinch runner or a late-inning defensive sub. By that time I was getting pretty close to Ryne Sandberg. We were having a good time, and Ryno was opening up a little bit.

I got into the game in the seventh or eighth inning – I didn't get an at-bat. We're in the ninth inning, and Randy Myers is pitching. He would always tell the outfielders to shade the hitters the opposite way because he threw everything away from hitters. So, if it was right-handers, they were going to hit it to right field. If it was left-handers, they were going to hit it the opposite way in left field.

I'm playing just shaded a little way into right-center field. Randy threw it, and he didn't get it away from the hitter. He laid it down the middle, and the guy just goes, "Boom!" and it's going to left-center. I think there was a runner on first base. It was like instinct. I just took off, looked at the ball, put my head down again just running full tilt. I raised my left arm, and the ball just went in the glove.

When I turned around I could see Ryno just jumping up in the air. All I can remember is that everyone was excited. Randy struck out the next guy to end the game, and we were all celebrating as we were coming off the field.

I wish that my catch had been the last out of the game because it would have been pretty cool to have that be the very last play of my career. It was still pretty cool to make that catch in my last game. It was a hard hit ball. It was a hell of a catch, then we went inside and it was all over.

After the game I'm sitting there in my big old leather chair, and José Martinez comes over to where I'm sitting. José was one of the first coaches and guys I met with the Royals so long ago back in rookie ball and the instructional league and then in my first few years with the Royals. Now he is coaching first base for the Cubbies, and I guess they thought José was more close to me than any other coach so they asked him to come and tell me that Trebelhorn wanted to see me upstairs.

He says, "Chili Bean" – that's what he called me – "Chili, the manager wants to see you."

I say, "OK, tell him after I take a shower and put my clothes on I'll be in there."

"No. No. He wants to see you now."

"Tell him I will take a shower and then come and see him." I wanted to be dressed to go upstairs and get the news. Then, I wouldn't have reporters standing around my locker while I was getting dressed after hearing I had been released.

I went in, took the shower, got dressed. And when I went up to his office, there was every coach just sitting in that room. They're just sitting there. I was thinking to myself, "What? Do they think I'm going to beat him up?" I guess they have the coaches there just in case someone goes crazy and wants to fight or that kind of stuff.

Trebelhorn says, "Willie we're going to have to release you." They had a young guy down in the minors who was a switch hitter. He told me the young guy could do what I had been doing for them. I think his name was Kevin Roberson.

I said, "OK, where do I sign?" The only thing I asked was, "Do I get paid for the rest of the year?" They said I would. I signed the papers, thanked everybody in the room, thanked the Cubs for having me.

You know 1994 was such a strange year. I was getting weird feelings coming to the ballpark. I had never been nervous about playing in games since about the first or second year I was in the majors. I was always excited, but never nervous. Then, one day I was driving to Wrigley and coming in through the back way through the neighborhood where you see the big Cubs emblem and my hands started sweating. That last week or so my hands started sweating every day I was coming to the ballpark. I didn't feel like I wanted to be there. I knew in my brain that I didn't want to be there. I always remember Hal McRae saying, "Don't take the uniform off. Make them take it off. That way you are still going to get paid."

For a few days I knew I didn't really want to be there. Maybe I knew I was done because we were playing Cincinnati one day, a right hander – I can't think of his name – he strikes me out three or four times that day. They were all fastballs. That's when I was like, "I don't miss fastballs. If I can't hit a fastball, I'm done." Mentally, I was just done and I was really ready to go.

I knew they were going to release me, so I just said, "Where do I sign?"

Of course, by that time all the reporters were gathered around my locker when I came back downstairs. I say goodbye to Gracie, say goodbye to (Mike) Morgan, say goodbye to Ryno. I just went to my locker, grabbed all my valuables out of the lock box and started to leave.

One of the reporters said, "That's it? That's all you are going to do?"

I turned around and said, "Nah ... goodbye" and I just left.

I walked to the car kind of in a little daze, and people were still hanging around and wanting autographs and this and that. I was living in an apartment building in downtown Chicago. There was a guy who parked your car. I got to the apartment, and the doorman – he called me Money because I would tip him well to do my car – he says, "Money, Money, what's going on?" I say, "Thank you, man. I'm going to be leaving in a few days." He was like, "Wow, you, too."

I had to wait three days to clear waivers to see if anybody wanted to put a claim on me. I sat up in the place for three days, and I didn't go outside. I basically didn't leave the apartment. It was almost surreal. In your brain you imagine what people are saying and what people are thinking about you. I remember getting in the elevator when I was taking my stuff down to pack my car and there were a couple of people in the elevator who had a little smirk on their face. I don't know what was said on the radio or the TV, but it just made me feel like crap when they were sort of smirking that I had lost my job. The emphasis is never on how the guy who is 38 or 39 years old feels when he loses his job.

I don't think I was really liked in Chicago. They never really got a chance to see me. They got to see the old me, the 39-year-old me.

I got a phone call from my agent, and he said the Texas Rangers wanted me and the Pittsburgh Pirates wanted me. I didn't want to stay in the National League, so I said to him let's see what happens with

Texas. A few hours later he called me back and said somebody blocked the deal.

I didn't really want to play for Pittsburgh, so I told my agent I was just going to go home. I didn't really want to play anymore anyway. I was done. Mentally, I was done. Physically, I was OK. It was frustrating to sit there and watch young kids play and young kids make mistakes and then at the end of the game they put the old guy in.

I packed everything in my car and waited for the appropriate moment and I drove home to Kansas City.

It was really kind of fitting. Chicago is a pretty good drive, nine or 10 hours. I was driving through the Midwest, coming through Iowa. I would see road signs, and it would say "Cedar Rapids" and I would start remembering A ball. Then Waterloo, Iowa, and all the A-ball stuff when I played in the Midwest League.

I kind of reflected all the way going home. At one point, I can remember thinking how ironic it was. Here you are just going back in time. Driving home was actually a peaceful drive. No more pressure. No more thinking about strikeouts or yelling or screaming. I was going home and remembering everything and thinking about everything.

… And basically going: "What am I going to do now?"

# 34
## WHAT'S
## NEXT?

**I** knew it was time to wrap up my baseball career, but I really didn't have a plan for what was going to come next. When I was growing up in Summit, I always thought I was going to college, study business, carry a briefcase and wear a tie. Those were the people with pretty big houses in Summit, so I wanted to do what they were doing.

When I chose baseball, that became my life. And it was a good life, but I wasn't really prepared for anything else. That's something people don't realize about guys who come straight out of high school and begin playing pro baseball, they aren't prepared for anything else because all they've done all their life is play baseball. You don't have a degree or any of those things that people want.

The other thing that was really different was that you had to learn how to do everyday things for yourself. People have been telling you what to do since you were in high school, so things as simple as going through an airport and doing your luggage is new. You never had to do that. Somebody always had your luggage. Going into a hotel and checking in was new. You never had to do that. You just popped off the bus and somebody gave you a key to your room. Those are little things. But they're little things in every facet of your life, and they eventually add up to big things.

I was in a funk. Every day I felt lost because I was living here in Kansas City, but I wasn't a Royal anymore. That's where I made my name. At the time, I think I still had a bad rap in their brain. I wasn't involved in anything at the stadium – and I might not have been ready for it right then. I just felt lost. I was used to going somewhere every day at 4 or 5:00 and was used to playing.

I still watched games. I still kept up with my friends. But it seemed like every time I watched TV a little bit that would just get me down a little more. So I stopped watching. It's kind of like you dropped off the map. It's like, "Thank you, now goodbye. We're not going to help you, not going to do anything. You're on your own."

I got released in May. Then I had June and July before they went on strike. I was just sitting around for a month or so and not doing anything, my family didn't know if I was depressed or what. I played a little golf, but I wasn't really into golf at the time like I am now. I was like a fish out of water. I didn't know what to do. I didn't know where to go. I didn't have a job. I didn't know how to go about getting a job.

I was in a pretty good place financially, but when you feel bad it doesn't matter how much money you have, you just feel bad. I found out later that when you don't have money and you feel bad, it's worse. But when you're lost, you're lost and how much money I had at the time wasn't a solution to any of the things I was feeling.

The only guy who really reached out was one of my former teammates from the A's, Dave Stewart. And that happened in 1994 when he was with Toronto. Stew just showed up one day, out of the blue. I was really depressed at the time. My wife knew they were in town and called him. He came over after a game – he called me "Bean," too. He says, "C'mon Bean! Let's go out (imitating Stewart's high-pitched voice)." I said I didn't want to go out anywhere, but he says, "Get your ass up, and let's go."

I think he took me down to Crown Center where some of the Blue Jays were staying, so we hung out there for a while. I talked to a few guys, hung out and pretended to feel better. So, he kind of got me out of my funk for a little bit, but it didn't really work.

The next spring, when it was time for spring training I went down to Arizona with my buddy Chet, Chester Shipps. We would play golf and do all kinds of stuff together. He was my best friend in Kansas City at the time. He still is a good friend. I think Chet is about 15 years older than I am. He was always kind of a mentor to me and the kind of guy who gave me some good advice.

We were in Arizona about the time that the strike was over in the spring of 1995. So, I said to Chet, "Let's go over to Phoenix and check out some of the boys with the A's and say hello before we go play golf. So, we get there, and Tony (LaRussa) sees me and calls me down to the sideline.

I didn't go on the field, just down to the first row on the right side of the field. He goes, "You still want to play?" I go, "Oh, wow. That wasn't a question I was expecting."

I thought about it for about 30 seconds then said, "Nah, that's OK, man." I had gotten used to not having to travel all the time. I was used to my time being my time and being around the kids. I was getting used to being away from the game.

And you know the first thing I thought of when he asked me that? I thought about getting yelled at. I just got a little knot in my stomach. Then Rickey (Henderson) comes over – he called me, Will Dog. He says, "Will Dog. Come on. You want to play? I'll play against lefties and you can play against righties."

Well, there are a lot more righties in the league than there are lefties and that means I would be playing. So, I say thanks, but no thanks. You guys have a great season. And then we went and played golf.

That was it. I think about it now and in hindsight sometimes wonder if maybe I should have gone back and played that one year for Tony.

I'm telling you, man. I was floundering for most of that year and the next two years before I got involved in a business that I thought would work.

# 35
# LOSING ALL
# MY MONEY

$S$o I was just hanging out in 1994, 1995 and 1996.

I didn't have any background to get into business. All I knew was playing baseball.

Dave Stewart had played with the Toronto Blue Jays in 1993 and 1994 and still had some ties up there. He invited me up there for this function some time in 1996, I believe. I got to meet Gord Ash, the Blue Jays general manager, and attended some parties and functions. My wife and children went up there with me because it was Toronto, and that's where she is from.

At one of these parties I also got introduced to this guy named Anthony Ramsaroop. He was from Trinidad, but he was living in Toronto. He had this telecommunications business, and I just fell for it – figuring, you know, I could make some money.

The company was Nutech Inc. based in Toronto. He sold me on it by saying he was with this company in Atlanta. Motorola was a part of what they did in that company, and that we could do this on our own. He said he had been on his own, and he told me the people he was dealing with and this and that. He came down and showed me his phone that was in the stores.

So, I'm trying to get the contract together, and checking him out. I'm thinking he is legit.

I had over a million dollars when I left baseball. When you have that kind of money you never think about running out. I never thought about running out, but when my agent and I looked at it, we were estimating that with bills and everything it would only last five years.

If you don't have any money coming in and all you are doing is giving it out, then the money is only going to last for so long. I was trying to make the same amount of money that I was making when I was playing.

I started off with about $300,000 that I invested with Nutech. My agent, Jack Sands, didn't want me to do it. He thought it was too much money. He and I had some words about it. But in my brain I was paying Jack, too, because he was paying my bills for me. So, I'm thinking how can he be critical of this deal when he is telling me he's going to get me this and that. But I haven't had a job, and I'm still paying him.

So, I'm thinking if I'm going to screw it up, I might as well screw it up myself – which I did (laughter). But if the money is only going to last for five yeas, I have to do something. So, I lose it all in five or lose it all in three or four. What's the difference? I'm going to go down trying to do something. I'm not going to sit here and not do anything and just keep spending.

Anthony wasn't guaranteeing I was going to double my money or anything at Nutech. It was a business where we sold phones. We sold DSS (digital spread spectrum) during the analog period. Digital was relatively unknown at the time. So, we couldn't really go to bankers to get loans because they didn't understand it.

When you are in my position, your friends are in baseball. They're not in business. It's not like the CEO of a company who can go to a bank and has a track record of making money in businesses. I have been a ballplayer. So, I have to put up collateral and money because I don't have a track record. And it wasn't like $1 million, all of a sudden. You would put in the initial investment, and then you get to a point where if you pull out, you would lose all that. So, what can you do? You put in another $150,000 here, another $100,000 there. After a while you get in so deep. What do you do?

We wanted to get the product in front of the people who would sell it, and in order to do that you have to give up a lot of money, buying product, going out and doing CES (Consumer Electronic Shows), buying a booth at those costs money.

And you have your employees – all that kind of stuff. I wasn't getting paid. I was paying it all out. In 1997, I got a job coaching in the minor leagues in Syracuse with the Blue Jays, but I was also trying to concentrate on getting this business off the ground. So, I was commuting between Syracuse and Toronto to try and keep this business going.

One of the things that messed us up is that since it was (Anthony's) company, I always allowed him to do the talking and negotiating. I wasn't all that up on electronics, so that seemed like the smart thing to do. But later, as I was talking to people we had done business with, they had offered to do deals and he had turned them down – things like turning down $250,000 because he wanted $2 million.

One day I'm up in Toronto, and we had a financial guy who paid all the bills. He has this big old check book, and he shows me all our expenses. Then, he turned to the back of the book and there were a bunch of checks missing. We found out that Anthony was writing checks from the bottom in cash. That really ticked me off, and I go storming in to his office. There were a couple of other guys who worked for us who were sports fans, and they were the ones who stopped me from throwing him out the window.

You know, he was one of those arrogant kind of guys who would just sit there while you are yelling at him. That made me even more furious and irritated that he was calm – all the while knowing that he was spending my money, not his money.

What I found out later is that Anthony owed a lot of people. He was taking the money I would give him and spreading it around to things that weren't necessarily in the business – paying his house off, stuff like that. He was a big-spending guy … on other people's money.

All this time I'm trying to make the business go. I'm traveling between Kansas City and Toronto, back and forth all the time. Syracuse and Toronto, back and forth. That's when all this stuff started happening. When you aren't always there (in Toronto) and you're trying to worry about money and you haven't got any money, and your wife is getting suspicious. It's not good.

By 1998 it's getting really bad. I had the minor-league job with the Blue Jays in 1997 to be with their AAA club in Syracuse. N.Y. Their GM Gord Ash hired me. He was a guy who came through the organization from the ticket department. That team had Roy Halladay and Chris Carpenter on it, so that was pretty cool. They ended up being pretty good guys. Then, in the last month of the season they had me go from

AAA down to rookie ball or A ball in Dunedin. I don't know. Then, that was it. It was just a one-year deal.

I had always had investments when I was playing that I bought through my agent. I owned apartment buildings in Texas, some oil rigs, and at one point I even owned some cows. So, I had stuff I had invested in, but when I got divorced, I lost some of that stuff. And I spent money on some things I probably didn't need to spend it on. You know, you might buy a car you probably don't need or something like that.

At one time, I invested in a restaurant back in Jersey with my friend Anthony Sereno. We had known each other since high school, and he was one of the guys who kept in touch with me through all the years – even when I was in prison. He came down and visited. So, he was a good friend – still is a good friend.

His family owned a restaurant called "Uncle Mike's" back there. So, he knew the business. I was going to provide most of the money, and he was going to run it. So, we got everything ready and we were opening. The day we opened they started doing some road construction right in front of the restaurant and nobody could get there easily. I think it lasted only about six or seven weeks.

The things I tried to do to keep money coming in just didn't really work out – for a variety of reasons.

You know, one of the hard things for me was that once I got to a certain position, financially, and a lifestyle I liked, there was a lot of pressure to stay there. I was trying to do everything possible to stay in that upper echelon of money, but I just couldn't get anything going. One of the biggest things for me was the embarrassment that I wasn't being successful, that I was losing money. So, I didn't really talk a lot about it or ask anybody for help who might have been able to help me.

And without a college education there weren't a lot of options of going to work for somebody else. In my brain, I was thinking if you're going to make money, you have to invest money. I mean, it isn't just going to be magically appearing. So, that was my thought process.

So by 1997, 1998, I was running out of money. My life was just in a shambles. By 1999 I was talking to somebody about bankruptcy because I was almost completely out of money.

# 36
# HOW THIS AFFECTED MY FAMILY

**I** don't think the women I married knew what they were getting into. Nobody knows how the pressure of being a professional athlete affects a marriage until after you're in it – how the media portrays you or how the fans try and grab your attention all the time.

I know there were times I was really hard to live with. If I had a bad day at the park, my wives knew when I came home – don't talk to me for two hours. It took that long just to calm down. I didn't forget about things that happened in the game, but I had to calm down. I mean, who wants to be around a mad guy all the time.

My first marriage was to a girl I dated in high school. I dated Kathy when I was in 12th grade, and she was in 11th. I took her to the senior prom in the spring of 1974. After I was drafted and playing in the minor leagues, we didn't date again until two years later and I was playing AA ball in Jacksonville. That's the year I got hurt and missed a lot of games.

She was back in Summit going to college and working. We got married in 1979. Later that same year our daughter, Shanice, was born. Our son Donnel (DJ) was born three years later in 1982 – the same year I won the batting championship.

We were two people who were nobodies when I first got into the big leagues. Within a couple of years, we had all the attention of the world – good and bad. You can't hide.

Being a pro athlete also affects your children. I can remember one instance when Shanice was about 4 years old; we were out having dinner after a Sunday afternoon game. We lived in Blue Springs, we were having dinner on the way home.

This fan came up, and he wanted an autograph. I had the fork right at my mouth, sitting there with my wife, my daughter and my son. I just wanted to hang with them. I can remember very clearly my daughter going, "He's MY daddy. He's not your father. He's MY daddy."

Kathy also went through all the drug stuff with me. I know me not being home for Christmas of 1983 when I was in jail was really hard on our family. Things started mounting up then as well. We weren't getting along the latter part of the 1984 season, and then we separated in 1985. We're actually really good friends now. We were in the hospital together when Shanice had her second child. Kathy cooked Thanksgiving dinner, and I was there. That makes it much better for everyone. I'm too old to be mad. We were both pretty young and naïve when we were married.

When Kathy and I were separated I met another woman and had a child with her: Mallori.

I met my second wife, Catherine, during the 1985 playoffs when we were in Toronto. I was separated from Kathy when I met Catherine. She didn't want anything to do with me until I was divorced. After the divorce, I started going out with her.

We were married in 1988. Our son Trevor James was born in 1992 and our son Maxwell James was born three years later in 1995. Catherine went through some stuff with me as well. She went through the business failures with me, the bankruptcy and all the downsizing we had to do with our homes.

We had a certain lifestyle when I was playing, and then the money stopped coming in. A lot of my frustration came from trying to cut down our spending and it seemed like no one even heard me talking about that. It's hard to change your lifestyle when you are use to a certain level.

I have five grandchildren. Shanice has two children, Anisa and Kayden. Mallori has two, Mikiya and Marie. Trevor has one, Trey Shawn. I attempt to stay in my kids' lives as much as they will let me. They each have unique qualities that I'm very proud of.

# 37
# I WASN'T READY TO COACH

The first time I signed on for a minor league coaching job, I don't think I was really ready to be a coach because I still thought I could play. But I was trying to get this business started in Toronto, and the only thing that was happening was money going out for the business.

I had met some of the Blue Jays people when I was up in Toronto with Dave Stewart, and they asked me if I wanted to coach in the minors. It was a way I could get some money coming in, so I decided to try it.

I was living in Kansas City at the time, and I had to go to Tampa for the interview. I had never really had a job interview before, and I wasn't used to getting up early. I had to catch an 8 a.m. flight to go down and meet Gord Ash, the Blue Jays general manager. I got caught in traffic, and I called and said I can't make it. They got me on another flight, but already I knew that wasn't a good thing because I had missed the flight.

I didn't really know what the deal was about coaching. I had always been a player. You show up, go through your preparation, play and leave. I didn't even think about it that as a coach you had to be there earlier than the players and then stay later than the players because you had to write up reports for the team.

When I finally got to Tampa, I met with several of the coaches and went to dinner that night. I met Gord Ash the next day while we are watching a game in the Instructional League. We talk, and he goes, "You sure you want this job." I said, "Yeah." So, we did our thing, then I flew back and got my stuff together.

During the interview Gord is just sitting there like he was top dog with his arms crossed across his chest. He was a big guy, and I'm giving him a lot of respect. I was dealing with another organization that I wasn't familiar with, I didn't know his background was that he had worked his way up through the organization from the grounds crew all the way up to being the GM.

I was coaching at AAA, in Syracuse. That's across the lake from Toronto. When I had a day off I was going back to Toronto to try and make a go of the business I'm working on. Then, I'd drive back to Syracuse to be there for a night game. I was going back and forth. I was worried about the business because all I could see was money going out.

I was the hitting coach and first base coach. I taught hitting the way Charley Lau had taught hitting. The whole thing was that you had to lead with your hands. I didn't teach that everybody had to hit a certain way – and if you look at Frank or George or Hal or me we all got to the set point in a different way. You had to get your hands to the right place when the ball was being pitched.

Garth Iorg was the manager, and I don't think he really liked me being there. He always kept mentioning – almost every day – that we had beaten them in the playoffs one year. After a few weeks, I had started to get what it meant to be a coach, and I was getting there earlier and staying later.

Then, it came to a head one day when I was dealing with the fourth outfielder on that team.

We had a really good team with Roy Halliday and Chris Carpenter. But we didn't have that good record. Anyway, this outfielder Lonell Roberts was called to be in as a pinch runner. He didn't have his spikes on while the game was going on. So he had to go inside and get them, and the whole game is being delayed.

He finally comes out, and the umpire says something to him. I said something to him, like, "Man, you are utility. You have to have your spikes and glove with you all the time." He gets mad about that, shouting at me, "I am not utility."

I'm thinking in my brain, "OK, you're the fourth outfielder. You haven't started for seven years. You've always been a fourth outfielder." So how is that not being utility.

Well, the next day I was getting on him in the locker room, and I finally left. He followed me out, running and just jumped on my back.

I flipped him over and had him on the ground and was like, "What the hell is wrong with you, man?"

Just then the brass walks out of the door and I have this kid lying on the ground. He apologizes, but they send me down from Syracuse to Bradenton or wherever it was in Florida –down to A ball. I don't know if it was punishment or not, must have been. The next year I didn't get a contract.

That's when I knew I wasn't ready to be a coach. I was treating him like it was the big leagues where we would get on each other all the time. I guess it embarrassed him in front of everybody else. I kept telling him, "you're utility, man. If you don't accept being a utility player what are you doing. These other guys are starting every day."

# 38
# JUST LOST

The first time I experimented with cocaine, I didn't get addicted. I just said "no" after a short while. The second time ... not so much.

The funny thing is that everybody knew about the first time, and not that many people knew about the second time even though it was a much more serious problem. That's because I didn't get caught. Nothing got in the papers about it.

My life was coming apart. I didn't feel good about anything. I don't know how many people get to that point in their life when they're just numb and they're trying to do anything to block it out. I was there, and I went to cocaine because I knew it would make me feel good – even though I also knew it wasn't the answer.

But I didn't care. It wasn't about whether it was right or wrong. I was using it to block out the numbness, and that just leads you to using it more. When you're doing it, you're not thinking about anybody else. The only person you're thinking about is yourself.

I didn't just snort it. Sometimes I smoked it. Sometimes I snorted it. Sometimes it was just whatever was available because I didn't care. I really didn't.

This was in 1999, I think. My life was in such a mess that I just didn't care. When you don't care, you don't care about anything. The drug is telling you, "Come hang out with me. Nobody understands you like me."

You wake up in the morning thinking about it. Everything else means less. Everything else doesn't matter. You're sleeping all frickin' day because you have been up all night. You get up, and it's almost afternoon or evening and you're going to go back to what you were doing.

People who knew about it were trying to talk to me sensibly, reasonably – I'm talking about my wife, even my mom. She had seen how disgusting I had become, how distracted I was, how small I was getting because I was losing weight. It was just really, really crappy.

And you are always thinking about stuff going on in your life, and then you get really emotional about it. And you're not doing the normal things in life.

One day, I needed some cash, so I went to a casino to use the ATM and get some money on a credit card. Then, I messed around and went to a gas station to get gas. You are paranoid about everything.

At the gas station, this lady rolled up beside me in a truck. She looked at me and she just shook her head side to side. That was sort of the thing that was the last straw. That's when I thought the police knew what I was doing. Shortly after that I told myself I either better get some help or go to jail, and I didn't want to go to jail.

I decided I had put people through enough. I had treated everybody badly enough. At some point – I don't even remember when – I just said I have had enough. I had felt sorry for myself enough. I had made it so bad I didn't know if I could get my marriage back together.

So, one day, late at night I was out and driving around, paranoid about everything. And I just drove myself to the emergency room at Shawnee Mission Medical Center and checked myself in. I didn't even know if they had a drug program. I just knew it was a hospital, and hospitals were supposed to help you. So, I went there, checked myself in and they sent me all the way upstairs. I probably slept for two days.

I don't really remember how Catherine knew. Either I called her or they called her to tell her where I was and that I was checking myself in. I don't know if she was relieved or not. I think she had already moved on mentally, but she came up and did all the stuff you need to do and talk about and all that kind of stuff.

But this was really for me. It wasn't for her or for anyone else. This was all for me. You end up losing things you don't want to lose. But in the end, you get yourself back.

The funny part of this was I was there for a week or so, and this other guy comes in – this young kid. So, I'm here going through all my stuff, and this kid's mother is asking me to talk to him. She recognized me and knew who I was and she asked me to talk to him. I talked to the kid, trying to help him get back. But that was really hard because I was going through what I was going through.

After I got out of Shawnee Mission I felt like everyone who looked at me knew that I had been abusing drugs. It didn't matter to me then because what else could they do to me, and I didn't care. I think I went to about four or five weeks as an outpatient. That was very helpful because you would have meetings with other people.

And it wasn't just dudes off the street. I was in sessions with people with money, people who would be blasted if they had been in the paper like I was every day. But they were just trying to get their lives together.

The thing that helped me the most didn't happen until a couple of years later when Catherine moved our family up to Canada. So, I went to Canada after the 2002 minor league season. I got away from everybody. I didn't know anybody up there. It was easier because I was only around people who didn't know me, who weren't making any real judgments.

When you are sober and healthy you see things a lot more clearly. When I do my clinics now or do my speaking engagements, I talk about the drugs. It's not something that I talk about with great enthusiasm, but it is something I talk about because I want them to know that we all go through bad stuff. It is either forced on us or we force it on ourselves. We all go through bad stuff.

The key is you can come out of it. That's the key to me. You have to be able to accept what people have to say about you – and it's mostly going to be bad.

I'm happy most of the time, about 95 percent of the time. I'm never 100 percent at accepting what people have to say about me. After I got out of rehab and was coaching with the Diamondbacks in 2001 and 2002 people were still bringing things up and reminding me. And sometimes a GM or somebody would look at you sort of funny, like they could pick up the tell-tale signs.

But I have been able to come to grips with it since 2004 or 2005.

# 39
# GETTING INTO THE ROYALS HALL OF FAME

$\mathbf{M}$y induction into the Royals Hall of Fame in 2000 was the start of re-establishing a good relationship with the team over the next several years. At the time, I had no money. I was going through problems in my marriage and a bankruptcy. I had just finished a drug rehab program at Shawnee Mission Medical Center.

I think through most of the '90s the Royals wanted nothing to do with me. Once you leave the game, you leave. I never felt like they really cared about me after they released me in 1990. It's basically that a team doesn't want you to embarrass the organization. They always categorized you the same way, and they never looked at whether you could change or how you could change.

I remember one trip back to Kansas City when I was with the A's, one of the Royals front-office people was in the elevator with me and says something like, "You are disgracing something by fighting and all of that." It was the same old crap. I just looked at him and dropped the F-bomb on him. He was probably thinking, "That's why we got rid of you."

In their brain, I was the angry guy, the guy who couldn't get along with anybody. I was the guy who embarrassed the team during the drug thing back in 1983 and 1984, and they wanted nothing to do with me.

Or maybe they just knew I was screwed up and didn't want to help. I'm not blaming them for anything that happened because I made whatever decisions were made in my life.

At the time, I did (blame them). At the time, I was still mad at them because they didn't sign me to four more years. I didn't understand why they hadn't let me end my career here. I didn't understand why George was so special and everybody else wasn't.

When I learned I was going to go in to their Hall of Fame I was at about the lowest of the low points in my life. I was just lost, considering bankruptcy, mad at the world, losing my wife. But nobody really knew any of that because if someone asked how I was doing, I lied. I didn't want anybody to know what was going on.

It came at a time when I really needed something positive to happen in my life.

But it was nerve wracking.

It was nerve wracking because I didn't know how everybody would accept me. I hadn't been a Royal since 1990. I was an Oakland A and then a Chicago Cub. You don't really know how deep the blue runs. So, I was apprehensive how people would accept me. I was worried that everybody kind of knew that I had been messed up. There were a lot of things going on in my head.

But it was good. It was surprisingly good. The fans are pretty appreciative of things. I didn't get any boos – at least I didn't get any I heard. I got to ride around in a car and wave at people.

I had been back to the stadium after I retired, but this was the first time I had been back down on the field. I was going in at the same time as Whitey Herzog, which surprised me. I didn't know how he would deal with stuff. He was the guy who was always saying I couldn't hit. I hadn't seen him in forever, but the funny thing was he tried to take credit for me becoming a good hitter.

We were at this press conference together, and they would ask me a question and I would start off answering it. I'd get three or four words out, and he would take over – you know just Whitey being Whitey. I was in such a messed up place in my life that I just let him do it because I didn't want them asking me about some of the things in my life. And in some ways he did make me the hitter I became because he was the one who said I should have been a switch hitter.

I was really nervous about my speech, and I really don't remember very much of what I said. I do remember it was hot as hell down on the field, and my whole shirt was just full of sweat. And they gave me a nice party afterwards up in one of the suites.

But the whole thing was kind of surreal to me because when you don't get a lot of accolades like that you don't know how to handle it. I was never a guy who was very good being out in the public eye because then everybody is looking at you, and I kind of shied away from that.

And my brain wasn't in a good enough place yet to think anything positive. I remember doing an interview with Fred White. I have seen that interview on television, and I can see how small I was because I had just gotten out of rehab for the cocaine. I don't remember if Fred even asked how my life was going or anything, and if he did, I lied. In a sense, that's bad because if you let people know what's going on they might have a way to help you, but you are embarrassed. You don't want people to know you have screwed up millions of dollars. I didn't screw up millions, but I screwed up the money I had left.

So, that day was pretty cool being back at the stadium.

But my life was still a wreck. I didn't have any money. I didn't have any job … I think it was a few weeks afterward that I went back to the Royals saying, "OK, I'm in your Hall of Fame now. Can I have a job?"

Basically, all they had was a scout position. I don't know if I talked to Allard Baird or his assistant. There were so many new people at that time that I didn't really know who to talk to. That's when they said they would send me to scout school down in Arizona that fall, and that led to me getting back on my feet when the Arizona Diamondbacks got in touch with me about a coaching job.

Getting into the Hall of Fame was really about the only good thing that had happened in my life for about eight or nine years. There is supposed to be a suite out there named after me. I haven't found it yet, but I haven't walked around the whole stadium. Supposedly, everyone who is in the Hall of Fame has a suite named after them.

Another step in the healing process was when I came back here in 2005 for a Negro Leagues event. I had been living in Toronto since 2002, and I hadn't been back to Kansas City. Bob Kendrick invited me to come to the Legacy Awards. I was really scared how the fans would receive me. When we pulled up in front of the museum there was about 18 inches of snow on each side of the street. All these people were standing there. When I got out of the car they started clapping and welcoming me back.

That's when I started talking to the Royals a little more. Several years later they named a minor league base-running award in my honor. That was pretty cool.

It's a responsibility, and I was really happy to accept it. Before I wouldn't want to accept any responsibility for anything because I didn't want anybody to know what I was doing. I wasn't that far from being out of trouble.

So those two honors are pretty cool. Those two things, getting into the Royal's Hall of Fame and the base-running award, mean more to me than any other thing I accomplished except for the World Series because they are – if I'm thinking right – going to be something that are there forever. Records are made to be broken. So, somebody may get more hits in a year than I had in 1980 or they may steal more bases than I did in 1979. But when you have an award named after you, that's there forever. Or if you are in the Hall of Fame, that's there forever. And it means a lot more to me now than it meant when I was playing.

I can say to my grandkids, "That's Papa." I signed a baseball for Kayden, my oldest daughter's son, the other day. It said, "I love you very much. Papa." Then I wrote 1982 batting champion, 100 hits from both sides, 668 stolen bases, second most hits in the '80s and 1985 World Series Champs.

When you are able to do that with pride it makes you feel really good. You can tell your grandkids you did some really good things. You also tell them the truth about some of the things you messed up. But it's a good feeling, man, when I can be proud of the things I have done.

# 40
# SELLING MY STUFF

The very first thing they asked me about when we declared bankruptcy was my World Series ring. The guy who was assigned our case wanted to know where it was, and he wanted it up in his office so he could take a photo of it.

So, I knew right away that I was going to have to give that up. All my memorabilia went into the bankruptcy auction: my high school football helmets, autographed baseballs, autographed bats, my Gold Glove I won in 1980, the trophy for winning the stolen base title in 1979, the Silver Slugger bat I won for the 1982 batting championship – though I have that one back. Fred White got that back somehow. Bob Turnaukas, who helped me get back to KC, found out about it and got it for me. Chuck Robinson, whose dad was the auctioneer, got my 1,500th hit baseball for me.

**Willie Wilson ring sold at auction to collector**

TONGANOXIE, Kan. - The World Series ring that once graced the hand of former Kansas City Royals outfielder **Willie Wilson** is now in the hands of a collector, sold at auction for more than $16,000.

But of all the stuff I wish I had, the World Series ring is the thing I would like to have most. That's what I think I treasure the most. All the other stuff, that's all right that I don't have it. A couple of trophies is just more stuff in my house that I don't have to put on a shelf.

But my ring is something I worked hard for. It was one of the highest accomplishments you can have in the sport. I know who bought it. I know where to get it. And we have had conversations with him about getting it back. But the guy who bought it at the auction wants too much money. He wants the cost of the ring, the cost of where he kept it in the safety deposit box all these years, season tickets.

I'm going to buy another one from the company that made it because it is less expensive for me. I had to get permission from Dan Glass to have another one made, and that took three years for him to agree to let me buy another one on my own, but I now have the permission.

So, I'm saving money for it. That's one of my goals right now. But every time I get a little bit of money saved up to get it, then something happens – you have to pay a bill or one of the kids need something.

But back to the bankruptcy. When I declared bankruptcy, the guy came out to the house, and he was going through all the rooms. Whatever was hanging up in the house could be taken, things in the drawers and the cabinets.

So, they took all the memorabilia. The furniture and all of that I could sell on my own. At that point I was just numb to it. I don't really know what all they took because I was at the point of "just take it."

I didn't go to the auction. That would have been too hard. I mean, it's embarrassing. And you also don't know how cruel people can be about that kind of stuff.

I remember one time this guy came up to me at a benefit bowling tournament. He was carrying the helmet that he bought at the bankruptcy, and he said, "OK, I got your helmet. Can you sign this for me?"

I'm like, "C'mon man. I'm at this benefit," but he didn't care that it was embarrassing or disheartening or anything like that. It was like a joke to him. Some people are just vindictive about stuff like that. They think it's a joke. For you, it's having your heart ripped out.

That's really only a small percent or so of the people, but those are the ones you remember. There are some really nice, nice people out there, too. They are the 99.9 percent nice people. I used to get all messed up on that other point-one percent. I used to let that part really bother me, but there are some really nice people.

This is the ball I hit for my 1,500th hit.

# 41
# FINDING
# MY WAY

**W**hen my stuff was being sold at auction, I was actually working for the Diamondbacks and at spring training by then. I think I was making about $25,000 then, and coaching their A-ball team in South Bend, Ind.

They had first talked to me about coaching when I was out in Arizona going through the scout school with the Royals. I was learning how to be a scout, and I was actually pretty good at it if you were talking about picking out talented players. But I didn't know how to file the scouting reports.

You were supposed to write about the player then put it in a limited number of lines: "Tall right-hander, three-quarter delivery" and then at the end is he a Major League prospect, who he reminds you of, is he a fifth starter or a reliever – you would do all of that.

The first time I was filing all those reports I would get them back marked up in yellow all over the page. What they would tell me is that "you know your stuff, but you just can't write it." I mean, I was picking the right guys.

So, we're down there in that instructional league thing in the fall. I was in Tucson. At the time there weren't too many teams, so you would see the same guys all the time because the teams would just play each other. I saw Andy Hassler's kid, Robin Yount's kid, J.J. Hardy. He was No. 1 on my sheet.

But I'm watching a game one day, and this guy came up to me while I was standing there with my (radar) gun and everything. He says, "Would you rather be on the inside of the fence or the outside of the fence?" I tell him I would rather be on the inside, and he says they will give me a call in a couple of weeks.

But you don't ever know if they will follow through. When I get back to Kansas City is when I was sitting there in my bathroom contemplating what else could go wrong in my life when they called. I went and met the guys, and I got the job. The really great thing at the time is when you signed the contract, you started to get paid. So, I was getting paid a little bit, which was really good because I was out of money.

I had an inkling I was going to be at South Bend with their A-ball team. Steve Scarcone was the manager. Royal Clayton, Royce Clayton's brother, was the pitching coach, and I was the hitting coach. The three of us got along like brothers.

This time I was ready to be a coach – maybe because I knew I had to be ready, but I knew I had to put in the time. I had to show up early. The three of us just clicked from spring training on.

They had a book of hitting, how you were supposed to teach it. I put the book in a drawer and closed it. My philosophy was that if the hitters trusted me they would do what I asked them. If they didn't trust me, you wouldn't get any results. I took Charley Lau's method again.

There were 12 teams in that league, and for five years in a row they had come in 12th in hitting. This year they were third, which made me feel really good. We were just two percentage points from the top. It was fun. They learned a few things from me about being aggressive as a hitter, going to the plate with a purpose, looking for zones, understanding pitch counts – which a lot of minor league coaches didn't teach when I was coming up.

It was pretty cool to see kids who were confused and then to see them get it about hitting. Certain guys needed early work before the others. Others didn't need as much work, but everybody needed some work. I remembered from all the times I was embarrassed while I was in the minor leagues, that I learned you got better results if you would take them off to the side and talk with them and not embarrass them.

We were in the playoffs that year, in 2001, and we made the finals. I think we were playing Kane County. We were all checked out of our apartments because the season was over, and we are all staying at a motel for the playoffs. We lose the first game, and the next morning 9/11 happens.

I wake up in the morning and turn the TV on, and I see the buildings on fire. I changed the channel and I go "Damn, the same movie is on." That shows how out of it I was, thinking the same movie was on all the channels. Then, all of a sudden the plane goes, "Boom!" My phone starts ringing. It's all my hitters who live in New York and their people are in the buildings.

They don't want to play. I mean, mentally, they are done. But we had to wait four or five days in that hotel before the games are finally cancelled. Within hours that place is cleared out. I was going to fly home, which of course wasn't happening. I rented a car and drove home to Kansas City.

That was a pretty good year. I really had fun. The next winter they wanted me to go back to South Bend without Royal and without Scarcone. I balked at that because I felt like they were punishing me. So, I gave them my opinion, "We worked good together. Why would you break that up?" Eventually they decided to send all three of us to Lancaster (Calif.) in high A-ball.

So, we're there in Lancaster and Scar has a financial problem at home and he has to go back for a couple of days. The third day they called him and told him to stay there for the season. They brought in Billy Plummer to manage our team. We had a bunch of the same players as the year before, but Billy was completely different than Scar. He was doing more yelling at the kids. I had learned from being with them the year before that you can't yell at them. You can't coach them old school. If you want to get the best out of them you just have to talk to them.

So, he is yelling and screaming. I remember Andy Green, a little second baseman. He had been with the AAA club and was sent back to the A club. So he is already angry, and here is Plummer just yelling at him because he didn't do something right. In the seventh inning, Greenie comes to me and says, "Willie, if he yells at me one more time I'm going to knock him out."

Well, I get him cooled down and say, "Just relax. Take it over to the side. I will talk to Plum for you, man." So, at the end of the game I go knock on the manager's door and go, "Plum, can we have a conversation."

We're in there filling out our reports at the end of the game, and I'm saying, "Plum, you can't yell at the kids like you are doing." He goes,

"I'M NOT YELLING." Then Royal walks in, and Plum says,"ROYAL, AM I YELLING?" Royal goes, "Yeah, you are."

That was a whole different experience for me. Then, I don't know what happens the last month of the season because I got fired when I grabbed a kid by the neck after he dropped the "N" word on me. Billy White, a left-handed pitcher, just thought he could drop the "N" word whenever he wanted.

This kid was from the South. He had been in South Bend the year before when I was coaching there, and we had no issues. He had been called up to Lancaster late in the season. When he first got to Lancaster, he walked right into the coaching room and turned on the television while we're sitting there doing reports. That's the first thing that kind of irritated me.

Then a couple of days before this incident he had said something else. My wife and I were going through the separation talks, and I wasn't in the greatest frame of mind with all that stuff going on.

The third time we were playing a game and one of the coaches is really on the catcher from the other team. I mean we're winning big, and he's yelling at the other team's catcher about being drafted in front of our catcher. I know that one of my hitters is going to get hit if keeps on yelling. So, I'm talking to our coach and this kid jumped in and said, "You think you know everything."

Then one of our hitters got hit. I said to the kid, "You know, you need to take yourself down to the other end of the bench and stay out of our conversation."

A few nights later, we're in extra innings and now our fourth outfielder is out there. There was this ball hit to right center, and I said, "Man, I wish we had more speed." The next thing I know this kid is behind me and he says, "Why are you always talking about black and white?"

I said, "Look man, you need to go to the other end of the bench and leave me and Royal alone. He goes "F--- you, nigger."

That's when I went off on him. I grabbed him and jammed him up against the wall and said: "You don't frickin' know me. You don't just say that …" By that time in the dugout they grabbed me. And I just got really quiet.

That night, when I'm at home, Ron Hassey, the head of their minor league operation, calls me and says, "We gotta fire you." He said to think how it would be if it was your son and we had to explain it to his dad. I said, "That's where he learned this crap. If you ever let this guy make to the big leagues you will have a lawsuit on your hands because one of the players is going to kill him."

So, they fired me.

I just went, you know, forget it. I don't want to coach any more. I was tired of organizations telling me what to do. I was tired of kids who don't respect their elders or ex-ball players. I just got tired of it. So, I started thinking about doing my own stuff.

And probably nobody else would have hired me. My reputation was that I was confrontational. I was probably black-listed again, but I didn't want to do it any more anyway. I knew I wasn't coaching material, I just knew it. I couldn't take kids yelling at me and calling me that and dissing me.

Maybe it would have worked if I had been in the big leagues. But in the minor leagues …

# 42
# FOUNDATION
# FOR MY LIFE

After getting fired from the Diamondbacks, I was up in Canada where Catherine had moved our family. She was from Toronto, and I think she wanted to be near her family while she worked out some things.

I drove from California to Toronto. We were living in the same house, but not really together, if you know what I mean. I was just sort of sitting around and doing nothing. I didn't know anybody up there.

One day, I think it was in 2004, some time after I had left the Diamondbacks, my buddy Anthony Serrano invited me to come down and visit in New Jersey. While I was there I was watching one of my friend's kids at a baseball camp.

*Youth from Farmland Foods participated in the youth clinic at the Willie Wilson Legends game at CommunityAmerica Ball Park.*

Most of the camps back there were being done by college kids. There was one that Don Mattingly held, but he showed up on a Thursday, and I don't know how long he really stayed there and worked with the kids.

Anthony suggested, "Wouldn't it be great if we could do a camp in Summit?" I decided why not try it. I went to a lawyer friend of mine to do all the legal stuff to get it right. We decided we would try to put on one camp in August of 2004. We didn't have any money to really promote anything, but we could print flyers on paper and take them all around town. Donald Davis, another friend, went around with me and we posted the flyers.

Mr. (Dominick) Guida wasn't working at the recreation center anymore, but he still had some pull there. He got me the fields for almost nothing. So, I had one field for August. People told me it wasn't going to work because a lot of people go on vacation in August.

That first year about 75 or 80 kids showed up. It worked.

The next year, in 2005, just spreading it by word of mouth, we had three camps. The year after that we did eight straight weeks of camps. I was doing it a little different. We would bring the camps to wherever you wanted to put it on. We were doing camps in Summit, New Providence, Orange, Edison … but mostly in Summit.

I was doing it with pro players. Bobby Dernier, who had been my neighbor back in Blue Springs, did every camp with me. He had gone to Raytown South and played 10 years in the Major Leagues with the Phillies and Cubs. I would also have Amos there, Mayberry, Fergie Jenkins, Steve Trout – a bunch of different guys.

Bobby saw how it was working in New Jersey, and the next year we did one in his hometown in Raytown.

So, in Jersey it was working well. We'd throw a golf tournament to help raise money so the kids wouldn't have to pay for all of it. Things seemed to be going well, then I found out the guy I was working with in New Jersey was doing the same thing I had run into with Anthony Ramsaroop. He was taking the money. So, we got rid of him.

Then the Republican mayor wanted me to take pictures with him and all of that. It started to get a little political, and I'm just not into that. I just wanted to help the kids. I didn't want to be political. It got harder and harder to do it in New Jersey after we had some success, because of longtime grudges. Sometimes, when you are doing things that try to help the community, people don't care about that. They just want to see you fail.

At one place, Donald Davis went in and tried to get people involved, he got a text message from one of the guys he knew in there, "Does Willie think he is coming back here to take over?" and that kind of stuff. I had a minister back in Summit tell me he was going to say to all the people at his church that they shouldn't go to the camps since we would not allow him to put out Christian literature.

I'm like, "What the heck man? That's just hurting the kids." But people are kind of leery about what you're trying to do and why you're trying to do it.

I know this seems strange that I like doing the clinics since I had decided that coaching wasn't for me, but what I realized is that I didn't want to be a *professional* coach. When you're dealing with 18, 19, 20-year-olds and their egos, it makes it really hard to be a minor-league coach.

The ego tells a kid he is making this amount of money, and no kid thinks they aren't going to make it to the big leagues. So, when you tell them something about what they'll have to improve the next year or the next level up they can't see it. Their egos are big enough to think they had gotten this far doing it their way, so why change. And if you say the wrong

Area youth participating in baseball clinic sponsored by Kansas City Sports Commission and Foundation.

thing they call their agent, the agent calls someone else, that person calls the manager, the manager calls you and says, "What did you say to the kid?" And you only told him he had a hitch in his swing or something.

I was probably a little bit the same way when I was a minor leaguer–you know, hard headed.

But when you have a 7- or 8-year-old, they do what you ask them to do and you can teach it to them. They don't have egos, they just do it. Think about it, if you tell a kid to throw, he just throws. If you tell him to swing, he just swings.

He might do it off the wrong foot, but he does everything you tell him. Then, you make it fun for them by telling them how to do it right. I love teaching the basics because when the basics are right and the light comes on it's like a different kid. Then the game becomes fun.

So, you teach them how to throw, how to find the seams on the ball so that it will go straight when they throw it, how to point their left hand, how to point their toe. For the guy who's waiting on the ball, don't wait like you are standing there catching a bus. When the ball comes to you, we want you to move your legs so you can get in front of the ball and catch it properly.

You tell a kid who is 18-, 19-years-old the same, and they say "Oh, I know that." Then they do it all wrong and start reaching for things. But those little kids … they go, "Oh, that works. Then, the game slooooooooows down for them. When you're doing everything wrong, you're doing it really quick. When you can slow the game down it becomes easy and fun.

That's why I love working with kids. When that light comes on their eyes get like saucers. I just love that.

The other thing you learn – and I found this out from my first rookie coach Billy Scripture – is that some people are visual and some are not. So, you take somebody and hold your hand out to the side and start counting down with your fingers as you say it. Five, four, three …

If the person maintains eye contact with you, that lets you know the kid can concentrate and understand. If the eyes dart back and forth between your hand and your face, you know he is visual. So, you have to coach them differently. If it's a visual person, you have to put your hands on them and show them how to do something. You can't just tell them. I was a visual person. So, when I had that breakthrough with my hitting in the Dominican League it was because Manny Mota put his hands on my body and showed me how my shoulders needed to go, where the bat needed to be.

And every time you make a correction with a kid on how to do something, you need to make a little joke or something at the end. You get your point across, and then perk him back up so he doesn't feel bad.

After all the on-field stuff is done, and then you give them a life-lesson story. For me, I can just tell them my story. I tell them that you can overcome anything you want to overcome, mentally and physically, if you have the right attitude. If the attitude isn't the right attitude it doesn't matter what I say. And then, you have to have fun.

I remember Dave Henderson when I was with the A's. He had fun playing baseball every day. It was just a joy to watch him. A couple of years ago, I had him back to one of my celebrity games. He told me, "You finally get it," which made me feel really good because for a long time I played the game mad. I didn't have any fun.

At the end of the clinic, I talk to them about the drugs. I don't say what drugs because the kids are all pretty smart about what drugs are out there. But you let them know that it's not something that will help them accomplish anything.

Then you can tell a baseball story about George Brett or Bo Jackson or somebody like that. So, that's really fun for me to do the clinics.

I was doing all those things in New Jersey, and we did a couple in Kansas City with Bobby Dernier, but I was still living in Toronto. I wasn't doing anything up there for two reasons. I wasn't a Blue Jay and I wasn't Canadian. So, it was pretty hard to get anyone excited about a clinic up there.

I started doing some things with the Negro Leagues Museum in 2005. I was still living in Toronto, but Bob Kendrick, Don Motley and Bob Turnauckas were having me come to Kansas City to do more things. I kept hearing from people that they really missed me and all that.

I came back and did more things from 2006 through 2008 and I kept hearing the same thing: "Willie, you should come back here." I decided I was going to come back in about 2009.

I met with Toby Cook of the Royals. I had breakfast with him one time, and I was just telling him about me and asking what I needed to do to get back in the Royals' good graces. Little by little, they would invite me to an event, then another event. Like anything else you gotta prove yourself.

This organization, this management, this group of front office people treat me so much better than the original ones when I was here as a player. Mr. K was great. I can't say enough good things about him. I always thought John Schuerholz was really straight with me. But some of the other people ... I think they always kind of thought of me as a troublemaker who couldn't get along with anyone.

When I found out I was really back with the team was at one of the Royals' "Diamond of Dreams" events when Dayton Moore came over to me. I don't remember the exact words, but I think he said, "I think you will be pleasantly surprised. We named an award after you for our minor leagues."

I said, "Really?"

He said, "Yeah," and then said that there was going to be the Paul Splittorff Pitcher of the Year, the George Brett Hitter of the Year, Frank White Defensive Player of the Year, Dan Quisenberry Special Achievement, Mike Sweeney Award and the Willie Wilson Baserunner of the Year. They have some others, but these were the ones named after former players.

I was really shocked, but also happy. And to know that as long as the Royals are around there is going to be an award with my name on it, makes me really proud. It makes me feel like I have really accomplished something and makes me feel like I'm back in the family.

Now, I do about five or six clinics that the Royals organize. They hire a couple of the alumni players, usually me or Dennis (Leonard) or John (Mayberry) or maybe Monty (Jeff Montgomery) or any of the alumni. It's a 90-minute event that they do out at the Little K. The kids go from station to station, and then we do an autograph session. I also participate as a coach at the Royals Fantasy Camp in Surprise, AZ.

I have some of my own events also. I have done several celebrity baseball games out at the T-Bones and a couple at the "K." I usually try to get a Royals team against another team of players who didn't play for the Royals. It's a way to get some money for the older players. We made pretty good money when we played, but we weren't making anything like the kind of money these guys are making today.

We'll do events wherever you want, at your ballpark .... or we do a lot of events out at CommunityAmerica Ballpark. For a kid, that's huge. It's not "the K," but it's a big deal for kids.

Another thing I do with the Royals is that they have an alumni batting practice day. It might be a company or fantasy camp players. They come out to "the K" and take batting practice and fielding, and we tell stories. At the end we get in the dugout and talk to them.

I have done speaking engagements with companies I'm involved with here in Kansas City. Some of them I met through Royals connections, some through the Negro Leagues Baseball Museum. Some during the (2012) All-Star festivities.

I know I made my own bed here before, so I lie in it. But now I see things a lot differently than I did before because I have stepped away from it. People might have told me things in the past, but I wasn't willing to listen. It just went in one ear and out the other. Nobody could tell me anything.

*Courtesy of Kansas City Royals*

*I was really proud, but really nervous, when I made the first "Baserunner of the Year" award. What an honor.*

Now when they stop me and talk with me, I realize they're genuine. So, why shouldn't I listen. That's just being older and having made a lot of mistakes. One thing I found out is if you keep doing the same thing over and over again thinking there is going to be a different result, then you're crazy.

A lot of people do that – I used to do that.

I'm also involved one-on-one with some people. I have a friend whose son has a drug problem. I have been trying to help him with that, sharing what I went through and what I learned.

We work with charities in the community when we do the baseball games, golf tournaments and other events. We don't make a lot of money, but it does help create awareness and donations for the charity. I do some things pro-bono to keep my name out there. Using my name to benefit the community makes me feel worthwhile!

I wish I could say that I learned all this when I was much younger.

I'm trying to learn it now. Everything isn't always great, but it's pretty good every day.

# 43
# A GOOD PLACE
# GOING FORWARD

I received a second chance – or a third chance depending on how you keep score.

The Royals gave me that first opportunity, and when you get an opportunity to sort of come back home you have to take full advantage of it. That's what I'm working to do, showing people what I'm capable of and what I can do.

But it wasn't just the Royals who have given me another chance, it was Kansas City.

Through the work with the Willie Wilson Baseball Foundation, I've been introduced to a lot of members of the Kansas City corporate community. They've been able to look past how I might have acted as a player and given me a chance to show them some things that I wasn't capable of showing them before. Through these relationships, I do corporate speaking engagements sharing my stories of success and failure.

The Negro Leagues Baseball Museum has also opened up many doors for me. It started with events at the museum, and I'll be forever grateful for

*I am involved with several charities and foundations such as Project Walk and try to help raise awareness and funding for them.*

*Wilson family photo*

*Flat Stanly made an appearance at Cubs Fantasy Camp with me and my friend Eddie Vedder.*

that. In 2006, I started co-hosting the Legends Luncheons with Al Fitzmorris, which gave me the confidence to do radio and TV broadcast spots. It's given me a chance to do some very fun things like walk the red carpet at the premiere of "42 The Jackie Robinson Story," when it was in Kansas City.

I got to meet Harrison Ford, one of the stars of the movie. I was waiting for the elevator when he stepped out of it, and he came up and said, "How are you doing?" I was sort of shocked, and I just sort of stammered out, "Hey, Harrison, how you doing?"

I've also been able to maintain and renew friendships with guys I played with and against – not just the Royals players. I have played in the Buck O'Neil Golf Tournament for the past seven years, serving as co-chair one year. At the premiere of the movie, I got a chance to see Bobby Bonilla and Tony Clark, who was with the Diamondbacks. They're both part of the MLBPAA (Major League Baseball Players Alumni) I usually do two or three events a year with MLBPAA such as clinics, legends games or golf outings.

I also work with other charities – not only the ones with the Willie Wilson Baseball Foundation. During spring training I go to Arizona and help Fergie Jenkins with his foundation raising money for charities for many of the teams who have spring training down there. We do autograph sessions at the spring training games, and the money we raise is given to different charities for each of the teams. When I'm down there I get to hang out with some of the other guys who won batting championships. And, of course, while in Arizona I get some golf in while Kansas City experiences cold wintery weather.

In 2012, when the All-Star Game was in Kansas City, I got to take part in a lot of the activities. That was pretty cool because the All-Star games I played in were some of the highlights of my playing career. I was just in awe of some of the players when I got selected to play, and it was an honor to be on the field with them. To be around the All-Star Game again was a very special experience.

I still don't like being entirely in the spotlight. Many people don't realize, but I'm really shy. I'm trying to get better about it. I tend to position myself near a door so I can make a quick escape from places if I need to. (Laughter)

Here's a perfect example of how I'm trying to change. I was on a flight recently coming back to Kansas City, and people were recognizing me on the plane. Before, I would have had my earphones on and stuck my nose into a magazine or a newspaper or something and never made eye contact. Now I'm a little more comfortable with the recognition, and I have some fun with it. It doesn't always work, and you can't please everybody with your actions, but I'm trying to be better about that.

I'm working some with Metro Sports on Time Warner Cable. Me … in the media … Who would have ever thought that? Right? (Laughter)

I'm working as an analyst on The Blue Zone, some college games, AAA games and AA games. That has been fun, and it's just low-key enough where I really like it.

That's actually shown me another side of the business. As a player, I never saw the media side, I would just hear a question and wonder sometimes, "Where in the hell did that come from?" I never thought about the job the reporters had to do. As a former player, I look at it a little differently than a reporter might. If I'm going to ask a difficult question, I tell the player beforehand that I'm going to ask it. I don't just turn on the camera and ask him because I always hated that as a player.

Good friend Frank White and I at the Willie Wilson Legends game in 2012.

265

*One of the more proud moments of my life is when I was selected to sit in the Buck O'Neil "Legacy" seat at a Royals home game.*

It makes me feel good to be a part of that, and it gives me something to look forward to whenever I have games that we're doing. And it keeps my face out there, keeps me out there.

Financially, I've started to get my life back together. I don't owe any money right now, and I'm not living check to check. That's one of the things that I try to emphasize with the kids when I talk with them at the clinics. With hard work you can get back on your feet. If you do things the right way, people will give you another chance.

Most days are good days. Not every day is a perfect day, but I'm enjoying my life right now – more than I ever did before. I'm in a good place in my life right now. I'm going to strive and keep it there.

I can't control the things that I did in my past. They're in the past. The only thing I can do is control the things I'm doing now.

I hope you have enjoyed my story and learning the highs and lows I have experienced to get to the level of success I'm at today. I had a lot of people who saw something in me that I did not see in myself. Thanks to each of them who took the time to talk, listen, show and teach.

I'd like to close with one of my quotes,

*"I tend to look at life like the game of baseball. What might happen in the first inning dictates how we handle the ninth."*

—Willie Wilson

# WILLIE WILSON FIELDING STATS

| Year | Tm | Lg | Age | Pos | G | GS | CG | Inn | Ch | PO | A | E | DP | Fld% | Rtot | Rtot/yr | RF/9 | RF/G | lgFld% | lgRF9 | lgRFG | Awards |
|---|---|---|---|---|---|---|---|---|---|---|---|---|---|---|---|---|---|---|---|---|---|---|
| 1976 | KCR | AL | 20 | CF | 6 | 1 | 1 | 18 | 8 | 6 | 1 | 1 | 0 | 0.875 | 0 | 33 | 3.5 | 1.17 | 0.984 | 3 | 2.98 | |
| 1976 | KCR | AL | 20 | OF | 6 | 1 | 1 | 18 | 8 | 6 | 1 | 1 | 0 | 0.875 | 0 | 33 | 3.5 | 1.17 | 0.981 | 2.45 | 2.48 | |
| 1977 | KCR | AL | 21 | CF | 9 | 6 | 5 | 73.1 | 26 | 25 | 0 | 1 | 0 | 0.962 | 1 | 15 | 3.07 | 2.78 | 0.983 | 2.82 | 2.81 | |
| 1977 | KCR | AL | 21 | OF | 9 | 6 | 5 | 73.1 | 25 | 24 | 0 | 1 | 0 | 0.96 | 1 | 15 | 2.95 | 2.67 | 0.978 | 2.34 | 2.32 | |
| 1977 | KCR | AL | 21 | DH | 2 | 0 | | | | | | | | | | | | | | | | |
| 1978 | KCR | AL | 22 | OF | 112 | 45 | 32 | 541.1 | 181 | 171 | 6 | 4 | 2 | 0.978 | 10 | 22 | 2.94 | 1.58 | 0.979 | 2.47 | 2.45 | |
| 1978 | KCR | AL | 22 | LF | 82 | 29 | 22 | 364.2 | 102 | 95 | 5 | 2 | 2 | 0.98 | 6 | 20 | 2.47 | 1.22 | 0.974 | 2.21 | 2.19 | |
| 1978 | KCR | AL | 22 | CF | 35 | 16 | 10 | 176.2 | 78 | 76 | 0 | 2 | 0 | 0.974 | 4 | 26 | 3.87 | 2.17 | 0.984 | 2.97 | 2.94 | |
| 1978 | KCR | AL | 22 | DH | 6 | 0 | | | | | | | | | | | | | | | | |
| 1979 | KCR | AL | 23 | OF | 152 | 135 | 122 | 1251.1 | 402 | 384 | 12 | 6 | 0 | 0.985 | 25 | 24 | 2.85 | 2.61 | 0.981 | 2.46 | 2.43 | MVP-17 |
| 1979 | KCR | AL | 23 | LF | 131 | 112 | 105 | 1037.1 | 322 | 308 | 10 | 4 | 0 | 0.988 | 21 | 24 | 2.76 | 2.43 | 0.98 | 2.22 | 2.2 | MVP-17 |
| 1979 | KCR | AL | 23 | CF | 24 | 19 | 15 | 180 | 74 | 70 | 2 | 2 | 0 | 0.973 | 4 | 24 | 3.6 | 3 | 0.983 | 2.92 | 2.88 | MVP-17 |
| 1979 | KCR | AL | 23 | RF | 5 | 4 | 2 | 34 | 10 | 10 | 0 | 0 | 0 | 1 | 0 | 7 | 2.65 | 2 | 0.98 | 2.25 | 2.22 | MVP-17 |
| 1979 | KCR | AL | 23 | DH | 2 | 1 | | | | | | | | | | | | | | | | MVP-17 |
| 1980 | KCR | AL | 24 | OF | 159 | 157 | 144 | 1401 | 497 | 482 | 9 | 6 | 1 | 0.988 | 24 | 20 | 3.15 | 3.09 | 0.979 | 2.47 | 2.46 | MVP-4,GG,SS |
| 1980 | KCR | AL | 24 | LF | 102 | 101 | 91 | 877 | 301 | 288 | 8 | 5 | 1 | 0.983 | 18 | 24 | 3.04 | 2.9 | 0.98 | 2.35 | 2.35 | MVP-4,GG,SS |
| 1980 | KCR | AL | 24 | CF | 63 | 56 | 53 | 524 | 195 | 193 | 1 | 1 | 0 | 0.995 | 6 | 15 | 3.33 | 3.08 | 0.983 | 2.92 | 2.91 | MVP-4,GG,SS |
| 1981 | KCR | AL | 25 | OF | 101 | 99 | 95 | 884.1 | 317 | 299 | 14 | 4 | 3 | 0.987 | 20 | 27 | 3.19 | 3.1 | 0.983 | 2.48 | 2.47 | |
| 1981 | KCR | AL | 25 | LF | 84 | 82 | 79 | 736.1 | 259 | 244 | 11 | 4 | 2 | 0.985 | 16 | 27 | 3.12 | 3.04 | 0.979 | 2.38 | 2.38 | |
| 1981 | KCR | AL | 25 | CF | 18 | 17 | 16 | 148 | 58 | 55 | 3 | 0 | 1 | 1 | 4 | 29 | 3.53 | 3.22 | 0.988 | 2.9 | 2.89 | |
| 1982 | KCR | AL | 26 | OF | 135 | 135 | 119 | 1162 | 385 | 376 | 4 | 5 | 0 | 0.987 | 23 | 24 | 2.94 | 2.81 | 0.982 | 2.47 | 2.46 | AS,MVP-15,SS |
| 1982 | KCR | AL | 26 | LF | 118 | 117 | 103 | 1002.2 | 315 | 307 | 3 | 5 | 0 | 0.984 | 16 | 19 | 2.78 | 2.63 | 0.981 | 2.29 | 2.28 | AS,MVP-15,SS |
| 1982 | KCR | AL | 26 | CF | 20 | 18 | 16 | 159.1 | 71 | 70 | 1 | 0 | 0 | 1 | 7 | 52 | 4.01 | 3.55 | 0.985 | 2.84 | 2.83 | AS,MVP-15,SS |
| 1983 | KCR | AL | 27 | OF | 136 | 132 | 117 | 1150 | 366 | 354 | 3 | 9 | 0 | 0.975 | -7 | -7 | 2.79 | 2.63 | 0.981 | 2.5 | 2.48 | AS |
| 1983 | KCR | AL | 27 | CF | 75 | 69 | 57 | 599 | 219 | 214 | 0 | 5 | 0 | 0.977 | -4 | -8 | 3.22 | 2.85 | 0.987 | 2.93 | 2.91 | AS |
| 1983 | KCR | AL | 27 | LF | 64 | 63 | 60 | 551 | 145 | 137 | 3 | 5 | 0 | 0.966 | -3 | -6 | 2.29 | 2.19 | 0.977 | 2.32 | 2.3 | AS |
| 1984 | KCR | AL | 28 | CF | 128 | 128 | 119 | 1129 | 388 | 378 | 6 | 4 | 2 | 0.99 | 6 | 6 | 3.06 | 3 | 0.986 | 3.01 | 2.99 | MVP-10 |
| 1984 | KCR | AL | 28 | OF | 128 | 128 | 119 | 1129 | 393 | 383 | 6 | 4 | 2 | 0.99 | 6 | 6 | 3.1 | 3.04 | 0.983 | 2.51 | 2.49 | MVP-10 |
| 1985 | KCR | AL | 29 | CF | 140 | 140 | 132 | 1244.2 | 386 | 380 | 4 | 2 | 1 | 0.995 | -2 | -2 | 2.78 | 2.74 | 0.988 | 2.91 | 2.88 | |
| 1985 | KCR | AL | 29 | OF | 140 | 140 | 132 | 1244.2 | 384 | 378 | 4 | 2 | 1 | 0.995 | -2 | -2 | 2.76 | 2.73 | 0.982 | 2.44 | 2.42 | |
| 1986 | KCR | AL | 30 | CF | 155 | 149 | 137 | 1305.2 | 421 | 413 | 5 | 3 | 3 | 0.993 | 5 | 5 | 2.88 | 2.7 | 0.986 | 2.83 | 2.8 | |
| 1986 | KCR | AL | 30 | OF | 155 | 149 | 137 | 1305.2 | 415 | 408 | 4 | 3 | 2 | 0.993 | 5 | 5 | 2.84 | 2.66 | 0.98 | 2.39 | 2.37 | |
| 1987 | KCR | AL | 31 | CF | 143 | 142 | 133 | 1221.1 | 346 | 342 | 3 | 1 | 1 | 0.997 | 1 | 1 | 2.54 | 2.41 | 0.986 | 2.7 | 2.68 | |
| 1987 | KCR | AL | 31 | OF | 143 | 142 | 133 | 1221.1 | 346 | 342 | 3 | 1 | 1 | 0.997 | 1 | 1 | 2.54 | 2.41 | 0.98 | 2.31 | 2.29 | |
| 1987 | KCR | AL | 31 | DH | 2 | 2 | | | | | | | | | | | | | | | | |
| 1988 | KCR | AL | 32 | CF | 142 | 140 | 122 | 1194 | 370 | 364 | 2 | 4 | 0 | 0.989 | -5 | -5 | 2.76 | 2.58 | 0.985 | 2.91 | 2.89 | |
| 1988 | KCR | AL | 32 | OF | 142 | 140 | 122 | 1194 | 370 | 365 | 1 | 4 | 0 | 0.989 | -5 | -5 | 2.76 | 2.58 | 0.979 | 2.47 | 2.45 | |
| 1989 | KCR | AL | 33 | CF | 108 | 95 | 81 | 831.2 | 260 | 252 | 2 | 6 | 0 | 0.977 | 3 | 4 | 2.75 | 2.35 | 0.984 | 2.78 | 2.75 | |
| 1989 | KCR | AL | 33 | OF | 108 | 95 | 81 | 831.2 | 260 | 252 | 2 | 6 | 0 | 0.977 | 3 | 4 | 2.75 | 2.35 | 0.98 | 2.42 | 2.39 | |
| 1989 | KCR | AL | 33 | DH | 1 | 0 | | | | | | | | | | | | | | | | |
| 1990 | KCR | AL | 34 | OF | 106 | 81 | 73 | 724.2 | 189 | 187 | 2 | 0 | 1 | 1 | -5 | -8 | 2.35 | 1.78 | 0.981 | 2.39 | 2.36 | |
| 1990 | KCR | AL | 34 | LF | 54 | 39 | 36 | 359.1 | 93 | 92 | 1 | 0 | 0 | 1 | -2 | -6 | 2.33 | 1.72 | 0.978 | 2.19 | 2.16 | |
| 1990 | KCR | AL | 34 | CF | 48 | 41 | 36 | 350 | 91 | 91 | 0 | 0 | 1 | 1 | -4 | -13 | 2.34 | 1.9 | 0.985 | 2.74 | 2.71 | |
| 1990 | KCR | AL | 34 | RF | 4 | 1 | 1 | 15.1 | 6 | 6 | 0 | 0 | 0 | 1 | 0 | 39 | 3.52 | 1.5 | 0.978 | 2.23 | 2.2 | |
| 1990 | KCR | AL | 34 | DH | 1 | 1 | | | | | | | | | | | | | | | | |
| 1991 | OAK | AL | 35 | OF | 87 | 63 | 55 | 597 | 181 | 176 | 2 | 3 | 0 | 0.983 | 10 | 20 | 2.68 | 2.05 | 0.983 | 2.37 | 2.37 | |
| 1991 | OAK | AL | 35 | LF | 41 | 26 | 25 | 258.1 | 84 | 81 | 1 | 2 | 0 | 0.976 | 6 | 26 | 2.86 | 2 | 0.978 | 2.17 | 2.16 | |
| 1991 | OAK | AL | 35 | CF | 33 | 23 | 21 | 212 | 67 | 66 | 0 | 1 | 0 | 0.985 | 3 | 18 | 2.8 | 2 | 0.989 | 2.76 | 2.76 | |
| 1991 | OAK | AL | 35 | RF | 19 | 14 | 9 | 126.2 | 30 | 29 | 1 | 0 | 0 | 1 | 1 | 10 | 2.13 | 1.58 | 0.98 | 2.19 | 2.19 | |
| 1991 | OAK | AL | 35 | DH | 9 | 1 | | | | | | | | | | | | | | | | |
| 1992 | OAK | AL | 36 | OF | 120 | 100 | 94 | 925 | 364 | 355 | 2 | 7 | 2 | 0.981 | 3 | 4 | 3.47 | 2.98 | 0.983 | 2.47 | 2.46 | |
| 1992 | OAK | AL | 36 | CF | 118 | 98 | 92 | 903 | 360 | 351 | 2 | 7 | 2 | 0.981 | 4 | 5 | 3.52 | 2.99 | 0.986 | 2.9 | 2.89 | |
| 1992 | OAK | AL | 36 | DH | 5 | 0 | | | | | | | | | | | | | | | | |
| 1992 | OAK | AL | 36 | RF | 3 | 2 | 2 | 22 | 5 | 5 | 0 | 0 | 0 | 1 | 0 | -16 | 2.05 | 1.67 | 0.982 | 2.25 | 2.23 | |
| 1993 | CHC | NL | 37 | CF | 82 | 39 | 33 | 411.2 | 112 | 110 | 1 | 1 | 0 | 0.991 | -2 | -5 | 2.43 | 1.35 | 0.985 | 2.75 | 2.73 | |
| 1993 | CHC | NL | 37 | OF | 82 | 39 | 33 | 411.2 | 111 | 109 | 1 | 1 | 0 | 0.991 | -2 | -5 | 2.4 | 1.34 | 0.979 | 2.34 | 2.33 | |
| 1994 | CHC | NL | 38 | CF | 10 | 3 | 3 | 39.2 | 9 | 9 | 0 | 0 | 0 | 1 | -2 | -57 | 2.04 | 0.9 | 0.982 | 2.63 | 2.61 | |
| 1994 | CHC | NL | 38 | OF | 10 | 3 | 3 | 39.2 | 9 | 9 | 0 | 0 | 0 | 1 | -2 | -57 | 2.04 | 0.9 | 0.98 | 2.25 | 2.23 | |
| | 19 Seasons | | | OF | 2031 | 1790 | 1617 | 16105.2 | 5203 | 5060 | 76 | 67 | 15 | 0.987 | 108 | 8 | 2.87 | 2.53 | 0.981 | 2.44 | 2.42 | |
| | 19 Seasons | | | CF | 1357 | 1200 | 1082 | 10721 | 3539 | 3465 | 33 | 41 | 11 | 0.988 | 29 | 3 | 2.94 | 2.58 | 0.986 | 2.86 | 2.84 | |
| | 8 Seasons | | | LF | 676 | 569 | 521 | 5186.2 | 1621 | 1552 | 42 | 27 | 5 | 0.983 | 78 | 18 | 2.77 | 2.36 | 0.979 | 2.28 | 2.26 | |
| | 4 Seasons | | | RF | 31 | 21 | 14 | 198 | 51 | 50 | 1 | 0 | 0 | 1 | 2 | 9 | 2.32 | 1.65 | 0.98 | 2.21 | 2.2 | |
| | 19 Seasons | | | TOT | 2031 | 1790 | 1617 | 16105.2 | 5203 | 5060 | 76 | 67 | 15 | 0.987 | 108 | 8 | 2.87 | 2.53 | 0.981 | 2.44 | 2.42 | |

# WILLIE WILSON'S CAREER STATS

| YEAR | AGE | TM | LG | G | PA | AB | R | H | 2B | 3B | HR | RBI | SB | CS | BB |
|------|-----|-----|-----|-----|------|------|------|------|-----|-----|-----|-----|-----|-----|-----|
| 1976 | 20 | KCR | AL | 12 | 6 | 6 | 0 | 1 | 0 | 0 | 0 | 0 | 2 | 1 | 0 |
| 1977 | 21 | KCR | AL | 13 | 37 | 34 | 10 | 11 | 2 | 0 | 0 | 1 | 6 | 3 | 1 |
| 1978 | 22 | KCR | AL | 127 | 223 | 198 | 43 | 43 | 8 | 2 | 0 | 16 | 46 | 12 | 16 |
| 1979 | 23 | KCR | AL | 154 | 640 | 588 | 113 | 185 | 18 | 13 | 6 | 49 | 83 | 12 | 28 |
| 1980 | 24 | KCR | AL | 161 | 745 | 705 | 133 | 230 | 28 | 15 | 3 | 49 | 79 | 10 | 28 |
| 1981 | 25 | KCR | AL | 102 | 465 | 439 | 54 | 133 | 10 | 7 | 1 | 32 | 34 | 8 | 18 |
| 1982 | 26 | KCR | AL | 136 | 621 | 585 | 87 | 194 | 19 | 15 | 3 | 46 | 37 | 11 | 26 |
| 1983 | 27 | KCR | AL | 137 | 611 | 576 | 90 | 159 | 22 | 8 | 2 | 33 | 59 | 8 | 33 |
| 1984 | 28 | KCR | AL | 128 | 588 | 541 | 81 | 163 | 24 | 9 | 2 | 44 | 47 | 5 | 39 |
| 1985 | 29 | KCR | AL | 141 | 642 | 605 | 87 | 168 | 25 | 21 | 4 | 43 | 43 | 11 | 29 |
| 1986 | 30 | KCR | AL | 156 | 675 | 631 | 77 | 170 | 20 | 7 | 9 | 44 | 34 | 8 | 31 |
| 1987 | 31 | KCR | AL | 146 | 653 | 610 | 97 | 170 | 18 | 15 | 4 | 30 | 59 | 11 | 32 |
| 1988 | 32 | KCR | AL | 147 | 628 | 591 | 81 | 155 | 17 | 11 | 1 | 37 | 35 | 7 | 22 |
| 1989 | 33 | KCR | AL | 112 | 423 | 383 | 58 | 97 | 17 | 7 | 3 | 43 | 24 | 6 | 27 |
| 1990 | 34 | KCR | AL | 115 | 345 | 307 | 49 | 89 | 13 | 3 | 2 | 42 | 24 | 6 | 30 |
| 1991 | 35 | OAK | AL | 113 | 318 | 294 | 38 | 70 | 14 | 4 | 0 | 28 | 20 | 5 | 18 |
| 1992 | 36 | OAK | AL | 132 | 437 | 396 | 38 | 107 | 15 | 5 | 0 | 37 | 28 | 8 | 35 |
| 1993 | 37 | CHC | NL | 105 | 237 | 221 | 29 | 57 | 11 | 3 | 1 | 11 | 7 | 2 | 11 |
| 1994 | 38 | CHC | NL | 17 | 23 | 21 | 4 | 5 | 0 | 2 | 0 | 0 | 1 | 0 | 1 |
| 19 Yrs | | | | 2154 | 8317 | 7731 | 1169 | 2207 | 281 | 147 | 41 | 585 | 668 | 134 | 425 |
| 162 Game Avg. | | | | 162 | 626 | 581 | 88 | 166 | 21 | 11 | 3 | 44 | 50 | 10 | 32 |
| KCR (15 yrs) | | | | 1787 | 7302 | 6799 | 1060 | 1968 | 241 | 133 | 40 | 509 | 612 | 119 | 360 |
| OAK (2 yrs) | | | | 245 | 755 | 690 | 76 | 177 | 29 | 9 | 0 | 65 | 48 | 13 | 53 |
| CHC (2 yrs) | | | | 122 | 260 | 242 | 33 | 62 | 11 | 5 | 1 | 11 | 8 | 2 | 12 |
| | | | | | | | | | | | | | | | |
| AL (17 yrs) | | | | 2032 | 8057 | 7489 | 1136 | 2145 | 270 | 142 | 40 | 574 | 660 | 132 | 413 |
| NL (2 yrs) | | | | 122 | 260 | 242 | 33 | 62 | 11 | 5 | 1 | 11 | 8 | 2 | 12 |

# WILLIE WILSON'S CAREER STATS

| SO | AVG | OBP | SLG | OPS | OPS+ | TB | GDP | HBP | SH | SF | IBB | POS | AWARDS |
|----|-----|-----|-----|-----|------|----|-----|-----|----|----|-----|-----|--------|
| 2 | 0.167 | 0.167 | 0.167 | 0.333 | -3 | 1 | 0 | 0 | 0 | 0 | 0 | /8 | |
| 8 | 0.324 | 0.343 | 0.382 | 0.725 | 97 | 13 | 1 | 0 | 2 | 0 | 0 | /8D | |
| 33 | 0.217 | 0.28 | 0.278 | 0.558 | 57 | 55 | 2 | 2 | 5 | 2 | 0 | *78/D | |
| 92 | 0.315 | 0.351 | 0.42 | 0.771 | 106 | 247 | 1 | 7 | 13 | 4 | 3 | *78/9D | MVP-17 |
| 81 | 0.326 | 0.357 | 0.421 | 0.778 | 113 | 297 | 4 | 6 | 5 | 1 | 3 | *78 | MVP-4,GG,SS |
| 42 | 0.303 | 0.335 | 0.364 | 0.7 | 104 | 160 | 5 | 4 | 3 | 1 | 3 | *78 | |
| 81 | 0.332 | 0.365 | 0.431 | 0.796 | 118 | 252 | 4 | 6 | 2 | 2 | 2 | *78 | AS,MVP-15,SS |
| 75 | 0.276 | 0.316 | 0.352 | 0.669 | 85 | 203 | 4 | 1 | 1 | 0 | 2 | *87 | AS |
| 56 | 0.301 | 0.35 | 0.39 | 0.74 | 105 | 211 | 7 | 3 | 2 | 3 | 2 | *8 | MVP-10 |
| 94 | 0.278 | 0.316 | 0.408 | 0.724 | 98 | 247 | 6 | 5 | 2 | 1 | 3 | *8 | |
| 97 | 0.269 | 0.313 | 0.366 | 0.679 | 84 | 231 | 6 | 9 | 3 | 1 | 1 | *8 | |
| 88 | 0.279 | 0.32 | 0.377 | 0.698 | 83 | 230 | 9 | 6 | 4 | 1 | 2 | *8/D | |
| 106 | 0.262 | 0.289 | 0.333 | 0.622 | 74 | 197 | 5 | 2 | 8 | 5 | 1 | *8 | |
| 78 | 0.253 | 0.3 | 0.358 | 0.657 | 85 | 137 | 8 | 1 | 6 | 6 | 0 | 8/D | |
| 57 | 0.29 | 0.354 | 0.371 | 0.725 | 106 | 114 | 4 | 2 | 3 | 3 | 1 | 78/9D | |
| 43 | 0.238 | 0.29 | 0.313 | 0.603 | 72 | 92 | 11 | 4 | 1 | 1 | 1 | 789/D | |
| 65 | 0.27 | 0.329 | 0.333 | 0.662 | 92 | 132 | 11 | 1 | 2 | 3 | 2 | *8/D9 | |
| 40 | 0.258 | 0.301 | 0.348 | 0.649 | 76 | 77 | 2 | 3 | 1 | 1 | 1 | 8 | |
| 6 | 0.238 | 0.273 | 0.429 | 0.701 | 80 | 9 | 0 | 0 | 1 | 0 | 0 | 8 | |
| 1144 | 0.285 | 0.326 | 0.376 | 0.702 | 94 | 2905 | 90 | 62 | 64 | 35 | 27 | | |
| 86 | 0.285 | 0.326 | 0.376 | 0.702 | 94 | 218 | 7 | 5 | 5 | 3 | 2 | | |
| 990 | 0.289 | 0.329 | 0.382 | 0.711 | 95 | 2595 | 66 | 54 | 59 | 30 | 23 | | |
| 108 | 0.257 | 0.313 | 0.325 | 0.637 | 83 | 224 | 22 | 5 | 3 | 4 | 3 | | |
| 46 | 0.256 | 0.298 | 0.355 | 0.654 | 77 | 86 | 2 | 3 | 2 | 1 | 1 | | |
| | | | | | | | | | | | | | |
| 1098 | 0.286 | 0.327 | 0.376 | 0.704 | 94 | 2819 | 88 | 59 | 62 | 34 | 26 | | |
| 46 | 0.256 | 0.298 | 0.355 | 0.654 | 77 | 86 | 2 | 3 | 2 | 1 | 1 | | |

# WILLIE WILSON'S BATTING STATS

| Year | Tm | Lg | Age | Pos | G | GS | CG | Inn | Ch | PO | A | E | DP | Fld% | Rtot | Rtot/yr | RF/9 | RF/G | lgFld% | lgRF9 | lgRFG | Awards |
|---|---|---|---|---|---|---|---|---|---|---|---|---|---|---|---|---|---|---|---|---|---|---|
| 1976 | KCR | AL | 20 | CF | 6 | 1 | 1 | 18 | 8 | 6 | 1 | 1 | 0 | 0.875 | 0 | 33 | 3.5 | 1.17 | 0.984 | 3 | 2.98 | |
| 1976 | KCR | AL | 20 | OF | 6 | 1 | 1 | 18 | 8 | 6 | 1 | 1 | 0 | 0.875 | 0 | 33 | 3.5 | 1.17 | 0.981 | 2.45 | 2.48 | |
| 1977 | KCR | AL | 21 | CF | 9 | 6 | 5 | 73.1 | 26 | 25 | 0 | 1 | 0 | 0.962 | 1 | 15 | 3.07 | 2.78 | 0.983 | 2.82 | 2.81 | |
| 1977 | KCR | AL | 21 | OF | 9 | 6 | 5 | 73.1 | 25 | 24 | 0 | 1 | 0 | 0.96 | 1 | 15 | 2.95 | 2.67 | 0.978 | 2.34 | 2.32 | |
| 1977 | KCR | AL | 21 | DH | 2 | 0 | | | | | | | | | | | | | | | | |
| 1978 | KCR | AL | 22 | OF | 112 | 45 | 32 | 541.1 | 181 | 171 | 6 | 4 | 2 | 0.978 | 10 | 22 | 2.94 | 1.58 | 0.979 | 2.47 | 2.45 | |
| 1978 | KCR | AL | 22 | LF | 82 | 29 | 22 | 364.2 | 102 | 95 | 5 | 2 | 2 | 0.98 | 6 | 20 | 2.47 | 1.22 | 0.974 | 2.21 | 2.19 | |
| 1978 | KCR | AL | 22 | CF | 35 | 16 | 10 | 176.2 | 78 | 76 | 0 | 2 | 0 | 0.974 | 4 | 26 | 3.87 | 2.17 | 0.984 | 2.97 | 2.94 | |
| 1978 | KCR | AL | 22 | DH | 6 | 0 | | | | | | | | | | | | | | | | |
| 1979 | KCR | AL | 23 | OF | 152 | 135 | 122 | 1251.1 | 402 | 384 | 12 | 6 | 0 | 0.985 | 25 | 24 | 2.85 | 2.61 | 0.981 | 2.46 | 2.43 | MVP-17 |
| 1979 | KCR | AL | 23 | LF | 131 | 112 | 105 | 1037.1 | 322 | 308 | 10 | 4 | 0 | 0.988 | 21 | 24 | 2.76 | 2.43 | 0.98 | 2.22 | 2.2 | MVP-17 |
| 1979 | KCR | AL | 23 | CF | 24 | 19 | 15 | 180 | 74 | 70 | 2 | 2 | 0 | 0.973 | 4 | 24 | 3.6 | 3 | 0.983 | 2.92 | 2.88 | MVP-17 |
| 1979 | KCR | AL | 23 | RF | 5 | 4 | 2 | 34 | 10 | 10 | 0 | 0 | 0 | 1 | 0 | 7 | 2.65 | 2 | 0.98 | 2.25 | 2.22 | MVP-17 |
| 1979 | KCR | AL | 23 | DH | 2 | 1 | | | | | | | | | | | | | | | | MVP-17 |
| 1980 | KCR | AL | 24 | OF | 159 | 157 | 144 | 1401 | 497 | 482 | 9 | 6 | 1 | 0.988 | 24 | 20 | 3.15 | 3.09 | 0.979 | 2.47 | 2.46 | MVP-4,GG,SS |
| 1980 | KCR | AL | 24 | LF | 102 | 101 | 91 | 877 | 301 | 288 | 8 | 5 | 1 | 0.983 | 18 | 24 | 3.04 | 2.9 | 0.98 | 2.35 | 2.35 | MVP-4,GG,SS |
| 1980 | KCR | AL | 24 | CF | 63 | 56 | 53 | 524 | 195 | 193 | 1 | 1 | 0 | 0.995 | 6 | 15 | 3.33 | 3.08 | 0.983 | 2.92 | 2.91 | MVP-4,GG,SS |
| 1981 | KCR | AL | 25 | OF | 101 | 99 | 95 | 884.1 | 317 | 299 | 14 | 4 | 3 | 0.987 | 20 | 27 | 3.19 | 3.1 | 0.983 | 2.48 | 2.47 | |
| 1981 | KCR | AL | 25 | LF | 84 | 82 | 79 | 736.1 | 259 | 244 | 11 | 4 | 2 | 0.985 | 16 | 27 | 3.12 | 3.04 | 0.979 | 2.38 | 2.38 | |
| 1981 | KCR | AL | 25 | CF | 18 | 17 | 16 | 148 | 58 | 55 | 3 | 0 | 1 | 1 | 4 | 29 | 3.53 | 3.22 | 0.988 | 2.9 | 2.89 | |
| 1982 | KCR | AL | 26 | OF | 135 | 135 | 119 | 1162 | 385 | 376 | 4 | 5 | 0 | 0.987 | 23 | 24 | 2.94 | 2.81 | 0.982 | 2.47 | 2.46 | AS,MVP-15,SS |
| 1982 | KCR | AL | 26 | LF | 118 | 117 | 103 | 1002.2 | 315 | 307 | 3 | 5 | 0 | 0.984 | 16 | 19 | 2.78 | 2.63 | 0.981 | 2.29 | 2.28 | AS,MVP-15,SS |
| 1982 | KCR | AL | 26 | CF | 20 | 18 | 16 | 159.1 | 71 | 70 | 1 | 0 | 0 | 1 | 7 | 52 | 4.01 | 3.55 | 0.985 | 2.84 | 2.83 | AS,MVP-15,SS |
| 1983 | KCR | AL | 27 | OF | 136 | 132 | 117 | 1150 | 366 | 354 | 3 | 9 | 0 | 0.975 | -7 | -7 | 2.79 | 2.63 | 0.981 | 2.5 | 2.48 | AS |
| 1983 | KCR | AL | 27 | CF | 75 | 69 | 57 | 599 | 219 | 214 | 0 | 5 | 0 | 0.977 | -4 | -8 | 3.22 | 2.85 | 0.987 | 2.93 | 2.91 | AS |
| 1983 | KCR | AL | 27 | LF | 64 | 63 | 60 | 551 | 145 | 137 | 3 | 5 | 0 | 0.966 | -3 | -6 | 2.29 | 2.19 | 0.977 | 2.32 | 2.3 | AS |
| 1984 | KCR | AL | 28 | CF | 128 | 128 | 119 | 1129 | 388 | 378 | 6 | 4 | 2 | 0.99 | 6 | 6 | 3.06 | 3 | 0.986 | 3.01 | 2.99 | MVP-10 |
| 1984 | KCR | AL | 28 | OF | 128 | 128 | 119 | 1129 | 393 | 383 | 6 | 4 | 2 | 0.99 | 6 | 6 | 3.1 | 3.04 | 0.983 | 2.51 | 2.49 | MVP-10 |
| 1985 | KCR | AL | 29 | CF | 140 | 140 | 132 | 1244.2 | 386 | 380 | 4 | 2 | 1 | 0.995 | -2 | -2 | 2.78 | 2.74 | 0.988 | 2.91 | 2.88 | |
| 1985 | KCR | AL | 29 | OF | 140 | 140 | 132 | 1244.2 | 384 | 378 | 4 | 2 | 1 | 0.995 | -2 | -2 | 2.76 | 2.73 | 0.982 | 2.44 | 2.42 | |
| 1986 | KCR | AL | 30 | CF | 155 | 149 | 137 | 1305.2 | 421 | 413 | 5 | 3 | 3 | 0.993 | 5 | 5 | 2.88 | 2.7 | 0.986 | 2.83 | 2.8 | |
| 1986 | KCR | AL | 30 | OF | 155 | 149 | 137 | 1305.2 | 415 | 408 | 4 | 3 | 2 | 0.993 | 5 | 5 | 2.84 | 2.66 | 0.98 | 2.39 | 2.37 | |
| 1987 | KCR | AL | 31 | CF | 143 | 142 | 133 | 1221.1 | 346 | 342 | 3 | 1 | 1 | 0.997 | 1 | 1 | 2.54 | 2.41 | 0.986 | 2.7 | 2.68 | |
| 1987 | KCR | AL | 31 | OF | 143 | 142 | 133 | 1221.1 | 346 | 342 | 3 | 1 | 1 | 0.997 | 1 | 1 | 2.54 | 2.41 | 0.98 | 2.31 | 2.29 | |
| 1987 | KCR | AL | 31 | DH | 2 | 2 | | | | | | | | | | | | | | | | |
| 1988 | KCR | AL | 32 | CF | 142 | 140 | 122 | 1194 | 370 | 364 | 2 | 4 | 0 | 0.989 | -5 | -5 | 2.76 | 2.58 | 0.985 | 2.91 | 2.89 | |
| 1988 | KCR | AL | 32 | OF | 142 | 140 | 122 | 1194 | 370 | 365 | 1 | 4 | 0 | 0.989 | -5 | -5 | 2.76 | 2.58 | 0.979 | 2.47 | 2.45 | |
| 1989 | KCR | AL | 33 | CF | 108 | 95 | 81 | 831.2 | 260 | 252 | 2 | 6 | 0 | 0.977 | 3 | 4 | 2.75 | 2.35 | 0.984 | 2.78 | 2.75 | |
| 1989 | KCR | AL | 33 | OF | 108 | 95 | 81 | 831.2 | 260 | 252 | 2 | 6 | 0 | 0.977 | 3 | 4 | 2.75 | 2.35 | 0.98 | 2.42 | 2.39 | |
| 1989 | KCR | AL | 33 | DH | 1 | 0 | | | | | | | | | | | | | | | | |
| 1990 | KCR | AL | 34 | OF | 106 | 81 | 73 | 724.2 | 189 | 187 | 2 | 0 | 1 | 1 | -5 | -8 | 2.35 | 1.78 | 0.981 | 2.39 | 2.36 | |
| 1990 | KCR | AL | 34 | LF | 54 | 39 | 36 | 359.1 | 93 | 92 | 1 | 0 | 0 | 1 | -2 | -6 | 2.33 | 1.72 | 0.978 | 2.19 | 2.16 | |
| 1990 | KCR | AL | 34 | CF | 48 | 41 | 36 | 350 | 91 | 91 | 0 | 0 | 1 | 1 | -4 | -13 | 2.34 | 1.9 | 0.985 | 2.74 | 2.71 | |
| 1990 | KCR | AL | 34 | RF | 4 | 1 | 1 | 15.1 | 6 | 6 | 0 | 0 | 0 | 1 | 0 | 39 | 3.52 | 1.5 | 0.978 | 2.23 | 2.2 | |
| 1990 | KCR | AL | 34 | DH | 1 | 1 | | | | | | | | | | | | | | | | |
| 1991 | OAK | AL | 35 | OF | 87 | 63 | 55 | 597 | 181 | 176 | 2 | 3 | 0 | 0.983 | 10 | 20 | 2.68 | 2.05 | 0.983 | 2.37 | 2.37 | |
| 1991 | OAK | AL | 35 | LF | 41 | 26 | 25 | 258.1 | 84 | 81 | 1 | 2 | 0 | 0.976 | 6 | 26 | 2.86 | 2 | 0.978 | 2.17 | 2.16 | |
| 1991 | OAK | AL | 35 | CF | 33 | 23 | 21 | 212 | 67 | 66 | 0 | 1 | 0 | 0.985 | 3 | 18 | 2.8 | 2 | 0.989 | 2.76 | 2.76 | |
| 1991 | OAK | AL | 35 | RF | 19 | 14 | 9 | 126.2 | 30 | 29 | 1 | 0 | 0 | 1 | 1 | 10 | 2.13 | 1.58 | 0.98 | 2.19 | 2.19 | |
| 1991 | OAK | AL | 35 | DH | 9 | 1 | | | | | | | | | | | | | | | | |
| 1992 | OAK | AL | 36 | OF | 120 | 100 | 94 | 925 | 364 | 355 | 2 | 7 | 2 | 0.981 | 3 | 4 | 3.47 | 2.98 | 0.983 | 2.47 | 2.46 | |
| 1992 | OAK | AL | 36 | CF | 118 | 98 | 92 | 903 | 360 | 351 | 2 | 7 | 2 | 0.981 | 4 | 5 | 3.52 | 2.99 | 0.986 | 2.9 | 2.89 | |
| 1992 | OAK | AL | 36 | DH | 5 | 0 | | | | | | | | | | | | | | | | |
| 1992 | OAK | AL | 36 | RF | 3 | 2 | 2 | 22 | 5 | 5 | 0 | 0 | 0 | 1 | 0 | -16 | 2.05 | 1.67 | 0.982 | 2.25 | 2.23 | |
| 1993 | CHC | NL | 37 | CF | 82 | 39 | 33 | 411.2 | 112 | 110 | 1 | 1 | 0 | 0.991 | -2 | -5 | 2.43 | 1.35 | 0.985 | 2.75 | 2.73 | |
| 1993 | CHC | NL | 37 | OF | 82 | 39 | 33 | 411.2 | 111 | 109 | 1 | 1 | 0 | 0.991 | -2 | -5 | 2.4 | 1.34 | 0.979 | 2.34 | 2.33 | |
| 1994 | CHC | NL | 38 | CF | 10 | 3 | 3 | 39.2 | 9 | 9 | 0 | 0 | 0 | 1 | -2 | -57 | 2.04 | 0.9 | 0.982 | 2.63 | 2.61 | |
| 1994 | CHC | NL | 38 | OF | 10 | 3 | 3 | 39.2 | 9 | 9 | 0 | 0 | 0 | 1 | -2 | -57 | 2.04 | 0.9 | 0.98 | 2.25 | 2.23 | |
| | 19 Seasons | | | OF | 2031 | 1790 | 1617 | 16105.2 | 5203 | 5060 | 76 | 67 | 15 | 0.987 | 108 | 8 | 2.87 | 2.53 | 0.981 | 2.44 | 2.42 | |
| | 19 Seasons | | | CF | 1357 | 1200 | 1082 | 10721 | 3539 | 3465 | 33 | 41 | 11 | 0.988 | 29 | 3 | 2.94 | 2.58 | 0.986 | 2.86 | 2.84 | |
| | 8 Seasons | | | LF | 676 | 569 | 521 | 5186.2 | 1621 | 1552 | 42 | 27 | 5 | 0.983 | 78 | 18 | 2.77 | 2.36 | 0.979 | 2.28 | 2.26 | |
| | 4 Seasons | | | RF | 31 | 21 | 14 | 198 | 51 | 50 | 1 | 0 | 0 | 1 | 2 | 9 | 2.32 | 1.65 | 0.98 | 2.21 | 2.2 | |
| | 19 Seasons | | | TOT | 2031 | 1790 | 1617 | 16105.2 | 5203 | 5060 | 76 | 67 | 15 | 0.987 | 108 | 8 | 2.87 | 2.53 | 0.981 | 2.44 | 2.42 | |

# ACKNOWLEDGEMENTS

**W**hen I first started this project I had no idea what it would entail. I hope that my story will inspire those that read it to never give up!

To the fans, the Kansas City Royals, the Kansas City T-Bones and the people of Kansas City – thank you for giving me the opportunity to return and be a part of our fine community.

My friends and family, you've stood by me when I didn't even want to stand by myself. Thank you for not giving up on me.

To my children, I pray that you will hold onto the memories of the love I have for each of you. Not growing up knowing my Dad made me want to be the best father I could to you. You are each my legacy! Let my life live on through each of you!

Thanks to Bob Snodgrass and Ascend Books, for picking me for this project.

I would like to thank the writer, Kent Pulliam for the many hours of work he has put into the book and telling my story through my eyes.

—Willie Wilson

**I**'d like to thank Willie Wilson for allowing me to tell his story. Although I follow sports in Kansas City closely and occasionally covered Royals games, I had no idea the path Willie took to the Major Leagues – and more importantly the path he walked afterwards and the trials he has overcome.

Research for this book could not have happened without great cooperation from the Royals, and particularly Mike Swanson, Colby Curry and Curt Nelson. Thanks also to Summit High School employees and teachers Sandra Soltis, Mary Beth Reardon and Don Standing for researching and making available photos from the Summit High School yearbook. Editor Jim Bradford did a masterful job of making sure the book's text remained true to Willie's voice.

And thanks to my wife Gina for allowing me to spend hours in front of the computer screen that could have been spent with her.

—Kent Pulliam

Royals Hall of Famer Willie Wilson played an integral part in the only two World Series appearances the Royals made, batting .311 against the St. Louis Cardinals in the Royals only World Series title in 1985. A superb lead-off hitter, Wilson led the American League in stolen bases his second full season in the Major Leagues in 1979, won the team's Player of the Year award in 1980 when he led the league in hits, runs, triples, singles and won the Gold Glove for defensive excellence. In 1982, Wilson was the Major League batting champion, hitting .332, winning his first trip to the All Star game. A speedster on the base path, Wilson led the league in triples five times and his 13 inside-the-park home runs is the most by any player in the modern-day era. He has 668 career stolen bases, ranking No. 10 in Major League baseball history. He was voted into the Royals Hall of Fame in 2000. Willie lives in Kansas City where he is head of the Willie Wilson Baseball Foundation. His on- and off-field experiences give him a unique opportunity to work with corporations for speaking engagements, team-building exercises and fund-raising events as well as offer baseball and life guidance for inner-city youth in clinics he conducts.

Kent Pulliam spent more than 30 years as a sports journalist for The Kansas City Star. He has won several writing awards from the Associated Press Sports Editors and the Missouri Press Association. He has written two other books: "For Wildcats Fans Only" and "Inside the Jayhawks Huddle." He lives in Kansas City, Missouri, with his wife Gina. This is his third book.

Visit www.ascendbooks.com for more great titles on your favorite teams and athletes.